Wittgenstein

To the memory
of
Ludwig Wittgenstein

WITTGENSTEIN

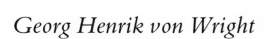

Georg Henrik von Wright

University of Minnesota Press
Minneapolis

Published by the University of Minnesota Press,
2037 University Avenue Southeast, Minneapolis MN 55414

Printed in Great Britain

ISBN 0-8166-1210-2
0-8166-1215-3 (pbk.)

Contents

Preface

THESE eight studies of different aspects of Ludwig Wittgenstein and his works have been revised, in places rewritten, and sometimes considerably expanded from papers published before, either *in toto* or in part. What has already been published is here reprinted with the kind permission of the respective copyright holders. I am greatly indebted to Heikki Nyman for his assistance in my work on revising the papers. I also wish to thank Norman Malcolm for help with the English.

Wittgenstein's German has a beauty and expressiveness which easily gets lost in translation. I have therefore preferred to quote his writings of a more personal nature, such as letters or 'general remarks', in the original language, giving the English translation in a footnote.

G. H. v. W.

Introduction

THE most important facts about Wittgenstein's life and the most outstanding traits of his character, as I saw them, form the subject matter of the first essay in this book. The last essay attempts an account of Wittgenstein's relations to his times as reflected in some of his writings of a more personal nature. Three of the papers deal with specific topics in his philosophy: probability, certainty, and modality as expressed in the *Tractatus Logico-Philosophicus*. This book has no pretensions, however, to be a full biographical or philosophical assessment of Wittgenstein. The remaining three essays are neither biographical nor philosophical, but consist of studies on Wittgenstein's *Nachlass* (the work unpublished at his death) and on the origin of his two great works, the *Tractatus* and the *Philosophical Investigations*. These studies may make difficult reading for the non-specialist, but I hope they have value as records of a number of facts which it would be hard or impossible for subsequent researchers to trace. The eight essays together, by casting narrow beams of light from different directions, may, it is hoped, help the reader towards a clearer understanding of the thoughts of one of the most fertile and original minds in the history of philosophy.

I wrote the 'Biographical Sketch' out of a sense of duty to Wittgenstein's memory. When Wittgenstein died in 1951, he was a 'celebrated' philosopher, but not much was commonly known about his life and false rumours and mystifying stories circulated about him. I had known him well and I thought it my duty to record available data and ascertain the factual basis of conflicting rumours – not so much perhaps with a view to enlightening the world as to be able to disprove false statements. The fact-collecting continued long after I had written the 'Sketch', and many later findings were used for my studies on the *Nachlass* and on the history of Wittgenstein's works.

I have often been asked whether I would write a full biography. But I have never contemplated this. I think, moreover, that the best pictures to be drawn of Wittgenstein as a man are impressionistic accounts of conversations and episodes – and I have little talent for this kind of writing. Two such accounts exist which seem to be superb, deserving the status of classics of biographical writing. They are Norman Malcolm's and Fania Pascal's memoirs.[1] If there is anything I miss in them it would be the overwhelming charm of Wittgenstein's imaginative powers; in conversation he could be very gay – *lustig*, as one would say in German.

Related to the genre of biography are literary efforts to assess Wittgenstein as *geistige Erscheinung*, that is, to view his personality and work in relation to phenomena outside the strictly professional sphere of philosophy – for example, trends in contemporary literature or art, or political and social ideas. One can try to trace *influences* to which he was himself subject or which he had on others. They belong to 'biography'. But one can also look for *similarities* which need have nothing to do with 'influence' but which may nevertheless illuminate the objects of comparison. Such studies might be called *morphological* or *physiognomic*. (The idea itself, of morphological comparisons in history, Wittgenstein found deeply interesting; we often talked about this.)

Literature about Wittgenstein in this genre was for a long time conspicuously absent. The vogue of 'Wittgensteinianism' of the first two postwar decades was rather narrowly 'professional'. It disregarded the broader cultural perspectives. An explanation for this is perhaps the fact that whereas Wittgenstein's influence then was mainly in the Anglo-Saxon

[1] Norman Malcolm, *Ludwig Wittgenstein: A Memoir*, Oxford University Press, London, 1958; Fania Pascal, 'Wittgenstein: A Personal Memoir', in C.G. Luckhardt (ed.), *Wittgenstein, Sources and Perspectives*, Cornell University Press, Ithaca, NY, 1979 and in R. Rhees (ed.), *Ludwig Wittgenstein: Personal Recollections*, Basil Blackwell, Oxford, 1981 (first published in a slightly different form in *Encounter* **41**, 1973).

world, his background was central European. The portrait of the man implicit in the writings of his British and American pupils and followers was – as an Italian writer put it – that of a cultural illiterate.[2] Partly as a consequence of the gradual reception of Wittgenstein's philosophy by the German-speaking and Latin worlds this portrait is now being corrected. The publication of the *Vermischte Bemerkungen* (1977)[3] will, I hope, contribute to a better understanding both of Wittgenstein's roots in European culture and of his significance to our times.

My own attitude to this kind of writing is ambivalent. I find it interesting when done with due knowledge and respect for facts and insight into the connections. When it does not meet these requirements I think it silly, even disturbing. I do not feel strongly tempted to contribute more myself to this genre, and I have no desire to act as arbiter between conflicting visions in these matters.

I first met and got to know Wittgenstein in 1939 when I was doing postgraduate research at Cambridge. Someone lent me a copy of the Blue Book to read. When war broke out I was in Finland. Wittgenstein wrote to me that he wanted to give me a copy of 'the MS of what would be the first volume of my book. I have an idea,' he said, 'that it shall never be published in my life time and might perhaps be entirely lost. I should like to know that you had read it and had a copy of it.' I arranged for it to be sent to Finland by diplomatic mail, but never received it. I assume that Wittgenstein after all decided not to dispatch it. Soon after, Finland's 'Winter War' broke out – and the country's future must have seemed hopeless to a foreign spectator.

When I came to England after the war in 1947 and renewed acquaintance with Wittgenstein, he gave me the then existing version of the *Philosophical Investigations* to read. I can no longer recall whether this was, more or less, what comprises

[2] Diego Marconi, *Il mito del linguaggio scientifico, Studio su Wittgenstein*, U. Mursia & C., Milan, 1971.

[3] Translated into English as *Culture and Value*, Basil Blackwell, Oxford, 1980.

Part I of the work as printed, or whether it was what I have later called the intermediate version. (See the study on the origin and composition of the *Investigations* below.) But I remember that the epigraph was that of the intermediate and not that of the final version.

Later, when I had succeeded Wittgenstein in the Cambridge chair and he came to visit Cambridge, he stayed for quite long periods in my house. We read together some portions of Part II, but it seems that he was then still improving the text of Part I. (See p. 130 below. The names 'Part I' and 'Part II' were not used by Wittgenstein.) Wittgenstein never discussed with me the publication of his work, nor did he give me any instructions in case he was not able to finish it in his lifetime. (It was a surprise to me when, after Wittgenstein's death, I was told that he had named me one of his three literary executors. The other two were Elizabeth Anscombe and Rush Rhees.) But some time in 1950 he told me that he contemplated a mimeographed edition, copies of which could be given to friends and students to read. I *think*, but I cannot be certain, that he had then abandoned hope of knitting together the two parts which make up the posthumous publication.

What Wittgenstein in the letter quoted above calls 'the first volume of my book' was evidently the first half of the pre-war version of the *Investigations*. The 'second volume' would have been a new version of the second half of the pre-war version, dealing with the philosophy of mathematics. After Wittgenstein's death, his literary executors knew that he had been working on this 'second volume', and then abandoned the writing but probably not the conception of a work in two volumes. It therefore seemed to us clear from the beginning that it was our duty to publish, in addition to the two manuscripts which make up the two 'parts' of the *Investigations*, also some of the unfinished writings on mathematics. Beyond this we had, to begin with, no publication plans. Besides, we had a very fragmentary conception of the *Nachlass* itself.

In the essay below on 'The Wittgenstein Papers' I have told the story of how the *Nachlass* gradually became disclosed to us. I had not had the faintest notion that its extent was so enormous.

The work, hardly yet finished, that we have undertaken as editors of Wittgenstein's posthumous papers, is open to criticism. The difficulties of the task, and our inexperience of this kind of scholarly work, may explain the shortcomings but cannot always excuse them. Perhaps we should have been more explicit about what we were doing, for example, by adding footnotes on variant readings or on the interpretation of corrupt passages in the texts. But I still think that our leading principle was right; that is, to give to the world those of Wittgenstein's writings which we considered to be of prime importance in as 'naked' a form as possible with a minimum of footnotes or other visible learned apparatus.

Revised editions of some of the volumes have already been published. Other volumes ought to be improved upon. The volume that most of all needed improved editing was the German text of *Zettel*; the work has now been completed and the results incorporated into the second edition in English (1981) but the German text still awaits publication.

It was not until some 15 years after Wittgenstein's death that I started what could be termed 'research' on his literary output. The impetus came from the distressing discovery that some items in the *Nachlass* which I knew had existed after his death in 1951 had since been destroyed or otherwise vanished. It was high time to bring together what was scattered and deposit it in a safe place. The best place, and one which would also have had Wittgenstein's approval, seemed to us to be the Wren Library of Trinity College, Cambridge. In May 1969 we gave all the manuscripts and typescripts in our possession to the college. After the death of the last survivor among the literary executors the copyright in possible further publications will also pass to the college.

The efforts to collect the *Nachlass* were not completely successful, however. A part of it existed in Austria and was outside the control of the literary executors. Some of this material later joined the collection in Trinity but the rest was sold to the Bodleian Library, Oxford, and the Österreichische Nationalbibliothek in Vienna.

Considering that some items belonging to the *Nachlass* came to light only recently, it cannot be regarded as totally impossible that there still exist 'originals' of Wittgenstein's writings in other places than the three here mentioned.

For the sake of making the Wittgenstein papers available to a broader circle of researchers, a microfilm of the *Nachlass* was made for Cornell University Library in 1967. Several libraries throughout the world subsequently acquired copies of the film.

The most surprising discovery in my search for items of the *Nachlass* was a notebook from the time of the First World War containing a complete handwritten manuscript of the whole of the *Tractatus* – although with some differences from the final printed text. This finding inspired my study of the origin and publication history of Wittgenstein's early masterpiece. Of crucial importance to this study became the accessibility of materials from the estate of the late C.K. Ogden relating to the translation and publication of Wittgenstein's book in England.

My research on the history of the *Tractatus* had essentially been a one-man job. Not so the research on the origin and composition of the *Investigations* on which I embarked in 1973 and which now, eight years later, has virtually come to an end (cf. below pp. 111–136). In this work I have had the invaluable help of my two research assistants, André Maury and Heikki Nyman. The most important fruits of this research are embodied in the central study of this collection. But I should like to give a brief account here also of the plan of the work in Helsinki on the *Investigations* and the path it has followed.

A first task was to try to trace all the printed remarks in the book back to their sources in the manuscripts. By a 'source' we understood a manuscript entry (probably) used by Wittgenstein in the dictation (or other construction) of the succession of typescripts leading up to the ones from which the book was eventually printed. The task of tracing these sources was accomplished, essentially, by Dr Maury. He also performed an analogous task for the remarks in *Zettel*. The resulting tables have recently been published.[4] A 'source' in the sense just defined may in its turn have one or several 'predecessors', that is, preliminary versions of a source entry may be found in

<hr />

[4] A. Maury, 'Sources of the Remarks in Wittgenstein's *Zettel*', *Philosophical Investigations* **4**, 1981.

other (earlier) manuscripts. We have so far *not* traced systematically these 'background sources', as they may also be called. This is a task still to be done.

The second main task concerned the typescripts. They had to be 'edited'. The meaning of this we have defined as follows: A 'clean' typed page is produced which does not show variant readings, words crossed out or changed or added, the author's indications of a change in the order of the remarks, etc. In a special apparatus of notes, or 'comments', the items on the original typescript page which are not shown on the clean page are then duly recorded – with the exception of such marks in the typescript which seemed to us too unimportant to deserve listing. In addition we mention in the comments the manuscript source of the typed remarks and *all differences between the typed text and the printed, 'final' text of the book.*

The texts that the literary executors have edited and published so far are also 'clean' in the sense that they do not usually show variants and changes made by Wittgenstein in the underlying typescripts or manuscripts. But these published texts are also edited in a stronger sense than ours, since a choice between variant readings has been made by the editors.

In the case of some of the early versions of Wittgenstein's *Investigations* being published – and I hope that this will happen – it would be easy to omit from our notes on the typescripts such comments that may be thought too heavy or pedantic.

The principles of editing and critical points in the comments have always been discussed and decided by joint agreement between Heikki Nyman and myself. But the producing of the clean text and the primary composition of the comments is the work of Mr Nyman alone. Both his devotion to the task and his skill in performing it seem to me exemplary.

For each of the texts edited and commented on we have written an editorial preface – sometimes not particularly short – which describes the history of this particular text and discusses problems connected with it. The Prefaces and all the editorial comments are in German.

To some of the edited texts there are Appendices (*Anhänge*) – mainly tables of correspondences between the various typescripts or between the typescripts and their manuscript sources. In some Appendices independent items from the *Nachlass* are reproduced.

The following are the Wittgenstein texts that we have thus edited and commented on:

(1) The typescripts numbered in the catalogue (p. 47 below) TS 220 and TS 221. They form a whole called by us the early or pre-war version of the *Investigations*. The principal manuscript source of the first is from the autumn of 1936 and that of the main bulk of the second from the autumn of 1937. At the end of the second there are some additions made early in 1939. With these two typescripts goes a separate, typed Preface (*Vorwort*), TS 225, which is dated 'Cambridge, August 1938'. It is in substance very like the Preface of the work as printed, but it also contains some rather puzzling remarks about the text on which we have commented in *our* editorial preface.

These two typescripts, 220 and 221, are the early forms of what Wittgenstein later speaks of as the *first* and the *second* volumes of his work. (Cf. the letter to me of September 1939 quoted above.)

(2) Typescript 239. This typescript, which, strangely, came to our knowledge as late as 1977, is a *Bearbeitung* (revision) of TS 220, Wittgenstein's 'first volume'. It contains a number of changes and a partial reordering of the material in 220 but does not substantially expand the content of 220. Wittgenstein made the revisions round the turn of the year 1942–43, working on copies of 220.

(3) A typescript of 195 pages and containing 300 numbered remarks, presumably made early in 1945. This we have called the intermediate version of the *Investigations*. The typescript begins with the Preface of the book as printed. This Preface, readers will remember, is dated 'Cambridge, im Januar 1945'. The typescript is based on TS 239 (220) to which has been added more than a hundred new remarks written in the second half of 1944.

This intermediate version has not survived in the form of one separate typescript. The greater part of it is the beginning of the typescript (TS 227) of Part I of the printed *Investigations*. A minor part has survived partly in the form of a collection of odd folios which Wittgenstein gave to me some time in 1949 or 1950, partly as 'old', renumbered folios among pages 144–195 of TS 227. The greater and the smaller part make up a complete whole. It should be born in mind, however, that this whole, the 'intermediate version', is a reconstruction.

(4)   TS 227. Later in the year 1945 Wittgenstein expanded the then existing intermediate version with some 400 remarks the manuscript sources of which are in his writings from almost the entire period after his return in 1929 to Cambridge. In a letter to Rush Rhees of June 1945 he still refers to this as 'my first volume'. As already said, this is the typescript of what the editors (Anscombe and Rhees) called 'Part I' of the book as printed. The copy of the typescript from which the printing took place is, regrettably, lost. The edited typescript with comments produced by us in Helsinki is made from the only surviving copy of 227. In editing we encountered some problems arising from the fact that many of the corrections and additions to it were not inserted into this copy by Wittgenstein himself but later transferred from the printer's copy.

(5)   Part II of the *Investigations*. No typescript at all has survived. Our edited text is based on a *manuscript* (MS 144) made by Wittgenstein himself using source material written in the three years from 1946 to 1949. When this manuscript is edited, following Wittgenstein's instructions in the margin about the reordering of remarks, a text is obtained which is practically identical with the printed text of Part II. There are some minor deviations which may be worth noting for future printings of the book.

Part II of the *Investigations* as we have it must not be confused with the projected second volume of Wittgenstein's work. This second volume was going to be a revised and probably also much expanded version of TS 221 or of the second half of the pre-war version of the *Investigations*. The volume, as we have seen, was to deal with the philosophy of mathematics. The greater part of Wittgenstein's work in the period 1937–44 was devoted to this theme. The only typescript existing, TS 222, is a revision of TS 221. It was printed posthumously as Part I of the work called by its editors *Bemerkungen über die Grundlagen der Mathematik (Remarks on the Foundations of Mathematics)*. The rest of that work is manuscript material from the period mentioned.

Copies of the edited and commented material have been deposited in the University Libraries of Cambridge and of Cornell, in the Wren Library of Trinity College, Cambridge, and in the Bodleian Library, Oxford. They are accessible to students who are interested in or wish to do research on the *Werdegang*, the origins, of Wittgenstein's *magnum opus*. In spite of all care, errors may have occurred in the comments. We shall be grateful if we are notified of any errors or inadequacies found.

It should be stressed once again that the research has been on the manuscripts and typescripts and *not* on the thoughts contained in them. Therefore this research, as such, is not a contribution to philosophy nor even to the history of ideas. At best it has been a necessary preparation for a clarification of the development of Wittgenstein's ideas in the *Investigations* and an aid to understanding his thoughts. If this has been achieved we regard our labour as amply rewarded.

As mentioned already, three of the essays concern aspects of Wittgenstein's philosophy. 'Wittgenstein on Probability' deals with one of the few topics that can be treated in relative isolation from the rest of his philosophy. The subject, moreover, has not been treated in detail before – its treatment in the paper may therefore be of interest both to students of Wittgenstein and to students of the history of probability. I have had some doubts about including the paper 'Wittgenstein on Certainty'. It was at the time of its composition perhaps the fullest presentation of the newly published *Über Gewissheit* (On Certainty) containing Wittgenstein's latest philosophical writings. Since then this wonderful little book has been widely read and also had a considerable influence. The expert will not find anything original in my study of it. But the uninitiated may still find it stimulating and useful as an introduction. The essay on modal logic and the *Tractatus*, finally, is an essentially new study, undertaken for this collection.

Wittgenstein influenced my intellectual development more than anyone else could have done. He did this partly by his teaching and writing, but mainly by *example*. I was not able to follow him very well in my own work – not only because my thinking cannot reach the standards he set, but also because his *style* of thought is so different from my own. I admire it but cannot (even try to) imitate it. Perhaps this explains why my constant preoccupation with Wittgenstein has been mainly with the externalities of his writings and not with the substance of his ideas. But this occupation too has kept alive the example, and I thought it fit, as a token of gratitude, to dedicate this collection of studies to the memory of Ludwig Wittgenstein.

LUDWIG WITTGENSTEIN
A Biographical Sketch

I wrote this biographical sketch not long after Wittgenstein's death. It was first published, in Swedish, in the yearbook *Ajatus* of the Philosophical Society of Finland in 1954. An English version appeared in the *Philosophical Review* one year later. It was reprinted in Norman Malcolm's *Ludwig Wittgenstein: A Memoir* (Oxford University Press, London) in 1958. For the reprint of this work in 1967 I made a number of corrections and revisions. A few remaining inaccuracies have now been removed. Some of them relate to Wittgenstein's life during the years immediately before the Second World War; another concerns my previous unqualified statement that Wittgenstein was not a pantheist. And a longish footnote has been added (note 15) on 'ancestors' in philosophy.

ON 29 April 1951 there died in Cambridge one of the greatest and most influential philosophers of our time, Ludwig Wittgenstein.

It has been said that Wittgenstein inspired two important schools of thought, both of which he repudiated. The one is so-called logical positivism or logical empiricism, which played a prominent role during the decade immediately preceding the Second World War. The other is an even more heterogeneous trend which cannot be covered by *one* name. In its early phase it was sometimes called the Cambridge School of analysis. After the war its influence came to prevail at Oxford and the movement became known as linguistic philosophy, or the Oxford School.

It is true that the philosophy of Wittgenstein has been of great importance to both of these trends in contemporary thought: to the first, his early work *Tractatus Logico-Philosophicus* and discussions with some members of the Vienna Circle; to the second, besides the *Tractatus*, his lectures at Cambridge and also glimpses of the works which he did not publish in his lifetime. It is also partly true that Wittgenstein repudiated the results of his own influence. He did not participate in the worldwide discussion to which his work and thought had given rise. He was of the opinion – justified, I believe – that his ideas were usually misunderstood and distorted even by those who professed to be his disciples. He doubted that he would be better understood in the future. He once said that he felt as though he were writing for people who would think in a quite different way, breathe a different air of life, from that of present-day men. For people of a different culture, as it were. [1] That was *one* reason why he did not himself publish his later works.

Wittgenstein avoided publicity. He withdrew from every contact with his surroundings that he thought undesirable. Outside the circle of his family and personal friends, very little was known about his life and character. His inaccessibility

[1] See his Foreword to *Philosophische Bemerkungen* (*Philosophical Remarks*) and my essay 'Wittgenstein in Relation to his Times' below.

contributed to absurd legends about his personality and to widespread misunderstandings of his teaching. The data published in his obituaries have often been erroneous and the atmosphere of most biographical articles on Wittgenstein that I have read has been alien to their subject.

Ludwig Josef Johann Wittgenstein was born in Vienna on 26 April 1889. The Wittgenstein family had migrated from Saxony to Austria. It is of Jewish descent. It is not, contrary to what has often been stated, related to the house of princes of the same name. Wittgenstein's grandfather was a convert from the Jewish religion to Protestantism. His mother was a Roman Catholic. Ludwig Wittgenstein was baptized in the Catholic Church.

Wittgenstein's father must have been a man of remarkable intelligence and willpower. He was an engineer who became a leading figure in the iron and steel industry of the Austro-Hungarian empire. Wittgenstein's mother was responsible for a strong artistic influence in the family. Both she and her husband were highly musical. The wealthy and cultured home of the Wittgensteins became a centre of musical life. Johannes Brahms was a close friend of the family.

Ludwig was the youngest of five brothers and three sisters. Nature was lavish to all the children both in respect of character and of artistic and intellectual talents. Ludwig Wittgenstein was undoubtedly a most uncommon man. Though he was free from that form of vanity which shows itself in a desire to seem different, it was inevitable that he should stand out sharply from his surroundings. It is probably true that he lived on the border of mental illness. A fear of being driven across it followed him throughout his life. But it would be wrong to say of his work that it had a morbid character. It is deeply original but not at all eccentric. It has the same naturalness, frankness, and freedom from all artificiality that was characteristic of him.

Wittgenstein was educated at home until he was 14. For three years thereafter he was at a school at Linz in Upper Austria. It seems to have been his wish to study physics with Boltzmann in Vienna. However, Boltzmann died in 1906, the same year that Wittgenstein finished school. Wittgenstein proceeded to the Technische Hochschule in Berlin-Charlottenburg.

That he chose to study engineering was a consequence of his early interests and talents, rather than of his father's influence. Throughout his life he was extremely interested in machinery. While a small boy he constructed a sewing machine that aroused much admiration. Even in his last years he would spend a whole day with his beloved steam-engines in the South Kensington Museum. There are several anecdotes of his serving as a mechanic when machinery that was out of order needed mending.

Wittgenstein remained in Berlin until the spring of 1908. Then he went to England. In the summer of 1908 he was experimenting with kites at the Kite Flying Upper Atmosphere Station near Glossop, in Derbyshire. The same autumn he registered as a research student in the department of engineering at the University of Manchester. He was registered there until the autumn of 1911, but spent substantial periods on the Continent. During those three years he was occupied with research in aeronautics. From his kite-flying experiments he passed on to the construction of a jet reaction propeller for aircraft. At first it was the engine that absorbed his interest, but soon he concentrated on the design of the propeller, which was essentially a mathematical task. It was at this time that Wittgenstein's interests began to shift, first to pure mathematics and then to the foundations of mathematics.

Wittgenstein once mentioned to me that the problems on which he worked during his Manchester years had since become very urgent. I regret that I was not curious enough to ask him more. I assume that he was thinking of the role which the reaction engine has come to play, especially in aeronautics.[2]

In Wittgenstein's life the years from 1906 to 1912 were a

[2] Data about Wittgenstein's time at Manchester have been recorded by Mr W. Eccles and Mr W. Mays. The design of the reaction engine and a number of other documents relating to this period in Wittgenstein's life have been deposited in the University Library at Manchester. I am told that Wittgenstein had patented some of his inventions in the field of aeronautics.

time of painful seeking and of final awakening to clarity about his vocation. He told me that in those years he was constantly unhappy. To his restlessness bear witness the several interruptions of work already begun and the flights to something new: the departure from Germany to England, the experiments with kites, the construction of the jet engine, the design of the propeller, the interest in pure mathematics and finally in the philosophy of mathematics.

It is said that Wittgenstein asked someone for advice about literature on the foundations of mathematics and was directed to Bertrand Russell's *Principles of Mathematics*, which had appeared in 1903. It seems clear that this book profoundly affected Wittgenstein's development, and was probably what led him to study the works of Frege. The 'new' logic which in Frege and Russell had two of its most brilliant representatives, became the gateway through which Wittgenstein entered philosophy.

If I remember rightly,[3] Wittgenstein told me that he had read Schopenhauer's *Die Welt als Wille und Vorstellung* in his youth and that his first philosophy was a Schopenhauerian epistemological idealism. I know nothing of how this interest was related to his interest in logic and the philosophy of mathematics, except that I remember his saying that it was Frege's conceptual realism which made him abandon his earlier idealistic views.

Having decided to give up his studies in engineering, Wittgenstein first went to Jena in Germany to discuss his plans with Frege. It was apparently Frege who advised Wittgenstein to go to Cambridge and study with Russell. He followed the advice.[4]

[3] The biographical information I acquired from conversations with Wittgenstein I did not record on paper until after his death. I felt very strongly that it would have been improper to write them down following our conversations. He did not often talk about his past and only rarely of his youth, which was to him a painful recollection. The idea that someone was collecting data for a biography would certainly have been deeply distasteful to him.

[4] This is how Wittgenstein related the matter to me. His account is confirmed by notes made by his sister Hermine. Russell seems, therefore, to

This was probably in the autumn of 1911.[5] At the beginning of the following year he was admitted to Trinity College and registered in the University, first as an undergraduate and later as an 'advanced student'. He was at Cambridge for all three terms of the year 1912 and the first two terms of 1913. At the beginning of the autumn of 1913 he visited Norway with David Pinsent, a young mathematician with whom he had made friends at Cambridge. After a short visit to England in October, he returned to Norway alone and took up residence on a farm at Skjolden in Sogn, north-east of Bergen. Here he lived for most of the time until the outbreak of war in 1914. He liked the people and the country very much and eventually learned to speak Norwegian fairly well. In an isolated place near Skjolden he built himself a hut, where he could live in complete seclusion.

The decade before the First World War was a period of exceptional intellectual activity at Cambridge. Bertrand Russell had arrived at the summit of his powers. He and A.N. Whitehead wrote *Principia Mathematica*, a milestone in the history of logic. The most influential philosopher was G.E. Moore. Wittgenstein soon became intimate with Russell,[6] and he saw much of Moore and Whitehead. Among Wittgenstein's friends during his early years at Cambridge should also be mentioned J.M. Keynes, the economist, G.H. Hardy, the mathematician, and the logician W.E. Johnson. Wittgenstein's *Tractatus* is dedicated to the memory of David Pinsent, who fell in the war.

Besides philosophy Wittgenstein did some experimental work in psychology at Cambridge. He carried out an inves-

---

be mistaken when in his memorial article in *Mind*, n.s., **60**, 1951, he says that Wittgenstein had not known Frege before he came to Cambridge.

[5] I have not been able to fix the exact dates of Wittgenstein's first visit to Frege and arrival at Cambridge. He was registered at Manchester for the Michaelmas term of 1911.

[6] Russell wrote, in his memorial article in *Mind*: 'Getting to know Wittgenstein was one of the most exciting intellectual adventures of my life.'

tigation at the psychological laboratory concerning rhythm in music. He had hoped that the experiments would throw light on some questions of aesthetics that interested him. Wittgenstein was exceptionally musical, even if judged by the highest standards. He played the clarinet, and for a time he wished to become a conductor. He had a rare talent for whistling. It was a great pleasure to hear him whistle through a whole concerto, interrupting himself only to draw the listener's attention to some detail of the musical texture.

An important source of our knowledge of Wittgenstein during these years is a series of letters he wrote to Russell. Another is Pinsent's diary of their Cambridge life and their travels to Iceland and Norway. The letters and the diary help to illuminate Wittgenstein's personality, not only as a young man, but also as he appeared to his friends of the 1930s and 1940s. The letters also contain interesting information about the gradual development of the work that first established Wittgenstein's fame as a philosopher.

Wittgenstein's earliest philosophical investigations were in the realm of the problems with which Frege and Russell had dealt. Concepts such as 'propositional function', 'variable', 'generality', and 'identity' occupied his thoughts. He soon made an interesting discovery, a new symbolism for so-called 'truth-functions' that led to the explanation of logical truth as 'tautology'.[7]

The oldest parts of the *Tractatus* are those dealing with logic. Wittgenstein had formed his principal thoughts on these matters before the outbreak of war in 1914, and thus before his 26th year. Later he became engrossed in a new problem. It was the question of the nature of the significant proposition.[8] There is a story of how the idea of language as a picture of reality occurred to Wittgenstein.[9] It was in the autumn of 1914, on

---

[7] The symbolism in question is much the same as that explained in *Tractatus* 6.1203. The now familiar truth-tables (*Tractatus* 4.31, etc.) he invented later.

[8] 'My *whole* task consists in explaining the nature of the proposition,' he wrote in one of the philosophical notebooks that he kept during the war.

[9] There exist several somewhat different versions of it. The story as told

the eastern front. Wittgenstein was reading in a magazine about a lawsuit in Paris concerning an automobile accident. At the trial a miniature model of the accident was presented before the court. The model here served as a proposition; that is, as a description of a possible state of affairs. It has this function owing to a correspondence between the parts of the model (the miniature-houses, -cars, -people) and things (houses, cars, people) in reality. It now occurred to Wittgenstein that one might reverse the analogy and say that a *proposition* serves as a model or *picture*, by virtue of a similar correspondence between *its* parts and the world. The way in which the parts of the proposition are combined – the *structure* of the proposition – depicts a possible combination of elements in reality, a possible state of affairs.

Wittgenstein's *Tractatus* may be called a synthesis of the theory of truth-functions and the idea that language is a picture of reality. Out of this synthesis arises a third main ingredient of the book, its doctrine of that which cannot be *said*, only *shown*.

At the outbreak of war, Wittgenstein entered the Austrian army as a volunteer, although he had been exempted from service because of a rupture. He served first on a vessel on the Vistula and then in an artillery workshop at Cracow. Later he fought on the eastern front. In 1916 he was ordered to Olmütz, in Moravia, to be trained as an officer. In 1918 he was transferred to the southern front. Upon the collapse of the Austro-Hungarian army in October, he was taken prisoner by the Italians. It was not until August of the following year that he could return to Austria. During the major part of his captivity, he was in a prison camp near Monte Cassino, in southern Italy.

---

here is based on an entry in Wittgenstein's philosophical notebooks in June 1930. It would be interesting to know whether Wittgenstein's conception of the proposition as a picture is connected in any way with the Introduction to Heinrich Hertz's *Die Prinzipen der Mechanik*. Wittgenstein knew this work and held it in high esteem. There are traces of the impression that it made on him both in the *Tractatus* and in his later writings.

When Wittgenstein was captured he had in his rucksack the manuscript of his *Logisch-philosophische Abhandlung*, which is generally known by the Latin title proposed for it by G.E. Moore, *Tractatus Logico-Philosophicus*. He had completed the work when on a leave of absence, in August 1918. While still in captivity he got in touch with Russell by letter and was able to send the manuscript to him, thanks to the aid of one of his friends of the Cambridge years, Keynes. He also sent Frege a copy and corresponded with him.

It was Wittgenstein's habit to write down his thoughts in notebooks. The entries are usually dated, and thus they comprise a sort of diary. The contents of an earlier notebook are often worked over again in a later one. Sometimes he dictated to colleagues and pupils. In the spring of 1914 he dictated some thoughts on logic to Moore in Norway. In the late 1920s and early 1930s he dictated to Schlick and Wais- mann. The so-called Blue Book was dictated in conjunction with lectures at Cambridge in the academic year 1933–34. The so-called Brown Book was dictated privately to some pupils in 1934–35.

Several of the notebooks which led up to the *Tractatus* have been preserved. These sketches and fragments of earlier versions are of great interest, partly because they show the development of his thoughts, partly because they illuminate many difficult passages in the extremely compressed final version. I have been especially impressed by a notebook of the year 1916. It deals chiefly with the ego, the freedom of the will, the meaning of life, and death. Thus the somewhat aphoristic remarks on these topics in the *Tractatus* are sifted from a quantity of material. The notes show how strong were the impressions   that   Wittgenstein   had   received   from Schopenhauer. An occasional Spinozistic flavour is also recog- nizable.

In the earliest notebooks a considerable part of the content is written in a code. Wittgenstein continued to use this code throughout his life. The notes in code are for the most part of a personal nature.

The period of the war was a crisis in Wittgenstein's life. To what extent the turmoil of the time and his experiences in war and captivity contributed to the crisis, I cannot say. A circumstance of great importance was that he became acquainted with the ethical and religious writings of Tolstoy. Tolstoy exercised a strong influence on Wittgenstein's view of life, and also led him to study the Gospels.

After the death of his father in 1912 Wittgenstein was in possession of a great fortune. One of his first steps after his return from the war was to give away all his money.[10] Henceforth a great simplicity, at times even an extreme frugality, became characteristic of his life. His dress was unconventional; it is impossible to imagine him with tie or hat. A bed, a table, and a few deckchairs were all he had of furniture. Ornamental objects of whatever kind were banished from his surroundings.

After the war Wittgenstein took up the vocation of schoolmaster. In 1919–20 he was trained at a college for teachers in elementary schools (*Lehrerbildungsanstalt*) in Vienna. From 1920 to 1926 he taught in various remote villages in the districts of Schneeberg and Semmering in Lower Austria. This suited his wish for a simple and secluded life. In other ways it did not suit him well. It appears that he was in constant friction with the people around him. Finally there a serious crisis. Wittgenstein resigned his post and quitted forever the career of schoolmaster. He went to work as a gardener's assistant with the monks at Hütteldorf, near Vienna.

In this period, Wittgenstein contemplated entering a monastery. The same thought occurred to him at other times in his life too. That it never came true was, partly at least, because for him the inner conditions of monastic life were not satisfied.

His service with the monks soon came to an end. In the

---

[10] Before the war Wittgenstein had made a large anonymous grant for the promotion of literature. Two poets of whom he was in this manner a benefactor were Georg Trakl and Rainer Maria Rilke. (For more details see Ludwig Ficker's article 'Rilke und der unbekannte Freund', in *Der Brenner*, 1954.) It may be remarked in passing that Wittgenstein had a high opinion of Trakl's talent, but that later in life, at least, he did not greatly admire Rilke, whose poetry he thought artificial.

autumn of 1926 Wittgenstein accepted a task that absorbed his
time and genius for two years. He built a mansion in Vienna
for one of his sisters. In the beginning he co-operated with his
friend, the architect Paul Engelmann. But soon Wittgenstein
took over entirely. The building is his work down to the
smallest detail and is highly characteristic of its creator. It is
free from all decoration and marked by a severe exactitude in
measure and proportion. Its beauty is of the same simple and
static kind that belongs to the sentences of the *Tractatus*. It does
not seem to me that the building can be classified as belonging
to some one style. But the horizontal roofs and the materials –
concrete, glass, and steel – remind the spectator of typically
'modern' architecture.[11] (In 1914 Wittgenstein had come to
know Adolf Loos, whose work he admired.)

During this same period Wittgenstein executed a sculpture
in the studio of his friend, the sculptor Drobil. It is the head of
a young woman. The features have the same finished and
restful beauty one finds in Greek sculptures of the classical
period and which seems to have been Wittgenstein's ideal. In
general, there is a striking contrast between the restlessness,
the continual searching and changing, in Wittgenstein's life
and personality, and the perfection and elegance of his finished
work.

The author of the *Tractatus* thought he had solved all
philosophical problems. It was consistent with this view that
he should give up philosophy.

The publication of the book was largely due to Russell. In
1919 the two friends met in Holland to discuss the manuscript.
The problem of finding a publisher caused difficulties and the
matter was further complicated by Wittgenstein's strong
disapproval of Russell's Introduction to the book. In July 1920
Wittgenstein wrote to Russell that he himself would take no

---

[11] Later the house was threatened by destruction. The garden adjoining it
was vandalized and the house eventually sold to the state of Bulgaria. For a
history and description of the building in its original shape, see Bernhard
Leitner, *The Architecture of Ludwig Wittgenstein, A Documentation with
Excerpts from the Family Recollections by Hermine Wittgenstein*, The Press of the
Nova Scotia College of Art and Design, Chatham (England), 1973.

further steps to have it published and that Russell could do with it as he wished. The German text was published in 1921 in the last issue of Ostwald's *Annalen der Naturphilosophie*. In the following year it was published in London with a parallel English translation.

During his years as schoolmaster and architect, Wittgenstein was not completely cut off from contact with the philosophical world. In 1923 a young man from Cambridge, Frank Ramsey, visited him at Puchberg, where he was then teaching. Ramsey had assisted in the translation of the *Tractatus* and had written, at the age of 20, a remarkably penetrating review of the book for *Mind*. The visit was repeated a year later. Ramsey tried to persuade Wittgenstein to come to England on a visit. He was helped in his efforts by Keynes, who even procured money for the purpose. In the summer of 1925 Wittgenstein finally did visit his English friends.

After Ramsey, Moritz Schlick, a professor in Vienna, managed to establish contact with Wittgenstein. The study of the latter's book had made a deep impression on this honest and intelligent man, who was to become famous as the founder and leader of the Vienna Circle. Wittgenstein's influence on the philosophical movement which the Vienna Circle started is thus in part due to a personal connection, lasting for a number of years, between Wittgenstein and Schlick. Another member of the Circle who was personally strongly influenced by Wittgenstein was Friedrich Waismann.

Wittgenstein said that he returned to philosophy because he felt that he could again do creative work. An external circumstance of this important step may have been that in March of 1928 he had heard Brouwer lecture in Vienna on the foundations of mathematics. It is rumoured to have been this which stirred him to take up philosophy again. [12] Early in 1929 Wittgenstein arrived at Cambridge. He was first registered as a research student, a somewhat unusual status for a man whom many already regarded as one of the foremost living representatives of his subject. The idea was that he should

[12] Cf. Herbert Feigl, 'The Wiener Kreis in America', *Perspectives in American History*, vol. 2, Harvard University Press, 1968, p. 639.

work for a Ph.D. It turned out, however, that he could count his pre-war residence at Cambridge as credit towards the degree and could present his book, published eight years earlier, as a thesis. He received his degree in June 1929. The following year he was made a Fellow of Trinity College.

Soon after his return to Cambridge Wittgenstein began to write down philosophical thoughts. His output in the years 1929–32 was, as always from then on, tremendous. From the manuscript notebooks he sifted remarks for two bulky typescripts. One is called *Philosophische Bemerkungen* (*Philosophical Remarks*); for the other he contemplated the names *Philosophische Betrachtungen* (*Philosophical Reflections*) or *Philosophische Grammatik* (*Philosophical Grammar*). They are virtually completed works.[13] But Wittgenstein did not publish them.

The only philosophical writing that Wittgenstein himself published subsequent to the *Tractatus* was the paper 'Some Remarks on Logical Form'.[14] This paper was supposed to have been read by him to the annual meeting of British philosophers – the Joint Session of the Mind Association and the Aristotelian Society – in 1929. The papers prepared for these meetings are printed and distributed to the participants in advance, and are subsequently collected in a Supplementary Volume to the Proceedings of the Aristotelian Society. Wittgenstein surprised his audience by talking to them on an entirely different topic – the notion of the infinite in mathematics – and not reading his paper at all. Wittgenstein himself thought this paper worthless.

[13] It was in reference to the *Philosophical Remarks* that Bertrand Russell, in 1930, reported to the Council of Trinity College, which was considering the award of a grant to Wittgenstein, as follows: 'The theories contained in this new work of Wittgenstein are novel, very original, and indubitably important. Whether they are true, I do not know. As a logician, who likes simplicity, I should wish to think that they are not, but from what I have read of them I am quite sure that he ought to have an opportunity to work them out, since when completed they may easily prove to constitute a whole new philosophy.' (Quoted with the permission of Lord Russell and the Council of Trinity College, Cambridge.)

[14] While he was a schoolmaster he published a German glossary for elementary schools, *Wörterbuch für Volks- und Bürgerschulen*, Holder-Piehler-Tempsky, Vienna, 1926.

Wittgenstein's writings of the period anterior to the Blue Book are of considerable interest, not least to the historian of philosophical ideas. Their intrinsic value is, I think, less than that of either the *Tractatus* or the *Philosophical Investigations*. This is natural, considering that they represent a transitional stage in Wittgenstein's development.

It will probably remain a matter of future debate to what extent there is continuity between the 'early' Wittgenstein of the *Tractatus* and the 'later' Wittgenstein of the *Investigations*. The writings from 1929 to 1932 testify to a continuous development and struggle – out of the former work and in the direction of the later. The Blue Book of 1933–34 conveys more the impression of a first, still somewhat rough version of a radically new philosophy. I myself find it difficult to fit the Blue Book into the development of Wittgenstein's thoughts. The Brown Book is a somewhat different case. It may be regarded as a preliminary version of the beginning of the *Investigations*. In August 1936 Wittgenstein began a revision, in German, of the Brown Book which had been dictated in English one year earlier. He called the revision *Philosophische Untersuchungen (Philosophical Investigations)*. He soon abandoned work on it as unsatisfactory, and made a fresh start in the autumn of the same year. What he then wrote is substantially identical with the first 188 sections of the *Investigations* in its printed form.

The young Wittgenstein had learned from Frege and Russell. His problems were in part theirs. The later Wittgenstein, in my view, has no ancestors in the history of thought. His work signals a radical departure from previously existing paths of philosophy.[15] But his problems grew to a great extent out of the *Tractatus*. This, I think, is the reason why Wittgenstein wanted the work which embodied his new

[15] I have seen this statement, and the one preceding it, contested. But I think they are substantially correct and also important. The *Tractatus* belongs in a definite tradition in European philosophy, extending back beyond Frege and Russell at least to Leibniz. Wittgenstein's so-called 'later philosophy', as I see it, is quite different. Its *spirit* is unlike anything I know in Western thought and in many ways opposed to aims and methods in traditional philosophy. This is not incompatible with the fact – about which

philosophy to be printed together with the work of his youth.[16]

It is sometimes said that the later Wittgenstein resembles Moore. This is hardly true. Moore's and Wittgenstein's ways of thinking are in fact utterly different. Although their friendship lasted until the latter's death, I do not believe that there is any trace of an influence of Moore's philosophy on Wittgenstein. What Wittgenstein appreciated was Moore's intellectual vitality, his love of truth and freedom from vanity.

Of great importance in the origination of Wittgenstein's new ideas was the criticism to which his earlier views were subjected by two of his friends. One was Ramsey, whose premature death in 1930 was a heavy loss to contemporary thought. The other was Piero Sraffa, an Italian economist who had come to Cambridge shortly before Wittgenstein returned there. It was above all Sraffa's acute and forceful criticism that compelled Wittgenstein to abandon his earlier views and set out upon new roads. He said that his discussions with Sraffa made him feel like a tree from which all branches had been cut. That this tree could become green again was due to its own vitality. The later Wittgenstein did not receive an inspiration from outside like that which the earlier Wittgenstein obtained from Frege and Russell.

From 1929 until his death, Wittgenstein lived – with some interruptions – in England. He became a British subject when, after the *Anschluss*, he had to give up his Austrian passport and make a choice between German and British nationality. But in

---

more is known now than when this essay was first published – that many of Wittgenstein's later ideas have *seeds* in works which he had read and conversations he had with others. It is interesting to note what Wittgenstein himself says about this in *Vermischte Bemerkungen* (edited by G.H. von Wright and translated into English by Peter Winch as *Culture and Value*, Basil Blackwell, Oxford, 1980), especially pp. 18 ff. and 36. In the latter place he says: 'I believe that my originality (if that is the right word) is an originality belonging to the soil rather than to the seed. (Perhaps I have no seed of my own.) Sow a seed in my soil and it will grow differently than it would in any other soil.'

[16] See the Preface to *Philosophical Investigations*.

general he was not fond of English ways of life and he disliked the academic atmosphere of Cambridge. When his Fellowship at Trinity College expired in 1935,[17] he had plans for settling in the Soviet Union. He visited Moscow and Leningrad in September and apparently was pleased with the visit. He did not go back, however, and from what he told me, I understood that the harshening of the political conditions in the Soviet Union in the mid-thirties had influenced his plans.[18] So Wittgenstein remained at Cambridge until the end of the academic year 1935–36. In the summer of 1936 he withdrew, after a holiday in France, to his hut in Norway. He stayed there, with an interruption around Christmas 1936, to nearly the end of the following year. In 1938 he returned to Cambridge. One year later he was elected to be Moore's successor in the chair in philosophy.

From the beginning of 1930 Wittgenstein lectured at Cambridge. As might be expected, his lectures were highly 'unacademic'.[19] He nearly always held them in his own room or in the college rooms of a friend. He had no manuscript or notes. He *thought* before the class. The impression was of a tremendous concentration. The exposition usually led to a question, to which the audience were supposed to suggest an answer. The answers in turn became starting points for new thoughts leading to new questions. It depended on the audience, to a great extent, whether the discussion became fruitful and whether the connecting thread was kept in sight from the beginning to end of a lecture and from one lecture to another. Many members of his audiences were highly qualified people in their various fields. Moore attended Wittgen-

[17] The Fellowship was prolonged to include the whole of the academic year 1935–36. When he became a professor, Wittgenstein was again made a Fellow of Trinity College.

[18] Fania Pascal doubts that thought of the political developments in the Soviet Union influenced Wittgenstein's plans. See her essay 'Wittgenstein: A Personal Memoir', in R. Rhees (ed.), *Ludwig Wittgenstein: Personal Recollections*, Basil Blackwell, Oxford, 1981, pp. 42 ff. and pp. 54 ff.

[19] A vivid and accurate impression of Wittgenstein as a teacher is conveyed by the memorial article, signed D.A.T.G.–A.C.J., in *Australasian Journal of Philosophy* **29**, 1951.

stein's lectures for some years in the early 1930s.[20] Several of
those who later became leading philosophers in England, the
United States, or Australia heard Wittgenstein lecture at
Cambridge. There exist good, more or less verbatim notes of
some of his lecture courses.

Before Wittgenstein assumed his chair, the Second World
War broke out. I think one may say that he wished for the war.
But, as in 1914, he did not want to watch it from an ivory
tower. For some time he served as a porter at Guy's Hospital in
London. Later he worked in a medical laboratory at Newcastle. It should be mentioned that Wittgenstein had been
strongly attracted to the medical profession and that once in
the 1930s he seriously considered leaving philosophy to take
up medicine. During his time at Newcastle he devised some
technical innovations that proved useful.

It need not surprise us that Wittgenstein's restless genius
was not happy in academic routine. It is likely that if the war
had not come his tenure of the chair would have been even
briefer. In the Easter term of 1947 he gave his last lectures at
Cambridge. In the autumn he was on leave, and from the end
of the year he ceased to be a professor. He wanted to devote all
his remaining strength to his research. As so often before in his
life, he went to live in seclusion. For the winter of 1948 he
settled on a farm in the Irish countryside. After that he lived
quite by himself in a hut beside the ocean, in Galway on the
west coast of Ireland. His neighbours were primitive fisher-
men. It is said that Wittgenstein became a legend among his
neighbours because he had tamed so many birds; they used to
come every day to be fed by him. The life in Galway,
however, became physically too strenuous for him, and in the
autumn of 1948 he moved to a hotel in Dublin. From then
until early spring of the following year he had an excellent
working period. It was then he completed the second part of
the *Investigations*.

[20] Moore published a full account and an interesting discussion of these
lectures in *Mind*, n.s., **63–64**, 1954–55. Moore's articles can be said to be a
commentary on some of the views that Wittgenstein held in the 'period of
transition' (1929–33) preceding the Blue Book.

During the last two years of his life Wittgenstein was severely ill. In the autumn of 1949 it was found that he suffered from cancer. Wittgenstein was then on a visit to Cambridge after his return from a stay in the United States. He did not go back to Ireland, but remained with friends in Oxford and in Cambridge. In the autumn of 1950 he visited Norway with a friend and even had plans for settling there again at the beginning of the following year. During part of his illness he was incapable of work. But it is remarkable that during the last two months he was not in bed and was apparently in the best of spirits. As late as two days before his death he wrote down thoughts that are equal to the best he produced.

Wittgenstein's very unusual and forceful personality exerted a great influence over others. No one who came in touch with him could fail to be impressed. Some were repelled. Most were attracted or fascinated. One can say that Wittgenstein avoided making acquaintances, but needed and sought friendships. He was an incomparable, but demanding, friend. I believe that most of those who loved him and had his friendship also feared him.

Just as there were many groundless legends concerning Wittgenstein's life and personality, so there grew up much unsound sectarianism among his pupils. This caused Wittgenstein much pain. He thought that his influence as a teacher was, on the whole, harmful to the development of independent minds in his disciples. I am afraid that he was right. And I believe that I can partly understand why it should be so. Because of the depth and originality of his thinking, it is very difficult to understand Wittgenstein's ideas and even more difficult to incorporate them into one's own thinking. At the same time the magic of his personality and style was most inviting and persuasive. To learn from Wittgenstein without coming to adopt his forms of expression and catchwords and even to imitate his tone of voice, his mien and gestures, was almost impossible. The danger was that the thoughts should deteriorate into a jargon. The teaching of great men often has a simplicity and naturalness which makes the difficult appear easy to grasp. Their disciples usually become, therefore, insignificant epigones. The historical significance of such men does not manifest itself in their disciples but through influences of a more indirect, subtle, and often unexpected kind.

Wittgenstein's most characteristic features were his great and pure seriousness and powerful intelligence. I have never met a man who impressed me so strongly in either respect.

It seems to me that there are two forms of seriousness of character. One is fixed in 'strong principles'; the other springs from a passionate heart. The former has to do with morality and the latter, I believe, is closer to religion. Wittgenstein was acutely and even painfully sensitive to considerations of duty, but the earnestness and severity of his personality were more of the second kind. Yet I do not know whether he can be said to have been 'religious' in any but a trivial sense of the word. Certainly he did not have a Christian faith. But neither was his view of life un-Christian, pagan, as was Goethe's. To say that Wittgenstein was not a pantheist is to say something important.[21] 'God does not reveal himself *in* the world,' he wrote in the *Tractatus*. The thought of God, he said, was above all for him the thought of the fearful judge.

Wittgenstein had the conviction, he sometimes said, that he was doomed. His outlook was typically one of gloom. Modern times were to him a dark age.[22] His idea of the helplessness of human beings was not unlike certain doctrines of predestination.

Wittgenstein was not, strictly speaking, a learned man. His temperament was very different from that of the typical scholar. 'Cool objectivity' and 'detached meditation' are labels which do not suit him at all. He put his whole soul into everything he did. His life was a constant journey, and doubt was the moving force within him. He seldom looked back on his earlier positions, and when he did so it was usually to repudiate them.

[21] This statement must be modified, but I do not know exactly how. From the *Notebooks 1914–1916* a view can be extracted which identifies God and the world, not unlike Spinoza's *Deus sive Natura*. I am here indebted to Brian McGuinness. Cf. his paper 'The Mysticism of the *Tractatus*', *Philosophical Review* **75**, 1966.

[22] See the Preface to *Philosophical Investigations*: 'the darkness of these times'.

Knowledge, for Wittgenstein, was intimately connected with doing. It is significant that his first studies were in the technical sciences. He had a knowledge of mathematics and physics not derived from extensive reading, but from a working familiarity with mathematical and experimental techniques. His many artistic interests had the same active and living character. He could design a house, make a sculpture, or conduct an orchestra. Perhaps he would never have achieved mastery in those fields. But he was no 'dilettante'. Every manifestation of his multi-dimensional spirit came from the same earnest drive to create.

Wittgenstein had done no systematic reading in the classics of philosophy. He could read only what he could wholeheartedly assimilate. We have seen that as a young man he read Schopenhauer. From Spinoza, Hume, and Kant he said that he could only get occasional glimpses of understanding. I do not think that he could have enjoyed Aristotle or Leibniz, two great logicians before him. But it is significant that he did read and enjoy Plato. He must have recognized congenial features, both in Plato's literary and philosophical method and in the temperament behind the thoughts.

Wittgenstein received deeper impressions from some writers in the borderland between philosophy, religion, and poetry than from the philosophers, in the restricted sense of the word. Among the former are St Augustine, Kierkegaard, Dostoievsky, and Tolstoy. The philosophical sections of St Augustine's *Confessions* show a striking resemblance to Wittgenstein's own way of doing philosophy. Between Wittgenstein and Pascal there is a trenchant parallelism which deserves closer study. It should also be mentioned that Wittgenstein held the writings of Otto Weininger in high regard.

An aspect of Wittgenstein's work which is certain to attract growing attention is its language. It would be surprising if he were not one day ranked among the classic writers of German prose. The literary merits of the *Tractatus* have not gone unnoticed. The language of the *Investigations* is equally remarkable. The style is simple and perspicuous, the construction of sentences firm and free, the rhythm flows easily. The form is sometimes that of dialogue, with questions and replies;

sometimes, as in the *Tractatus*, it condenses to aphorisms. There is a striking absence of all literary ornamentation, and of technical jargon or terminology. The union of measured moderation with richest imagination, the simultaneous impression of natural continuation and surprising turns, leads one to think of some other great productions of the genius of Vienna. (Schubert was Wittgenstein's favourite composer.)

It may appear strange that Schopenhauer, one of the masters of philosophical prose, did not influence Wittgenstein's style. An author, however, who reminds one, often astonishingly, of Wittgenstein is Lichtenberg. Wittgenstein esteemed him highly. To what extent, if any, he can be said to have learned from him I do not know. It is deserving of mention that some of Lichtenberg's thoughts on philosophical questions show a striking resemblance to Wittgenstein's.[23]

It is fairly certain that both the work and personality of Wittgenstein will provoke varying comments and different interpretations in the future. The author of the sentences 'The riddle does not exist' and 'Everything that can be said can be said clearly' was himself an enigma, and his sentences have a content that often lies deep beneath the surface of the language. In Wittgenstein many contrasts meet. It has been said that he was at once a logician and a mystic. *Neither* term is appropriate, but each hints at something true. Those who approach Wittgenstein's work will sometimes look for its essence in a rational, matter-of-fact dimension, and sometimes more in a supra-empirical, metaphysical one. In the existing literature on Wittgenstein there are examples of both conceptions. Such 'interpretations' have little significance. They must appear as falsifications to anyone who tries to understand Wittgenstein in all his rich complexity. They are interesting only as showing in how many directions his influence extends. I have sometimes thought that what makes a man's work *classic* is often just this multiplicity, which invites and at the same time resists our craving for clear understanding.

[23] See my paper, 'Georg Christoph Lichtenberg als Philosoph', *Theoria* **8**, 1942.

THE WITTGENSTEIN PAPERS

This study of Wittgenstein's *Nachlass* (the work unpublished at his death) was originally published in the *Philosophical Review* **78**, 1969. Drafts of it were read by several persons. I am particularly indebted to Mr Rush Rhees and Mr Brian McGuinness for their invaluable help in my efforts to make accurate both the catalogue and the comments on individual items in it.

In the progress of my research on the *Nachlass* various errors were discovered and my opinion on the dates of some of the items changed. A number of typescripts I had not known of before came to light only late in the 1970s. A reissue of the catalogue became urgent. When preparing the present volume in 1981, I rewrote and expanded the essay. All my efforts notwithstanding, mistakes and lacunae may be found in it. I shall be grateful for any additional information and corrections that students of the Wittgenstein papers might want to suggest.

EARLY in February 1951, Wittgenstein moved to the house of Dr Edward Bevan at Cambridge, where he died on 29 April. During the last six weeks of his life he was working continuously. He had with him a number of manuscript notebooks containing his last writings. Other manuscripts and typescripts he had left in the house of Miss Anscombe at Oxford, where he had been living, with minor interruptions, since April 1950.

At the time of Wittgenstein's death his literary executors did not know for certain whether there existed papers other than those just referred to. We knew, however, that Wittgenstein on his last visit to Vienna, from Christmas 1949 to March 1950, had ordered a great many papers, belonging to all periods of his work, to be burned.[1] We also knew that, when living in Ireland after giving up his chair at Cambridge, Wittgenstein destroyed old material which he considered useless for his work. It was therefore not without surprise that we gradually realized that our initial estimate of the scope of the *Nachlass* was much mistaken.

In December 1951, the executor of Wittgenstein's will, Mr Rush Rhees, received a box which had been left by Wittgenstein in Trinity College. It was thought to contain some of his books, but turned out to contain a huge number of manuscripts. Professor G.E. Moore returned to us a typescript which Wittgenstein had left with him, probably in 1930, and showed us verbatim notes of dictations made in Norway in 1914. From Bertrand Russell we received copies of Wittgenstein's letters to him and of the 1913 'Notes on Logic'.[2] An early inquiry addressed to Dr Friedrich Waismann produced no answer, but after Dr Waismann's death in 1959 much material consisting of notes on conversations and also of some verbatim dictations came to light.[3]

[1] See Editors' Preface to the first edition of *Notebooks 1914–1916*, Basil Blackwell, Oxford, 1961 (2nd edition, 1979).

[2] Published as an Appendix in ibid.

[3] For an account of this material see the Preface by B. F. McGuinness to

In the summer of 1952 the literary executors visited Austria. At Gmunden in the house of Wittgenstein's sister, Mrs M. Stonborough, we were shown some manuscripts and typescripts, among them the three notebooks (1914–16) from the time of the germination of the *Tractatus*. Later the same year seven big manuscript volumes were discovered at the family estate, Hochreit. The literary executors had photographic copies made for them in England of the pre-*Tractatus* notebooks and of the Hochreit manuscripts.

Thirteen years later I revisited Vienna with the purpose of checking the Austrian material and obtaining copies of some of the items which, in addition to the 1914–16 notebooks, had been at Gmunden in 1952. Of this last material I found, alas, no trace. But in addition to the manuscript volumes 1 to 7 (items 105–111 of the catalogue), I found also volumes 8 and 9 (items 112 and 113). This filled the gap which had up to then existed between the Austrian material and the manuscript volumes in England, the earliest of which was numbered 10. An entirely unexpected discovery was that of a manuscript book containing a complete early version of the *Tractatus*.[4] A typescript of the *Tractatus* was also discovered.

Further searching for the missing items in the Gmunden material was without result. But in the course of this search a number of hitherto unknown typescripts were found in 1967.

In 1976 and 1977 further typescripts came to light. They are listed here as items 235–245 of the catalogue. The most interesting one among them is a revision of the first half of the pre-war version of the *Philosophical Investigations*.

In the summer of 1967 the part of the *Nachlass* which was then known to exist in England was temporarily collected at Oxford and microfilmed for Cornell University. The process was supervised by Professor Norman Malcolm and myself. Later in the same year copies of papers in the Austrian part of

---

F. Waismann, *Wittgenstein and the Vienna Circle*, Basil Blackwell, Oxford, 1979 (German edition, 1967). Cf. also the comment on items 302–308 of the catalogue below.

[4] Published under the title *Prototractatus*, with a facsimile of the author's manuscript, Routledge and Kegan Paul, London, 1971.

the *Nachlass* were filmed at Cornell. The material thus filmed is available to students and scholars. Some items belonging to the *Nachlass* that were found after 1967 are not on the film.

In May 1969 Wittgenstein's literary executors gave all their originals of the Wittgenstein papers to Trinity College, Cambridge. The originals are kept in the Wren Library. Wittgenstein himself had deposited his papers there during the Second World War; and later he indicated to one of us that he regarded the Library as a suitable place for their permanent custody. The typescripts that were found after 1969 are now also in Trinity.

Seven manuscript books of the Austrian *Nachlass* have been donated to the Wren Library. These are items 101, 102, 103, 108, 109, 110, and 111 in the catalogue. The early *Tractatus* manuscript (104) was sold to the Bodleian Library, Oxford, and items 105, 106, 107, 112, 113, and 203 to the Öster-reichische Nationalbibliothek in Vienna.

On a visit to Israel in 1964, I met Mr Paul Engelmann. He showed me a typescript, from which apparently Wittgenstein's *Logisch-philosophische Abhandlung* had first been printed (in Germany in 1921). This typescript too is now in the Bodleian.

CLASSIFICATION AND DESCRIPTION OF THE PAPERS

The papers of which this essay gives an account can be divided into three main groups: manuscripts, typescripts dictated to a typist or otherwise prepared by Wittgenstein himself, and verbatim records of dictations to colleagues or pupils. Comprising a fourth group are the notes, more or less verbatim, of conversations and lectures, of which there exist a good many. Wittgenstein's correspondence constitutes a fifth group of papers.

Nearly all the manuscripts are written in bound manuscript books and only a few on loose sheets. The manuscript books I have classified in the catalogue given below as either 'volumes', 'large notebooks', 'notebooks', or 'pocket notebooks'. All the volumes are solidly bound in hard covers.

They vary considerably in size. Some of the biggest are ledgers measuring 21 by 31 cm; a few of the smaller ones measure 18 by 21 cm. What I have called large notebooks are all of uniform size (22 by 29 cm) and have soft covers. The pocket notebooks normally measure 10 by 16 cm, and most of them have hard covers.

One can, broadly speaking, distinguish two strata of writings in manuscript form. I shall refer to them as 'first drafts' and 'more finished versions'. But the distinction between the strata is by no means clearcut, and there is no one-to-one correlation between them. Some of the more finished writings are revisions of earlier, draftlike material, but others are revisions of material itself classified here as 'more finished'. Some of the most finished manuscripts have the nature of 'fair copies' of remarks which have been extracted from earlier writings. Others definitely have the character of manuscripts for a planned book.

All manuscripts here classified as 'volumes' are of the more finished type, but to the same category belong also some notebooks, pocket notebooks, and writings on loose sheets. Particularly difficult to classify are some of the manuscripts from the last two years of Wittgenstein's life.

In the more finished manuscripts the entries are often dated. This makes a chronological arrangement of these manuscripts relatively easy. In many cases the books are running diaries in which apparently every day on which an entry was made is recorded. In other manuscripts of this category there are only a few dates and large sections are undated. Some of the manuscript volumes contain parts separated by long intervals of time. (A case in point is 116 which spans the period from the mid-1930s to 1945.) Sometimes two or more manuscript volumes have been written during the same, or during largely overlapping, periods (114 and 115 are one example; another is 117, the first half of which stretches over roughly the same time as 118–121). The chronological order of the volumes is thus not entirely linear.

The more draftlike notebooks sometimes have a date at the beginning and sometimes dates in the text. But often they contain no dates at all. The chronology of the manuscripts of this kind and their relations to the more finished writings are to some extent a matter for conjecture.

The main bulk of the more finished manuscripts can be divided into two 'series'. The first series consists of 18 volumes written in the years 1929–40. Wittgenstein referred to them as *Bände* (volumes) with a number. Usually he also gave them a title – for example, '*Philosophische Bemerkungen*' ('Philosophical Remarks').

The second series consists of 16 manuscript books, some few of which are pocket notebooks and not 'volumes'. It is impossible to tell exactly which writings should count as belonging to this series and whether it, like the first, is complete. It covers the years 1940–49. The books are not numbered. The last three in the series Wittgenstein called '*Band Q*', '*Band R*', and '*Band S*'. One of the earlier members in the series, a pocket notebook, he marked '*F*'. I have not found any indications that Wittgenstein thought of the unnamed members of the series as volumes *A*, *B*, *C*, and so forth. But if one arranges the existing manuscript books in a chronological order and assigns to each of them a letter, one is struck by the following fact. The notebook called '*F*' becomes correlated with the letter *E* and the volume called '*Q*' with the letter *N*. If we assume that *one* of the first five manuscript books of the series,[5] and *two* books after the one called '*F*',[6] are lost or have been destroyed, then we have a perfect alphabetical order for the manuscripts in the second series. This observation is of some interest in connection with the conjectured existence of, and the search for, missing manuscripts.

Not all of the more finished manuscripts have a place in either series.

From the more finished manuscripts Wittgenstein dictated to typists. In the course of dictation he evidently often altered the sentences, added new ones, and changed the order of the remarks in the manuscripts. Usually he continued to work with the typescripts. A method which he often used was to cut up the typed text into fragments (*Zettel*) and to rearrange the order of the remarks. Conspicuous instances of this method of

[5] But see the comment on item 163 of the catalogue.
[6] It is also possible that there never was a '*Band J*' or a '*Band O*'.

work are items 212, 222–224, and 233 of the catalogue. A further stage was the production of a new typescript on the basis of a collection of cuttings. One case of this procedure is represented by item 213, a typescript of 768 pages, evidently made in 1933. In an outward sense it is one of the most finished of all Wittgenstein's writings after the *Tractatus*. It is divided into 19 main chapters which are themselves subdivided into larger sections. Each chapter and section has a heading – a unique occurrence in Wittgenstein's literary output. The literary executors used to refer to this item as the Big Typescript. It was in our hands from 1951. But it was not until 1967 that the *Zettel* from which it was made and the typescripts from which these fragments are cut were discovered.

The typescript of the *Philosophical Investigations* probably had a similar history. The beginning of the book as we have it, up to Section 189, is a revision of a typescript (220 of the catalogue) which was composed probably in 1937 on the basis of a manuscript volume (142) now lost. The history of the origin of the final typescript for the book remains to a certain extent obscure.[7] It is reported that there existed in September 1944 a typescript of Part I consisting of cuttings (perhaps partly from the 1937 typescript) clipped together in bundles.[8] The final typescript of Part I was probably finished in the academic year 1945–46. Part II of the *Investigations* has a more straightforward history. Its first version was a manuscript extracted by Wittgenstein from the manuscripts which were themselves of the kind here called 'more finished'. From this manuscript he composed, with some omissions, the typescript from which the book was printed.

The papers listed as verbatim dictations to colleagues and pupils can be regarded as on a level with the rest of Wittgenstein's own writings. Eleven (or twelve)[9] items of this kind are known: the dictations to G.E. Moore in Norway in 1914; seven (or eight) dictations to Schlick; and the so-called

---

[7] See 'The Origin and Composition of the *Philosophical Investigations*' below.

[8] Report by R. Rhees.

[9] See the comment on items 302–308 below.

Blue and Brown and Yellow books. It is important to distinguish these verbatim dictations from the more or less verbatim notes taken by various people of conversations and lectures.[10] Many of these notes are of great interest and evidently very faithful to their source. Several of them have been published.

CATALOGUE

To make reference easier I have numbered the items in the catalogue as follows: manuscripts beginning at 101, type-scripts at 201, and dictations at 301. In some cases several items are grouped under the same number and distinguished as a, b, c, and so forth. The names in quotation marks are Wittgenstein's own titles. Names invented by the editors and executors are not enclosed in quotation marks and are prefixed 'called' or 'so-called'. The language of the writings is German, except when otherwise indicated. For each manuscript and typescript the number of pages it contains is also given. The actual pagination is not always by Wittgenstein himself. There is some vacillation; sometimes, for example, the title page has a number, sometimes it has not. Also errors occasionally occur. Some comments on individual items follow after the catalogue.

Manuscripts

101 Notebook. 9 August–30 October 1914. 106 pp.
102 Notebook. 30 October 1914–22 June 1915. 265 pp.
103 Notebook. 7 April 1916–10 January 1917. 118 pp.
104 Notebook. The so-called *Prototractatus*. 1918. 122 pp.
105 Volume I. *'Philosophische Bemerkungen.'* Begun 2 February 1929. 135 pp.
106 Volume II. Undated, 1929. 298 pp.
107 Volume III. *'Philosophische Betrachtungen.'* Last entry 15 February 1930. 300 pp.
108 Volume IV. *'Philosophische Bemerkungen.'* 13 December 1929–9 August 1930. 300 pp.
109 Volume V. *'Bemerkungen.'* 11 August 1930–3 February 1931. 300 pp.

[10] See the comment on item 311 below.

110   Volume VI. *'Philosophische Bemerkungen.'* 10 December 1930–6 July 1931. 300 pp.
111   Volume VII. *'Bemerkungen zur Philosophie.'* 7 July–September 1931. 200 pp.
112   Volume VIII. *'Bemerkungen zur philosophischen Grammatik.'* 5 October–28 November 1931. 270 pp.
113   Volume IX. *'Philosophische Grammatik.'* 28 November 1931–23 May 1932. 286 pp.
114   Volume X. *'Philosophische Grammatik.'* First entry 27 May 1932. 288 pp.
115   Volume XI. *'Philosophische Bemerkungen.'* First entry 14 December 1933. *'Philosophische Untersuchungen.'* August 1936. 292 pp.
116   Volume XII. *'Philosophische Bemerkungen.'* 1936–?; May 1945. 347 pp.
117   Volume XIII. *'Philosophische Bemerkungen.'* 1937; 1938; 1940. 263 pp.
118   Volume XIV. *'Philosophische Bemerkungen.'* 13 August–24 September 1937. 238 pp.
119   Volume XV. 24 September–19 November 1937. 295 pp.
120   Volume XVI. 19 November 1937–26 April 1938. 293 pp.
121   Volume XVII. *'Philosophische Bemerkungen.'* 26 April 1938–9 January 1939. 186 pp.
122   Volume XVIII. *'Philosophische Bemerkungen.'* 16 October 1939–3 February 1940. 238 pp.
123   Notebook. *'Philosophische Bemerkungen.'* 25 September–23 November 1940; 16 May–6 June 1941. 138 pp.
124   Volume. 6 June–4 July 1941; 5 March–19 April 1944; 3 July 1944–?. 292 pp.
125   Pocket notebook. 28 December 1941–16 October 1942. 156 pp.
126   Pocket notebook. 20 October 1942–6 January 1943. 155 pp. (Missing.)
127   Pocket notebook. *'F. Mathematik und Logik.'* 6 January–4 April 1943; 27 February–4 March 1944; undated part. 175 pp. (Missing.)
128   Volume. *Circa* 1944. 52 pp.
129   Volume. First entry 17 August 1944. 221 pp.
130   Volume. Undated part; 26 May–9 August 1946. 294 pp.
131   Volume. 10 August–9 September 1946. 206 pp.
132   Volume. 9 September–22 October 1946. 212 pp.
133   Volume. 22 October 1946–28 February 1947. 190 pp.

134   Volume. 28 February 1947–?. 184 pp.

135   Volume. 12 July–18 December 1947. 192 pp.

136   Volume. '*Band Q.*' 18 December 1947–25 January 1948. 288 pp.

137   Volume. '*Band R.*' 2 February 1948–9 January 1949. 286 pp.

138   Volume. '*Band S.*' 15 January 1949–20 May 1949. 66 pp.

139a   The Lecture on Ethics. 1929. Written in English on loose sheets. 23 pp.

   b   The same. (Missing.)

140   '*Grosses Format.*' Approximately 1934. Large sheets. 42 pp.

141   The beginning of an early version in German of the Brown Book. Large sheets. 1935 or 1936. 8 pp.

142   Volume. '*Philosophische Untersuchungen.*' November—December 1936. (Missing.)

143   Notes on Frazer's *The Golden Bough*. Loose sheets of varying size. 1936 or later. 21 pp.

144   Volume. Fair manuscript copy containing Part II of the *Investigations*. 1949. 118 pp.

145   Large notebook. Called $C1$. 1933. 96 pp.

146   Large notebook. Called $C2$. 1933–34. 96 pp.

147   Large notebook. Called $C3$. 1934. 96 pp. Partly in English.

148   Large notebook. Called $C4$. 1934–35. 96 pp. Mainly in English.

149   Large notebook. Called $C5$. Immediate continuation of 148. 1935–36. 96 pp. Mainly in English.

150   Large notebook. Called $C6$. 1935–36. 96 pp. Mainly in English.

151   Large notebook. Called $C7$. 1936. 47 pp. Mainly in English.

152   Large notebook. Called $C8$. 1936. 96 pp.

153a   Pocket notebook. '*Anmerkungen.*' 1931. 339 pp.

   b   Pocket notebook, immediately continuing 153a. 122 pp.

154   Pocket notebook. 1931. 190 pp.

155   Pocket notebook. 1931. 189 pp.

156a   Pocket notebook. *Circa* 1932–34. 121 pp.

   b   Pocket notebook, immediate continuation of 156a. 116 pp.

157a   Pocket notebook. 1934; 1937. 142 pp.

   b   Pocket notebook, immediate continuation of 157a. 1937. 81 pp.

158   Pocket notebook. 1938. 94 pp. Partly in English.

159   Pocket notebook. 1938. 80 pp. Partly in English.

160   Pocket notebook. 1938. 63 pp. Partly in English.

161   Pocket notebook. 1939–?. 140 pp. Partly in English.

162a   Pocket notebook. Begun and probably also completed in
        January 1939. 103 pp.
   b   Pocket notebook, immediate continuation of 162a. Ends in
        August 1940. 140 pp.
163   Pocket notebook. 22 June–29 September 1941. 156 pp.
164   Pocket notebook. *Circa* 1941–44. 172 pp.
165   Pocket notebook. *Circa* 1941–44. 230 pp.
166   Pocket notebook. 'Notes for the "Philosophical Lecture".'
        Written in English. Probably 1935–36. 65 pp. (At the end,
        transcriptions of some poems in Russian.)
167   Pocket notebook. Probably 1947–48. 64 pp.
168   Notebook. Fair manuscript copy of some remarks from the
        years 1947–49 on general subjects. 12 pp.
169   Pocket notebook. Probably first half of 1949. 161 pp.
170   Pocket notebook. Probably 1949. 10 pp.
171   Pocket notebook. 1949 or 1950. 14 pp.
172   Manuscript on loose sheets. Probably 1950. 24 pp.
173   Notebook. 24 March–12 April 1950; undated part. 200 pp.
174   Notebook. 1950. 78 pp.
175   Pocket notebook. 1950; 10–21 March 1951. 156 pp.
176   Notebook. 1950; 21 March–24 April 1951. 160 pp.
177   Notebook. 25–27 April 1951. 21 pp.
178   Undated fragments:
   a   '*Man könnte die (ganze) Sache. . . .*' 10 pp.
   b   '*Ich verstehe es. . . .*' 9 pp.
   c   '*Das Bild der Cantorschen Überlegung. . . .*' 6 pp.
   d   '*Unter Logik versteht man. . . .*' 6 pp.
   e   '*darfst Du Dich nicht. . . .*' 4 pp.
   f   '*Ich möchte sagen. . . .*' 2 pp.
   g   '*Diese Sicherheit ist eine empirische. . . .*' 2 pp.
   h   '*folgt? ist das Verstehen?. . .*' 1 p.
179   Notebook. 1944 or 1945. 72 pp.
180a   Notebook. 1944 or 1945. 80 pp.
   b   Notebook. 1944 or 1945. 56 pp.
181   'Privacy of sense data.' Probably 1935–36. Loose sheets.
        6 pp. In English.
182   List of the remarks from TS 228 which were included in the
        final version of Part I of the *Investigations*. Loose sheets. 2 pp.

Typescripts
201a   'Notes on Logic.' September 1913. The so-called Russell

Version. English. 7 typescript pages dictated by Wittgenstein and 23 manuscript pages in Russell's hand.

b The same. The so-called Costello Version. English.

202 The so-called Engelmann TS of the *Tractatus*. 1918. 53 pp.

203 The so-called Vienna TS of the *Tractatus*. 1918. 56 pp.

204 The so-called Gmunden TS of the *Tractatus*. 1918. (Missing.)

205 'Geleitwort zum Wörterbuch für Volksschulen.' 1925. 6 pp.

206 An Essay on Identity. English. 1927. 3 pp.

207 The Lecture on Ethics. 1929. 10 pp.

208 Typescript based on 105, 106, 107, and the first half of 108 (MS Volumes I, II, III, and IV). 1930. 97 pp.

209 'Philosophische Bemerkungen.' Typescript based on 208. 1930. 139 pp.

210 Typescript based on the second half (p. 133 ff.) of 108. *Circa* 1930. 87 pp.

211 Typescript based on 109, 110, 111, 112, 113, and the beginning of 114. Probably 1932. 771 pp.

212 Typescript consisting of cuttings from 208, 210, and 211. 1932 or 1933.

213 The so-called Big Typescript. Probably 1933. viii + 768 pp.

214 Three essays. Probably 1933. 15 pp.

a 'Komplex und Tatsache.'

b 'Begriff und Gegenstand.'

c 'Gegenstand.'

215 Two essays. Probably 1933. 20 pp.

a 'Unendlich lang.'

b 'Unendliche Möglichkeit.'

216 An essay, 'Gleichungen und Ungleichungen sind Festsetzungen oder die Folgen von Festsetzungen.' Probably 1933. 6 pp.

217 An essay, 'Allgemeinheit einer Demonstration.' Probably 1933. 5 pp.

218 An essay, 'Wie kann uns ein allgemeiner Beweis den besonderen Beweis schenken?' Probably 1933. 3 pp.

219 Typescript beginning 'Muss sich denn nicht. . . .' Probably 1932 or 1933. 24 pp.

220 Typescript, probably based on 142, of approximately the first half of the prewar version of the *Investigations*. 1937 or 1938. 137 pp.

221 Typescript, based on 117–120 (MS Volumes XIII–XVI) and 162a of the second half of the pre-war version of the *Investigations*. 1938. 134 pp.

222 Typescript composed of cuttings from 221.

223 Typescript beginning '*Man kann sich leicht eine Sprache denken. . . .*', composed of cuttings from 221. 10 pp.

224 Typescript beginning '*Das Überraschende in der Mathematik . . .*', composed of cuttings from 221. 7 pp.

225 Typescript of Preface to the prewar version of the *Investigations*. August 1938. 4 pp.

226 Translation into English by R. Rhees with corrections by Wittgenstein, of the beginning of the pre-war version of the *Investigations*. 1939. 72 pp.

227 Typescript of Part I of the final version of the *Investigations*. (1944)–45–(46). 324 pp.

228 '*Bemerkungen* I.' 1945 or 1946. 185 pp.

229 Typescript, being a continuation of 228. 1947. 272 pp.

230 '*Bemerkungen* II.' Probably 1945 or 1946. 155 pp.

231 Two lists of corresponding remarks in '*Bemerkungen* I' and '*Bemerkungen* II'. Probably 1945 or 1946. 8 pp.

232 Typescript based on MS Volumes 135–137. 1948. 174 pp.

233 '*Zettel*.' Cuttings from various typescripts from the period 1929–48, but mostly from 1945–48 (items 228–230 and 232).

234 Typescript of Part II of the final version of the *Investigations*. Probably dictated in 1949. (Missing.)

235 Typescript of a Table of Contents to an unidentified work. Date unknown. 9 pp.

236 Typescript consisting of 17 non-consecutive pages from 210 and one page from 211. 18 pp.

237 Typescript of fragments, partly as cuttings, from pp. 80–92 of 220, with additions and changes. 5 pp.

238 Typescript of revisions of pp. 77–93 of 220. 1942 or 1943. 16 pp.

239 Typescript of a revised version of 220. 1942 or 1943. 134 pp.

240 Typescript of fragments, partly as cuttings, from 221 with changes. 3 pp.

241 Typescript based on 129. 1944–45. 33 pp.

242 Typescript of pages between pp. 149–195 of the so-called Intermediate Version of the *Investigations*. 1944–45. 23 pp.

243 Typescript of a Preface to the *Investigations*, dated 'Cambridge im Januar 1945'. 4 pp.

244 Typescript of an 'overlapping' part of 228 and 229. 11 pp.

245 Typescript beginning in the middle of remark 689 of 244 and containing the rest of 244 and the whole of 229. Date unknown. 192 pp.

Dictations

301 Notes dictated to G.E. Moore in Norway, April 1914. English. 31 pp.
302 The so-called *Diktat für Schlick*. Approximately 1931–33. 42 pp.
303 Dictation to Schlick beginning '*Die normale Ausdrucksweise. . . .*' Date uncertain. 11 pp.
304 Dictation to Schlick beginning '*Hat es Sinn zu sagen., . . .*' Date uncertain. 4 pp.
305 Dictation to Schlick beginning '*Fragen wir diese. . . .*' Date uncertain. 1 p.
306 Dictation to Schlick beginning '*Was bedeutet es denn. . . .*' Date uncertain. 2 pp.
307 Dictation to Schlick. The so-called *Mulder* II. 6 pp.
308 Dictation to Schlick. The so-called *Mulder* V. 57 pp.
309 The so-called Blue Book. English. Dictated to the class at Cambridge in the academic year 1933–34. 124 pp.
310 The so-called Brown Book. English. Dictated to Alice Ambrose and Francis Skinner at Cambridge in the academic year 1934–35. 168 pp.
311 The so-called Yellow Book. Dictated to Margaret Masterman, Alice Ambrose, and Francis Skinner in the year 1933–34.

COMMENTS ON INDIVIDUAL ITEMS IN THE CATALOGUE

105 and 106. Only the first few entries in 105 are dated; they are from 2 to 6 February 1929. In 106 there are no dates. It is, however, apparent that the left-hand pages number 8, 10, and so forth up to 132, and from there to the end (p. 135) of 105 continue the text in 106. The text in 106 again first runs through the right-hand pages up to 296 and then continues on the left-hand pages up to and including right-hand page 298.

107. The first date occurs on page 87. The date is 11 September 1929. The next date, 6 October 1929, is on page 153. From here on dating is regular. After the entry made on 4 December 1929, which ends on page 229, the writing continues in 108 (Volume IV), pages 1–64. Wittgenstein was in Vienna during the Christmas vacation and did not bring 107 (Volume III) with him from Cambridge. The writing in 107 (p. 229) was resumed on 10 January 1930 and continued to 15

February, which is the date of the last entry in 107. On the next day the writing continues in 108 on page 64.

109 and 110. The same sort of 'jump' from one manuscript volume to the next, and back, occurs in 109 and 110. The reason is probably the same as in the case of 107 and 108. Pages 1–31 of 110 were written in the period 10 December 1930–28 January 1931. These pages follow chronologically after page 271 of 109. The writing in 109 from page 272 to the end are from 29 January to 3 February 1931. Then the writing continues on page 31 in 110.

111. The last date in this volume is 13 September. It is on page 166.

114 and 115. These each fall into two parts. The first part of 114 consists of 60 pages, not paginated by the author, and written in the period from 27 May to 5 June 1932. The second part of 114 is paginated by the author 1–228. There are no dates at all in it. It may be regarded as of one piece with the first part (pp. 1–117) of 115 and with MS 140 on large sheets ('*Grosses Format*'). 115 was commenced on 14 December 1933, but there are no further dates in the first part of 115, either. 140 is essentially a revision of pages 1–56 of the second part of 114. There are numerous insertions from the first part of 115 into the second part of 114. The revisions and 'jumps' back and forth between the manuscripts means that the reading of them is not easy. From the point of view of their content, however, they form a close unity. It is clear that Wittgenstein is here attempting to write a *book*, to give a consecutive and coherent statement of his philosophical position at the time. It is a plausible conjecture that this piece of writing dates from the academic year 1933–34 and that it is at least partly contemporary with the dictation of the so-called Blue Book.

The second part of 115 (pp. 118–292) is dated as of the end of August 1936 and called '*Philosophische Untersuchungen. Versuch einer Umarbeitung*'. It is an attempt at a revision, in German, of the so-called Brown Book. It ends with the words '*Dieser ganze "Versuch einer Umarbeitung" von Seite 118 bis hierher ist* NICHTS WERT.' A little later in the same year (1936) Wittgenstein wrote a first version of what are now sections 1–188 of the *Investigations* (MS 142).[11]

116.[11] In 116 – the largest volume in the series – four parts can be distinguished. The first (pp. 1–135) begins as a revision of material in the early portions of 213 (the Big Typescript), but becomes more and more unlike 213, moving, so to speak, in the direction of the

[11] For a fuller account of this volume and the problems connected with it, see 'The Origin and Composition of the *Philosophical Investigations*' below, pp. 122–125.

Investigations. In places there are strong similarities to the Blue Book. The second part of 116 (pp. 136–264) contains revisions of writings from the academic year 1937–38, and the third (pp. 265–315) again seems related to some writings which presumably date from 1944. Finally, the fourth part (pp. 316–347) contains a good many remarks which occur at the very end of Part I of the printed version of the *Investigations*.

The manuscript volume 116 is from Bergen, Norway. It is not known that Wittgenstein visited Norway after his return to Cambridge in 1929 and before 1936. This is a strong indication that the earliest entries in the volume cannot have been made before some time in the summer of 1936. It is therefore not an implausible conjecture that the first part of the volume was written in 1936, and before the end of August, when Wittgenstein began writing (in 115) the revision of the Brown Book which he called '*Philosophische Untersuchungen*'. The fact, however, that 116 begins with a revision of the Big Typescript from 1933 speaks against this conjecture. So also does the length of these writings in 116. Since there are no dates either in the first, second or third part of 116 the question when these parts were written must, for the time being, remain open. Maybe we shall have to conclude that Wittgenstein acquired the manuscript volume some years before he went to Norway in 1936. There is some internal evidence that the revisions on the Big Typescript in 140 are later than the revisions in 116.[12] There is, further, some indication that 140 immediately preceded the first manuscript draft (142) of the *Investigations*. I find these problems very intriguing, and would not despair of the possibility of eventually solving them.

The only date in MS 116 stands at the beginning of the fourth part and reads (in English) 'May 1945'. There is every reason for thinking that the whole of the fourth part dates from 1945. This is, incidentally, the only preserved writing in manuscript form which is known with certainty to be from this year.

117. Several parts of 117 can be distinguished. Pages 1–97 is manuscript material for 222 and 223 – that is, Part I of the *Remarks on the Foundations of Mathematics*. The first entry is dated 11 September 1937; there are no further dates in this part of the volume. Pages 97–110 are headed '*Ansätze*'. They are printed as Part II of the *Remarks* (the revised edition). There are no dates. Pages 110–126 contain three drafts of a Preface to the *Investigations*. The third is

[12] See Anthony Kenny, 'From the Big Typescript to the Philosophical Grammar', Jaakko Hintikka (ed.), *Essays on Wittgenstein in Honour of G.H. von Wright*, Acta Philosophica Fennica **28**, 1976, p. 52.

dated Cambridge, August 1938. Pages 127–148 are undated but were probably written in the second half of 1938. In this section there are references to a typescript which is evidently item 221 – that is, the typescript of the second half of the prewar version of the *Investigations*. My conjecture is that this typescript was made in the autumn of 1938. Pages 148–273, finally, are an immediate continuation of the material in 122. The entries are dated 3 February–18 April 1940. There is a gap in the pagination between pages 209 and 220, evidently due to a mistake.

118–121. This is manuscript material from the same period, and dealing with much the same topics, as pages 1–148 of 117. Roughly the second half of 121 was written in the period 25 December 1938–9 January 1939.

122. This is the last in the series that Wittgenstein called '*Bände*' (volumes), giving each a number. But it is continued in 117 (pp. 148–273). Thus it is there, on 18 April 1940, that the writings in the numbered '*Bände*' which had begun on 2 February 1929 come to an end (not counting the section from 1945 in 116). There are no manuscripts preserved from the period 18 April–25 September 1940, when Wittgenstein began 123. This is the first volume in the series of manuscripts, some of which were called by Wittgenstein '*Bände*' and given a letter from the alphabet.

125–127. These are pocket notebooks written during the war when Wittgenstein was working first at Guy's Hospital in London, from November 1941 to April 1943, and later in a medical laboratory in Newcastle. In the autumn of 1944 he resumed his teaching at Cambridge. The general character of the notebooks makes it reasonable to classify them with the second series of manuscript volumes of a more finished kind. (Cf. the comment on 163 below.) Photocopies exist of 126 and 127; the originals are missing.

128. This volume contains no dates and its classification is problematic. Near the end there is a draft of what eventually became the Preface to the final version of the *Investigations*. This links 128 with the next volume in the catalogue.

129. This begins with several undated drafts of the Preface to the *Investigations*. In these drafts, as also in the draft at the end of 128, Wittgenstein speaks of the results of his philosophical investigations in 'the last 16 years'. The same phrase occurs in the printed Preface to the *Investigations* which is dated Cambridge, January 1945. The drafts therefore seem to be from the same period as the final version (in 227) of the Preface – that is, late 1944 or early 1945. Since the drafts in 129 are written on special sheets at the beginning of the volume, it is quite possible that they were written *after* the rest of the material in the volume, for the first entry (after the drafts of a preface) is dated 17 August 1944. There are no other dates in the volume.[13]

130. The first dated entry here, of 26 May 1946, is halfway through the book. The entries after that are dated. The undated first half of the book could have been written, or at least begun, one or two years earlier.

134. The last dated entry in this volume is of 27 June 1947. There are a few entries at the end which are presumably later.

138. The consecutive writings in this volume end on 22 March 1949, but there is an additional entry dated 20 May.

139. Two manuscripts of this lecture are known to exist or to have existed. The one listed as 139a differs in some interesting respects from the typescript (207) from which the lecture was posthumously printed in the *Philosophical Review* **74**, 1965. The manuscript listed as 139b is now missing. It was in Gmunden in 1952.

140. See comments on 114 and 115 above.

142. This manuscript volume, dedicated to Wittgenstein's sister, Mrs M. Stonborough, was in Gmunden in 1952. It is now missing.

143. This was published, together with some other comments on Frazer in 110, under the title 'Bemerkungen über Frazers *The Golden Bough*' in *Synthese* **17**, 1967, 233–253, with an Introductory Note by R. Rhees. The editor's comment on the date is 'not earlier than 1936 and probably after 1948'. (Republished in book form as *Remarks on Frazer's* Golden Bough, ed. by Rush Rhees, Brynmill, Retford, 1979.)

145 and 146. These contain material in draft form for 114 and 115 (Volumes X and XI).

147. Commenced in February 1934. The latter part of this notebook consists of drafts for the Blue Book.

148. Mainly notes for lectures in the academic year 1934–35.

149. Mainly notes for lectures, 1935–36.

150. Mainly notes for Part II of the Brown Book.

151. Largely notes for lectures, 1936.

152. Drafts for the beginning of the *Investigations*. Probably written in Norway in the second half of 1936.

---

[13] In the printed Preface of the *Inverstigations* it is said: 'Four years ago I had occasion to re-read my first book (the *Tractatus Logico-Philosophicus*) and to explain its ideas to someone.' This sentence makes reference to conversations that Wittgenstein had been having in 1943 with Nicholas Bachtin, linguist and classical scholar (d. 1950). The typescript has, correctly, 'Vor zwei Jahren'.

153a and b. Drafts for 111 (Volume VII). Notebooks have been grouped, a and b, under the same item, when the second book is an immediate continuation of the material in the first.

154 and 155. These contain no dates. They contain draft material for 111 and 112 (Volumes VII and VIII), and probably date from 1931.

156a and b. These likewise contain no dates.

157a. This begins with an entry dated 4 June 1934 and has (p. 90) an entry dated 9 February 1937. The first entry in 157b is dated 27 February 1937.

159. This ends with what is evidently the first draft of the Preface to the (pre-war version of the) *Investigations*. Cf. the comment on 117.

161. This falls into two distinct parts. Pages 1–32 are written in English, the rest in German. The first part contains drafts for Wittgenstein's lectures on the philosophy of mathematics given in the winter and spring of 1939. The second half seems to consist of drafts written in 1941 for the first part of MS 124.

163. The entries in this pocket notebook are dated throughout. It is arguable that it should perhaps be placed after 124 in the second series of more finished manuscripts. The draftlike nature of the contents, however, speaks against this classification. (Cf. the comment on 125–127 above).

168. The remarks, entered in the reverse order (1949–47), are from 136–138 (MS volumes Q–S).

172. These manuscript pages – dealing with the topics of colour and of certainty – were probably written by Wittgenstein during his last visit to Vienna in the early months of 1950.

201. There exist two versions of these notes. Both are in English and both date from the autumn of 1913. Their origin and mutual relation were for a long time obscure, but have eventually been clarified in what seems a conclusive manner by Brian F. McGuinness in 'Bertrand Russell and Ludwig Wittgenstein's "Notes on Logic"', *Revue Internationale de Philosophie* **26**, 1972. What is called the Russell Version in the catalogue consists of a 'Summary' evidently dictated by Wittgenstein (in English) and four 'Manuscripts' which Russell had translated into English from notes in German by Wittgenstein. The so-called Costello Version is apparently a subsequent rearrangement of the text made by Russell alone.

202. In all probability, this is the typescript from which Wittgenstein's *Logisch-philosophische Abhandlung* was printed by Ostwald in Germany in 1921. (The printing of the book in England seems to have been from an offprint of the publication by Ostwald.) The manuscript was later given by Wittgenstein to his friend, the architect Paul Engelmann. (See p. 39 above.)

203. This is not a second copy of 202, but a different typescript. The last page is lost.

204. This was in Gmunden in 1952. With it was also a typescript of Russell's Introduction. They are now missing. (Cf. p. 38 above.) It is not possible to tell at present whether 204 is a second copy of 202 or 203.

206. This 'essay' is an extract from a communication from Wittgenstein to Ramsey in June 1927. The extract exists in a carbon copy of a typescript, found among Waismann's papers. The copy is headed '*Wittgenstein an Ramsey, Juni 1927. Durchschlag*'. The communication was evidently a letter which is now lost. There is some evidence that the letter had, in fact, been written by Schlick. The extract, and probably the rest of the communication, is in English. It is possible that the communication was dictated by Wittgenstein to Schlick (in German) and that Schlick translated the dictation into English. One hesitates therefore over whether to classify this item among the typescripts or among the dictations. There can be no doubt, however, that the thoughts stem directly from Wittgenstein.

208. The typescript originally had 144 pages. The missing ones were used by Wittgenstein himself, chiefly for the composition of 211.

209. The original, which is now lost but of which there exist photocopies, was put together from cuttings from a carbon copy of 208 pasted into a black ledger book.

210. A few pages at the end of this typescript seem to be missing.

211. A few pages are missing, but can be identified in 213. Photocopies of the missing pages have been inserted.

212. The cuttings from the 'underlying' typescripts are arranged and clipped together in chapters. The chapters are grouped in 'parts' and enclosed in folders.

213–218. These represent the content of 212 typed out, following the arrangement into chapters and parts. The reason for separating, in the catalogue, 214–218 (what I have called the Essays) from 213 (the Big Typescript) is that the essays are already placed apart in 212 and that their pagination does not follow on from the pagination of 213. The reason again for separating the essays from each other in the manner done in the catalogue is that the pagination of the three essays in 214 and of the two in 215 is consecutive, whereas the three essays 216, 217, and 218 are three distinct typescripts.

220 and 221. The pagination of the two typescripts is consecutive from 1 to 271. TS 220 ends with page 137. The page numbered 1 is lost and has been replaced in the typescript, as we have it, by three pages with Roman numerals i, ii, and iii. The actual number of paginated sheets in the existing typescript 220 is thus 139.

It is possible but not certain that the two typescripts were typed at the same time. The manuscript material for 220 must already have existed in the first half of 1937; that for 221 was not ready until some time in 1938. (A few remarks at the very end of 221 are from January 1939.)

Roughly the second half of 220 is a top copy; the first half a second copy. The remainder of the top copy is actually preserved in the typescript with the catalogue number 239, found in 1977. Of TS 221 two copies exist more or less intact. Neither of them is a top copy. The top copy was evidently used for composing 222.

222–224. The reason for distinguishing these as three different items, although they all stem from 221, is that Wittgenstein himself separated 223 and 224 from the main body of cuttings comprising 222.

228 and 229. The pagination is consecutive from 1 to 457, and the remarks are numbered consecutively from 1 to 1804. The typescript nevertheless clearly falls into two parts. Wittgenstein made some corrections and revisions to the remarks (1–698) of the first part; the second part is unrevised. At the beginning of the second part there seems to be some confusion in the numbering of the remarks. The first remark has the number 699. Then follows 670, which probably is a mistake and ought to be 700. Thus the total number of remarks in 228 and 229 together is not 1,804 but 1,834. An additional typescript of the remarks with overlapping numbers 670–698 (in 229) was found later, in 1976. It was given the catalogue number 244.

230. This is a collection of 542 numbered remarks, practically all of which are in 228 ('*Bemerkungen* I'). There is a complete list of correspondence between the remarks in the two collections in 231.

232. This is a collection of 736 numbered remarks written in the period 9 November 1947–23 August 1948. The pages of the typescript are numbered 600–773. The explanation for this pagination is not known.

233. Concerning the arrangement of the cuttings, see the Editors' Preface to *Zettel* (Basil Blackwell, Oxford, 1967).

302–308. Eight typescripts are known of dictations by Wittgenstein to Schlick. One of them, however, is essentially a typescript version of 140 (the manuscript, to which Wittgenstein referred by the name '*Grosses Format*'). This typescript I have not listed in the catalogue. (Cf. also the comment on 206 above.) The dictations cannot be dated with accuracy. None, however, can be earlier than 1926. It is improbable that any of the listed typescripts is later than 1933.

309–310. The Blue Book was dictated in the period from 8

November 1933 to the first week in June 1934, the Brown Book in the period from mid-October 1934 to late April or May 1935. Of the first, a number of copies were taken and circulated to friends and pupils by Wittgenstein himself. The second was not meant for circulation and originally existed in only three copies. Clandestinely made copies of both dictations came into circulation against Wittgenstein's wishes. In some of the original copies of the Blue Book, which Wittgenstein gave away, he inserted minor corrections. In future scholarly editions of the text, attention should be paid to variations between the copies. I am indebted to Professor Ambrose-Lazerowitz for information concerning the origin and history of 309 and 310.

311, also known as the Yellow Book, consists of verbatim notes taken by Margaret Masterman, Alice Ambrose, and Francis Skinner in 1935. It is doubtful whether it should be classified with the other dictations or with the notes of conversations and lectures (cf. p. 43 above).

THE POSTHUMOUS PUBLICATIONS

In his will, dated 29 January 1951, Wittgenstein gave to Mr R. Rhees, Miss G.E.M. Anscombe, and myself the copyright in all his unpublished writings with the intention that we should publish from the papers as many of them as we considered fit.

Wittgenstein did not give us specific instructions concerning the publication and preservation of his unpublished writings. (It was, in fact, not until after his death that I learned that he had named me in his will as one of his literary executors.) We knew, of course, that he had for many years been writing a major work to which he had never been able to give an absolutely finished form but which he certainly wanted to be published and read. Of this work, the *Investigations*, there had, moreover, existed an earlier version from the late 1930s, the second half of which dealt with the philosophy of mathematics. This second half Wittgenstein had later 'laid aside' and it formed no part of the book in the final form he gave it.[14] Yet it somehow belonged there, perhaps after the

[14] See Editors' Preface to *Remarks on the Foundations of Mathematics* (Basil Blackwell, Oxford, 1956; 3rd edition, in German, 1974, and in English, 1978).

discussion of the philosophy of psychology in Part II of the *Investigations*.[15] To have published the most mature fruits of Wittgenstein's labours after his return to philosophy in 1929, but none of his writings on the philosophy of mathematics, would have been to give to the world a seriously truncated picture of his life's work. When Anscombe and Rhees had finished their work as editors of the text of the *Investigations* in 1951, the literary executors therefore immediately proceeded to supplement it with a volume of Wittgenstein's writings on the philosophy of mathematics from the period 1937–44.

The *Remarks on the Foundations of Mathematics* occupy a nearly unique, and not altogether happy, position among the posthumous publications. In addition to the relatively finished Part I, corresponding to typescripts 222, 223, and 224 of the catalogue and constituting the second half of the pre-war version of the *Investigations*, the *Remarks* contain *selections* from several manuscripts (117, 121, 122, 124, 125, 126, and 127). In the revised edition of 1974 (English translation 1978) the selections from those manuscripts were somewhat enlarged and a further manuscript (164) which was not known to the editors at the time of the first edition was added, practically without omissions. A publication of the manuscripts *in toto*, however, seemed to us excluded even at the time of preparing the new edition.

The 1930 typescript (209) called *Philosophische Bemerkungen* (*Philosophical Remarks*), which had been in the custody of G.E. Moore, was a nearly completed work. It could be published (1964) with a minimum of editorial interference. As Appendices to it, 214a and 215a and 215b were included.

A much more complicated case was presented by the so-called Big Typescript (213) of 1933 (cf. p. 42 above). The last third of it, on the philosophy of mathematics, existed in a relatively finished form. But on the earlier parts Wittgenstein had started to make extensive revisions. The revisions were first made in the typescript, but the work was continued in new manuscripts from the years 1933 and 1934, and perhaps even later (see comment on item 116 above).

Rush Rhees, the editor of the *Philosophische Grammatik*,

[15] Cf. the concluding remark in Part II, section xiv, of the *Investigations*.

which was published in German in 1969 and in English translation as *Philosophical Grammar* in 1974, decided to include the part on the philosophy of mathematics (five chapters in all) and two chapters dealing with logic practically unchanged from TS 213. They form Part II of the printed book. Four chapters of the typescript were omitted altogether and the remaining ones printed in the revised form that Wittgenstein gave to them, mainly in new manuscripts (114, 115, 140). TS 214 was now included *in toto* in an Appendix between the two parts of the volume.

From the time of the composition of the *Investigations* (1936–49) there were several typescripts in addition to the two which embodied the final versions of Part I and Part II of Wittgenstein's *chef d'oeuvre*. Among Wittgenstein's papers there was also a box containing a huge collection of cuttings from various typescripts but mainly from the time after 1945. The fragments were partly loose, partly clipped in bundles. An arrangement of the cuttings made by Peter Geach was published in 1967 under the title *Zettel*.

From May 1946 to May 1949 Wittgenstein wrote consecutively on the philosophy of psychological concepts (MSS 130–138). Three typescripts of his were based on these writings; the last of the three being the now lost typescript for Part II of the *Investigations*. The other two can with some justification be regarded as preliminary studies for Part II of Wittgenstein's main work. They were published in two volumes in 1980 under the title *Remarks on the Philosophy of Psychology* in German and English parallel texts.

Wittgenstein's writings in the last two years of his life (after May 1949) never advanced to the typescript stage. In these writings three main themes can be clearly distinguished. The one which is treated most fully concerns knowledge and certainty, and what Wittgenstein wrote on this theme was published under the title *On Certainty* in 1969. A second main theme was the philosophy of colour concepts. A small volume *Remarks on Colour* appeared in print in 1977. The remaining bulk of the writings can be placed under the heading 'The "Inner" and the "Outer" ' and is due to appear as the second of two volumes of *Last Writings* – the first volume consisting of writings in the 1946–49 manuscripts which never advanced to the typescript stage.

In nearly all Wittgenstein's manuscripts, from 1914 to 1951, there occur scattered remarks which do not directly belong to his philosophical work but deal with art, religion, philosophy of history, questions of value, *Lebensweisheit*, and other 'general topics'. It was long clear to us that a collection of these remarks had to be published. I was entrusted with the task of compiling it. The *Vermischte Bemerkungen* eventually appeared in German in 1977, and three years later in a bilingual edition with the title *Culture and Value*. In the Preface to the book I have explained the principles I followed in making the selections.

It has taken us 30 years to make the full body of Wittgenstein's philosophy accessible to the public. All the works of major interest have, in my view, now been published or are due to appear shortly. The availability of copies of the Cornell film in public libraries has opened the door to research by everybody who is interested in the details of the development of Wittgenstein's thought and the relation between the various 'layers of composition' of his works. The student will also be able to judge, by comparing the published texts with the originals, the editors' choices between variants in the formulations and the selections they have made when, as in the *Remarks on the Foundations of Mathematics*, the complete manuscripts have not been published.

In the course of continued and careful study of the manuscripts and typescripts (as I explained in the Introduction above) corrections and improvements to the editions have turned out to be necessary. Sometimes the editors have misread words or been too rash in the choice of alternative readings or interfered, in a way that now seems unwarranted, with Wittgenstein's own punctuation or with details of his spelling of words. A thorough revision of the bulk of already published writings seems to me called for. Although I think we adopted a basically sound policy in avoiding, as much as possible, editorial and scholarly comments on the texts, a few more indications of variants and explanations of otherwise obscure references would, in my opinion, now be appropriate.

For some time there have been plans for a *complete* publication of the *Nachlass*. This would record all information which the manuscripts and typescripts provide about deletions and insertions, variant readings, and the author's own comments, cross-references, and other textual marks.

APPENDIX I. THE WRITINGS OF LUDWIG WITTGENSTEIN PUBLISHED BY HIM IN HIS LIFETIME

Review of P. Coffey, 'The Science of Logic', *Cambridge Review* **34**, No. 853 (6 March 1913).

Logisch-philosophische Abhandlung, Annalen der Naturphilosophie, edited by Wilhelm Ostwald, Band XIV, Heft 3/4, 1921.

Tractatus Logico-Philosophicus, with an Introduction by Bertrand Russell, Kegan Paul, London, 1922.

Wörterbuch für Volks- und Bürgerschulen, Hölder-Pichler-Tempsky, Vienna, 1926. An Introduction to this dictionary, 'Geleitwort zum Wörterbuch für Volksschulen' (TS 205 of the catalogue), was published posthumously in a reprint of the *Wörterbuch* issued by the original publishing firm in 1977, edited with an Introduction by A. Hübner and W. and E. Leinfellner.

'Some Remarks on Logical Form', *Proceedings of the Aristotelian Society*, Supp. Vol. 9 (1929), pp. 162–171.

A Letter to the Editor, dated Cambridge, 27 May 1933, *Mind* **42**, No. 167 (July 1933), pp. 415–416.

APPENDIX II. WITTGENSTEIN'S LETTERS

Over the years the following collections of letters by Wittgenstein have been published:

W. Eccles, 'Some Letters of Ludwig Wittgenstein', *Hermathena* **97**, 1963.

Paul Engelmann, *Letters from Ludwig Wittgenstein. With a Memoir*, trans. by L. Furtmüller, ed. by B.F. McGuinness, Basil Blackwell, Oxford, 1967. The German original, *Ludwig Witt-*

genstein, Briefe und Begegnungen, ed. by B.F. McGuinness, was published by R. Oldenbourg, Vienna and Munich, 1970.

Ludwig Wittgenstein, Briefe an Ludwig von Ficker, ed. by G.H. von Wright in collaboration with W. Methlagl, Otto Müller Verlag, Salzburg, 1969.

Ludwig Wittgenstein, Letters to C.K. Ogden with Comments on the English Translation of the Tractatus Logico-Philosophicus, ed. with an Introduction by G.H. von Wright and an Appendix of Letters by Frank Plumpton Ramsey, Basil Blackwell, Oxford, and Routledge & Kegan Paul, London, 1973.

Ludwig Wittgenstein, Letters to Russell, Keynes and Moore, ed. with an Introduction by G.H. von Wright assisted by B.F. McGuinness, Basil Blackwell, Oxford, 1974, 2nd edit. with corrections 1977.

Ludwig Wittgenstein, Briefwechsel mit B. Russell, G.E. Moore, J.M. Keynes, F.P. Ramsey, W. Eccles, P. Engelmann und L. von Ficker, ed. by B.F. McGuinness and G.H. von Wright, Suhrkamp Verlag, Frankfurt am Main, 1980. This volume also contains all the letters that have been preserved to Wittgenstein from his correspondents.

At least from his return to Cambridge in 1929 Wittgenstein preserved letters from his friends – except casual communications and notes. It should therefore be possible to publish, at some future date, a more complete collection of exchanges of letters than the collection already published by Suhrkamp.

THE ORIGIN OF THE
TRACTATUS

Work on this study was begun after I found the manuscript notebook for the complete *Tractatus* in Vienna in 1965 in the Wittgenstein–house in Kundmann-gasse. The essay first appeared as a 'Historical Introduction' to the volume *Prototractatus, An Early Version of* Tractatus Logico-Philosophicus *by Ludwig Wittgenstein,* edited by B.F. McGuinness. Tauno Nyberg, and G.H. von Wright (Routledge & Kegan Paul, London, 1971). Preliminary versions of the paper were read by several persons. I am greatly indebted to them for comments and corrections and also to all those who patiently answered my inquiries on particular points. In particular I should like to express my thanks to Brian McGuinness. McGuinness also translated into English the numerous German passages quoted in the text, with the exception of the letters to Engelmann, which were translated by Dr L. Furtmüller.

After the first publication of the essay valuable additional information came to my notice. Some concerns the Wittgenstein–Frege correspondence. For this I am indebted to Prof. Dr. Friedrich Kambartel and Prof. Dr. Gottfried Gabriel. A much greater amount of new information relates to the publication, in a series edited by C.K. Ogden, of the *Tractatus* in England and to the first English translation of the German text. For a full record of this information the reader is referred to *Ludwig Wittgenstein, Letters to C.K. Ogden with Comments on the English Translation of the* Tractatus Logico-Philosophicus, edited with an Introduction by G.H. von Wright (Basil Blackwell, Oxford, and Routledge & Kegan Paul, London, 1973). I am indebted to Mr Mark Haymon for his unfailing helpfulness in the course of my work on this part of the publication history of the *Tractatus*.

The original study was republished with minor revisions in *Wittgenstein: Sources and Perspectives,* edited by C.G. Luckhardt (Cornell University Press, Ithaca, NY, 1979). It has been thoroughly revised and expanded for the present collection.

I

In September 1965 I found in Vienna a hitherto unknown manuscript in Wittgenstein's hand. It contains an early, but essentially complete, version of his *Logisch-philosophische Abhandlung*. The manuscript is written in pencil in a hardcover notebook measuring 20 × 24½ cm.

An examination of the manuscript shows that it consists of two parts and a Preface. The first, and by far the longer, part is by itself a complete work; this is the early version, mentioned above, of the *Tractatus*. For the sake of convenience, I shall henceforth refer to it by the label 'Prototractatus'.

The second part has the character of additions to and further elucidations of the thoughts contained in the 'Prototractatus'. With few exceptions, remarks[1] in this part have the same number as the corresponding remark in the *Tractatus*. In most cases there is also complete identity of formulation; the differences that exist are insignificant.

At the very end of the manuscript there is a Preface (*Vorwort*). It differs from the Preface of the *Tractatus* only in not giving any date or place (or the author's initials) *and* in containing an additional paragraph at the very end. This paragraph reads: 'Meinem Onkel, Herrn Paul Wittgenstein, und meinem Freund Herrn Bertrand Russell danke ich für die liebevolle Aufmunterung die sie mir haben zuteil werden lassen.'[2]

Since the Preface must have been written after the second part of the manuscript, it cannot be regarded as a preface specifically for the 'Prototractatus'.

There are in the 'Prototractatus' 30 remarks and 6 'loose' or unnumbered paragraphs which do not occur in the *Tractatus*. There is also one loose paragraph which does. In approxi-

[1] By a 'remark' I here understand a paragraph, or section consisting of several paragraphs, with a number – either in the 'Prototractatus' or in the *Tractatus*.

[2] I wish to thank my uncle Mr Paul Wittgenstein and my friend Mr Bertrand Russell for the kind encouragement they have extended to me.

mately 400 places the actual wording of the text of the 'Prototractatus' differs from the corresponding place in the text of the *Tractatus*. Often, however, the difference is insignificant. In addition to differences of formulation there are also differences in the arrangement of the thoughts. These last are probably the most interesting differences between the two works.

2

The manuscript thus discovered begins with a page which reads: 'Zwischen diese Sätze werden alle guten Sätze meiner anderen Manuskripte gefügt. Die Nummern zeigen die Reihenfolge und die Wichtigkeit der Sätze an. So folgt 5.04101 auf 5.041 und auf jenen 5.0411 welcher Satz wichtiger ist als 5.04101.'[3]

Then follows the page with the title, the page with the epigraph and the dedication, and the first page of the text, which lists the six principal 'theses' of the work and some of the main 'sub-theses' under them.[4]

A student of the manuscript is struck by the use of the *accusative* in 'Zwischen diese Sätze' and by the phrase 'werden alle guten Sätze . . . gefügt'. The question arises which are the sentences, of which it is said that in between them all the good sentences of Wittgenstein's other notes will be inserted. My conjecture is that they are the sentences listed on the first text-page, or possibly first few text-pages. Perhaps the note at the very beginning was written after Wittgenstein had on the first text-page written down the remarks which so to speak constitute the backbone of the entire work.

It is, unfortunately, no longer possible to identify exactly the manuscripts from which the remarks that constitute the 'Prototractatus' were selected.

[3] In between these sentences will be inserted all the good sentences from my other manuscripts. The numbers indicate the order and the importance of the sentences. Thus 5.04101 follows after 5.041, and 5.0411 follows after and is more important than 5.04101.

[4] Thesis 7 is found on page 71 of the manuscript.

Of Wittgenstein's writings prior to the completion of the *Tractatus* the following items, in addition to the present manuscript, have been preserved:

(1) Three notebooks from the time of the First World War. The first two are continuous and cover the period 9 August 1914 to 22 June 1915; the third covers the period 15 April 1916 to 10 January 1917. These notebooks also contain a diary written for the most part in code. In 1952, when I first saw them, the notebooks were in the house of Wittgenstein's youngest sister, Mrs M. Stonborough, at Gmunden. I shall here call them the Gmunden notebooks. The philosophical content of the notebooks was, with a few slight omissions, edited by Miss Anscombe and me and published in 1961.

(2) The 'Notes on Logic' of September 1913 which Wittgenstein sent to Bertrand Russell. There exist two versions of the 'notes'. The version that the editors of the *Notebooks 1914–1916* included as an Appendix to the first edition (1961) is presumably a rearrangement of the material made by Russell. The other version is slightly earlier and consists of a part called 'Summary' and of four sections called the first, second, third, and fourth 'Manuscript'. The Summary was evidently dictated by Wittgenstein himself to a typist, and the manuscripts were translated by Russell from the German text, which is no longer preserved. This second, and more 'authentic', version of the 'Notes' replaced the other version in the new edition (1979) of the *Notebooks 1914–1916*.[5]

(3) The notes dictated to G.E. Moore on the occasion of Moore's visit to Wittgenstein in Norway in April 1914. They, too, are printed as an Appendix to the *Notebooks 1914–1916*.

Wittgenstein's last visit to Vienna before his death was from December 1949 to March 1950. Miss Anscombe, who saw him in Vienna, testifies that Wittgenstein had then ordered several notebooks which still existed from the time of the germination of the *Tractatus* to be destroyed. (She thinks it was only by accident that the notebooks at Gmunden were

---

[5] The problems connected with the two versions of 'Notes on Logic' have been thoroughly investigated and probably conclusively solved by Brian McGuinness. See his essay 'Bertrand Russell and Ludwig Wittgenstein's "Notes on Logic"', *Revue internationale de Philosophie* **26**, 1972.

preserved.) I have not been able to confirm that the order was carried into effect, but there seems no strong reason for doubting that it was.

In a letter, dated 23 April 1953, to Professor F.A. Hayek, giving biographical information about Wittgenstein, the late Mr Paul Engelmann writes: 'Seine Manuskriptbücher waren große, in schwarz und grün gestreiftes Leinen gebundene Geschäftsbücher, wie man sie in Österreich als Hauptbücher verwendete. . . . Der Tractatus ist der endgültige Extrakt aus 7 solchen Büchern, die er nach dem Erscheinen des Buches vernichtet hat.'[6]

This report gives rise to many questions. Were the three Gmunden notebooks among the seven to which Engelmann refers? In which case it would not be true that they were all destroyed.[7] The Gmunden notebooks were composed at an average speed of one notebook in six months. Between the second and the third there is a gap of a little less than a year. Assuming that the final composition of the *Tractatus* took place in the summer of 1918, there is a gap of a year and a half between the third notebook and this final stage. Assuming further the same writing speed throughout the whole war period, it is reasonable to suppose that there existed at least four wartime notebooks which are now lost and which were of a similar character to the three that we have.

In a letter without date, which Russell received in January 1915, Wittgenstein writes: 'Sollte ich in diesem Krieg umkommen, so wird Dir mein Manuskript, welches ich damals Moore zeigte, zugeschickt werden; nebst einem,

[6] His manuscript volumes were large office-books bound in black and green striped cloth, of the kind used in Austria as ledgers. . . . The *Tractatus* is the final selection from seven books of this kind, which he destroyed after the appearance of the book.'

[7] In a later letter to Hayek (12 June 1953), Engelmann says that he saw the manuscript books only at Olmütz and not later in Vienna. Engelmann's friendship with Wittgenstein dates from the autumn of 1916, when Wittgenstein was in an officers' training school at Olmütz. Wittgenstein also visited Olmütz later in the war when on leave from the army. But we have no evidence that he came to Olmütz to visit Engelmann after his return from captivity in Italy after the end of the war.

welches ich jetzt während des Krieges geschrieben habe.'⁸

From this it is evident that Wittgenstein in April 1914, when Moore came to visit him in Norway, had a manuscript. As indicated above, there also existed a manuscript in September the year before from a copy of which Russell had made translations.⁹ Whether this was the same manuscript as the one Moore saw, or a different one, we cannot tell. The other manuscript to which Wittgenstein refers and which he says was written during the war is probably the first (or first two) of the Gmunden notebooks. The way he speaks of the two manuscripts would indicate that they were of a roughly similar character, that is, that the second was a continuation of, rather than superseding, the first.

The above letter is a reply to a letter from Russell, which is dated 28 July 1914 but which reached Wittgenstein only much later. It seems that Russell had complained that Moore had not been able to explain to him Wittgenstein's ideas. 'Daß Moore meine Ideen Dir nicht hat erklären können, ist mir unbegreiflich. Hast Du aus seinen Notizen irgend etwas entnehmen können?? Ich fürchte, Nein.'¹⁰

On 22 May 1915 Wittgenstein wrote to Russell in reply to a letter dated 10 May:

Daß Du Moores Aufschreibungen nicht hast verstehen können tut mir außerordentlich leid. Ich fürchte, daß sie ohne weitere Erklärung sehr schwer verständlich sind, aber ich halte sie doch im Wesentlichen für endgültig. Was ich in der letzten Zeit geschrieben habe wird nun, wie ich fürchte, noch unverständlicher sein; und, wenn ich das Ende dieses Krieges nicht mehr

⁸ 'If I should not survive the present war, my manuscript, which I showed to Moore in the past, will be sent to you along with another which I have now written, during the war.'

⁹ See the essay by McGuinness and the letters numbered 17–20 to Russell in *Ludwig Wittgenstein, Letters to Russell, Keynes and Moore*, ed. with an Introduction by G.H. von Wright assisted by B.F. McGuinness, Basil Blackwell, Oxford, 1974, 2nd edit. with minor revisions 1977. References to the letters to Russell will henceforth be given with the letter *R* followed by a numeral.

¹⁰ 'I find it inconceivable that Moore has not been able to explain my ideas to you. Have you been able to understand anything at all from my notes?? I am afraid the answer is: no.'

erlebe, so muß ich mich darauf gefaßt machen, daß meine
ganze Arbeit verloren geht. – Dann soll mein Manuskript
gedruckt werden, ob es irgend einer versteht, oder nicht.[11]

At the time that Wittgenstein wrote this letter, he had nearly
completed the second of the Gmunden notebooks.. What he
here calls 'my manuscript' is, I conjecture, the manuscript or
manuscripts he had in Norway *and* the first two wartime
(Gmunden) notebooks.

On 22 October the same year, Wittgenstein wrote again to
Russell. He now says:

Ich habe in der letzten Zeit sehr viel gearbeitet und, wie ich
glaube, mit gutem Erfolg. Ich bin jetzt dabei das Ganze
zusammenzufassen und in Form einer Abhandlung niederzu-
schreiben. Ich werde nun keinesfalls etwas veröffentlichen, ehe
Du es gesehen hast. Das kann aber natürlich erst nach dem
Kriege geschehen. Aber, wer weiß, ob ich das erleben werde.
Falls ich es nicht mehr erlebe, so laß Dir von meinen Leuten
meine ganzen Manuskripte schicken, darunter befindet sich
auch die letzte Zusammenfassung mit Bleistift auf losen
Blättern geschrieben. Es wird Dir vielleicht einige Mühe
machen alles zu verstehen, aber laß Dich dadurch nicht
abschrecken.[12]

Here Wittgenstein evidently is referring to something
which is *not* of the same character as the notebooks but which

---

[11] 'I am extremely sorry that you weren't able to understand the notes that
Moore took down. I am afraid they are very hard to understand without
further explanation; yet I consider them essentially as definitive. And now
I'm afraid that what I've written recently will be still more incomprehensible
and if I don't live to see the end of the present war I must be prepared for all
my work to go for nothing. – In that case my MS must be printed whether
anyone understands it or not.'
[The notes are evidently those published with the *Notebooks 1914–1916*.]
[12] 'I have recently done a great deal of work and, I think, quite
successfully. I'm now in the process of summarizing it all and writing it
down in the form of a treatise. Now whatever happens I won't publish
anything before you've seen it. But of course that can't happen until after the
war. But who knows whether I shall survive it. If I don't survive, get my
people to send you all my manuscripts: among them you'll find the final
summary written in pencil on loose sheets of paper. It will probably cost you
some trouble to understand it all, but don't be put off by that.'

is a *Zusammenfassung* (synopsis) of their content – to something like the 'Prototractatus' in fact. Could it be the 'Prototractatus' itself? An affirmative answer is excluded if only by the fact that the 'Prototractatus' also contains remarks from the third Gmunden notebook, which was written in 1916. The letter, moreover, speaks of a 'letzte Zusammenfassung' on loose sheets. It does not, in my opinion, follow that there must at that time have existed *two Zusammenfassungen*. The *Zusammenfassung* to which Wittgenstein refers with the words 'Ich bin dabei das Ganze zusammenzufassen' can be the same as the one on loose sheets. But we may safely conclude that the 'Prototractatus' had *at least one* predecessor.[13]

It is thus certain that, in addition to the manuscripts that have been preserved, there existed at least one manuscript from before the war (spring 1914), probably of the same nature as the Gmunden notebooks, and at least one *Zusammenfassung* from the autumn of 1915, perhaps of similar character to the 'Prototractatus'. This is all we know for certain. But it seems to me a reasonable conjecture that there also existed one or two notebooks from the period June 1915–April 1916, and two or three notebooks from the time January 1917–August 1918 which have been lost. If this is right, there once existed seven to nine notebooks in all, from which the content of the *Tractatus* is an extract. This squares relatively well with the information in Engelmann's letter to Hayek.

We also know[14] that when Wittgenstein in the autumn of 1913 left Cambridge and moved to Norway, he deposited with a furniture dealer (Jolley) a number of belongings, including some books, diaries, and manuscripts. The diaries and manuscripts Wittgenstein ordered to be burned and the other things to be sold. Russell writes in his *Autobiography*[15]

[13] Dr Heinrich Groag, who knew Wittgenstein during the first war, remembers a manuscript lent to him in the winter of 1917–18 which was written in pencil on loose sheets with numbered propositions. It is not unlikely that this manuscript was another 'predecessor' of the 'Prototractatus'. (I am indebted to Mr B.F. McGuinness for this item of information.)

[14] *R* 40.

[15] *The Autobiography of Bertrand Russell 1914–1944*, Allen & Unwin, London, 1968, p. 100.

that he himself bought the books and furniture; of the fate of the manuscripts nothing is said. The money from the sale was evidently used to finance Wittgenstein's visit to Holland and meeting with Russell in December 1919.

When was the 'Prototractatus' and the rest of the manuscript book in which it appears written?

In a postcard to Russell, dated 9 February 1919, from Cassino in Italy, Wittgenstein says that he has been a prisoner in Italy since November (1918) and that he hopes to be able to communicate with Russell 'after three years' interruption'.[16] He adds: 'I have done lots of logical work which I am dying to let you know before publishing it.'

On 10 March Wittgenstein again wrote a postcard – in reply to a card from Russell which had reached him in the meantime. Here he says: 'I've written a book which will be published as soon as I get home.' And he adds: 'I think I have solved our problems finally.'

Later in March Wittgenstein sent a letter to Russell from the prison camp. In it he describes more fully the work he had done:

> I've written a book called 'Logisch-philosophische Abhandlung' containing all my work of the last six years. I believe I've solved our problems finally. This may sound arrogant but I can't help believing it. I finished the book in August 1918 and two months after was made Prigioniere. I've got the manuscript here with me. I wish I could copy it out for you; but it's pretty long and I would have no safe way of sending it to you. . . . I will publish it as soon as I get home.

Soon after, however, Wittgenstein was able to send his work to Russell. In his next letter, Cassino, 12 June 1919, we read: 'Vor einigen Tagen schickte ich Dir mein Manuscript durch Keynes's Vermittelung. . . . Es ist das einzige korrigierte Exemplar, welches ich besitze und die Arbeit meines Lebens. Mehr als je brenne ich jetzt darauf es gedruckt zu sehen.'[17]

[16] There seems to have been no communication between the two friends in the period 22 October 1915– 9 February 1919.

[17] 'Some days ago I sent you my manuscript through Keynes's intermediacy. It is the only corrected copy that I possess and is my life's work. I long more than ever to see it printed.'

The next letter is the last one written in the prison camp. Its date is 19 August 1919. Here Wittgenstein repeats a wish which he had already earlier expressed that Russell and he should meet and discuss the work. As a possible meeting place he suggests Holland or Switzerland. 'Please write to Vienna IV, Alleegasse 16. As to my MS, please send it to the same address; but only if there is an absolutely safe way of sending it. Otherwise please keep it. I should be very glad though, to get it soon, as it's the only corrected copy I've got.'

Wittgenstein continues: 'I also sent my MS to Frege. He wrote me a week ago and I gather that he doesn't understand a word of it all.' Then in a long postscript to the letter he proceeds to answer a number of questions concerning his work which Russell had raised.[18]

The only date which is significant for the dating of Wittgenstein's work and which is mentioned in the correspondence with Russell from the prison camp is that he finished the book in *August* 1918.

At the beginning of the second part of the manuscript there is a puzzling footnote. It says that the numbers of the remarks in this part are the numbers in the *'Korrektur'*. The word *Korrektur* could mean the proofs of a printed text. It is extremely unlikely that this is what it means here. The earliest possible printed proofs would have been those of the publication in Ostwald's *Annalen* in 1921; and we have no evidence that Wittgenstein ever saw these proofs. What the word *Korrektur* probably refers to is a corrected MS- or TS-copy of the *Tractatus* or 'Prototractatus'.

I here make the following conjecture. After having written down in the manuscript book all the remarks that constitute the 'Prototractatus', Wittgenstein copied it out, or had it copied out, with the remarks arranged in their proper number order. Probably either this copy was a typescript or a typescript copy of it was made (see below). Then he worked with this text (the *Korrektur*) changing the formulations, grouping remarks which carried separate numbers under one single number, rearranging the order in places. Having done this (or when doing this) he also made some additions. These additional entries he noted down in handwriting in the same

[18] *R* 37.

notebook as the 'Prototractatus'. When he had finished with
the additions, he wrote the *Vorwort*, and probably transferred
it too to the *Korrektur*. Another possibility is that the *Korrektur*
simply was the copy of the work which he sent to Russell from
Cassino and of which he said that it was 'the only corrected
copy'.

If the above reconstruction of what took place is correct, it
still does not answer the question when the 'Prototractatus' was
composed. We know that Wittgenstein was on a longish leave
in the summer of 1918. He spent it partly at the family estate
Hochreit, partly, it seems, with his uncle (the Paul Wittgenstein referred to in the *Vorwort* at the back of the 'Prototractatus' notebook) at Hallein near Salzburg, and partly in
Vienna. Did he do *all* the work of finishing the book then,
beginning with the extracting of the 'Prototractatus' from the
earlier notes? Or did he start then with the composition of the
Korrektur, having already extracted the 'Prototractatus' –
perhaps in the winter and spring of that same year?

Engelmann, in his letter to Professor Hayek of 12 June 1953,
says: 'Vor seinem Abgang an die italienische Front hat er sein
Manuskript in die Maschine diktiert.'[19] Wittgenstein was
transferred to the Italian front in March 1918. It is not certain,
however, that this dictation for the typewriter took place
before Wittgenstein went there for the first time. Nor is it
certain that the manuscript referred to by Engelmann was the
'Prototractatus'.

The dedication to the memory of David Pinsent is already in
the 'Prototractatus'. There seems no reason to think that it had
been added to the MS later. Pinsent was killed in the war on 8
May 1918. News could hardly have reached Wittgenstein until
a month or so later. The most likely conjecture seems to me to
be that work on the 'Prototractatus' immediately preceded the
final composition of the book in the summer of 1918.

[19] 'Before going to the Italian front he dictated his manuscript for the
typewriter.'

3

Three different typescripts of the *Tractatus* are known to exist, or to have existed. One later belonged to Wittgenstein's friend Engelmann, who died in Tel Aviv early in 1965. It is now in the Bodleian Library at Oxford. Another typescript, from which the last page is missing, I found in Vienna in 1965. A third, to which was also attached a typescript of Russell's Introduction, I saw in 1952 at Gmunden. This typescript is now missing. Attempts to find it have so far proved unsuccessful. I shall refer to these typescripts as the Engelmann TS, the Vienna TS, and the Gmunden TS respectively.

Engelmann, to whom Wittgenstein had given the typescript as a gift, believed that his was the copy from which the book had actually been printed. On the grounds partly of annotations on the typescript and partly of the correspondence which took place between Wittgenstein and C.K. Ogden in 1922, it seems certain that the printing of the book in Ostwald's *Annalen* (1921) was from this typescript. But the subsequent printing of the book by Kegan Paul in London (1922) evidently was from (an offprint of) the publication by Ostwald (see p. 98 below).

The Gmunden TS, as I remember it, contained a great number of corrections and marks in pencil. I cannot recall whether Russell's 'Introduction' was a part of the *same* typescript – nor even whether it was in English or German. I listed it among my notes, at the time when it was shown to me, as a 'typescript (with corrections) of the whole *Tractatus* with Russell's Introduction'.[20]

The Vienna TS is, surprisingly, not a carbon copy of the Engelmann TS. It contains relatively few corrections in pencil, and no substantial additions. It does not, for example, contain the remark 6.1203, which has been added to the Engelmann TS in handwriting on a separate sheet. I have found one difference in substance between it and the Engel-

[20] In 1952 there also existed, at Gmunden, a handwritten version, dated November–December 1936, of the first 188 remarks of the *Philosophical Investigations* and a manuscript and a typescript of the Lecture on Ethics. These are now missing.

mann TS. This is the remark 6.241 which in the Engelmann TS and the printed text is a proof of the proposition that $2 \times 2 = 4$ but which in the Vienna TS is the much simpler proof that $2 + 2 = 4$.

There is at present no way of telling whether the Gmunden TS is a second copy of either the Engelmann or the Vienna TS, or whether it is a third typescript 'original'.

As we have seen, Wittgenstein in his letters from Cassino to Russell speaks of his work as a 'manuscript'. This, however, cannot be taken as proof that it was, in fact, a *manu*script and not a *type*script. There is good evidence for thinking that it was the latter. Thus Ludwig Hänsel, who was with Wittgenstein in the prison camp at Cassino and remained a close friend of his ever after, writes in a letter to Hayek of 28 January 1953: 'Er hatte ein maschingeschriebenes fertiges Exemplar in seinem Rucksack bereits mit. (Er hat es mir damals zu lesen gegeben, auch mit mir sehr ausführlich besprochen.) Hinzugefügt hat er in der Gefangenschaft nur einige Stellen, so die Schemata von 6.1203.'[21]

In his first letter (after the two postcards) to Russell from Cassino Wittgenstein says he wishes he could copy the thing out for Russell. This speaks in favour of thinking that he had only *one copy* of it with him. In the next letter, dated 12 June 1919, Wittgenstein says that the 'manuscript' which he had just sent to Russell was his only *corrected* copy. In the letter after that (19 August 1919) he says that he had also sent a copy to Frege and that he now has no copy with him at Cassino.

The copy to Frege had in fact been sent already in December 1918, that is, nearly half a year before he sent his only corrected copy to Russell. We know this from records of communications to Frege from one of Wittgenstein's sisters (see p. 80 below). The copy had been sent by this sister and not 'directly' by Wittgenstein. Perhaps it was a copy which Wittgenstein had left behind at home when going back to the front. We know, moreover, from the same records that, when Frege

---

[21] 'He already had a complete typescript copy with him in his rucksack. (He gave it to me to read at the time and also discussed it with me in great detail.) He added only a few passages while a prisoner, as, for example, the schemata in 6.1203.'

received the copy, one page was missing from it. This may be regarded as slight evidence for thinking that the copy in question was in fact the Vienna TS. The missing page, however, was later, in March 1919, sent separately to Frege. Whether it was eventually returned with the typescript we do not know. Nor do we know when the typescript was sent back. But we know that Wittgenstein had a copy of his work in Vienna on his return from captivity in the middle of August 1919 (cf. the letter to Russell of 20 August 1919, quoted below). Perhaps this was a third typescript – possibly the Gmunden TS.

The remark 6.1203 and the diagrams mentioned in the letter from Hänsel quoted above are missing from the Vienna TS. They have been added to the Engelmann TS, as it now exists, in handwriting. The fact that the remark had not been added to the Vienna TS is additional evidence that Wittgenstein had only *one* copy, probably the Engelmann TS, with him at Cassino and that two other copies, probably the Vienna and the Gmunden TSS, had been left by him in Austria.

4

Towards the end of the summer of 1918, when still on leave from the army, Wittgenstein had offered his book to the Viennese publisher, Jahoda & Siegel, for publication.[22] When back in the army, he was impatiently waiting for an answer.[23] He got it on 25 October, a few days before the end of the war. The answer was negative. Wittgenstein wrote to his friend Paul Engelmann: 'Heute erhielt ich von Jahoda die Mitteilung, daß er meine Arbeit nicht drucken kann. Angeblich aus technischen Gründen. Ich wüßte aber gar zu gern, was Kraus zu ihr gesagt hat. Wenn Sie Gelegenheit hätten es zu erfahren, so würde ich mich sehr freuen. Vielleicht weiss Loos etwas. Schreiben Sie mir.'[24]

[22] See the letters to Engelmann of 14 July, 9 October, 22 October, and 25 October 1918.

[23] Letters to Engelmann of 9 October and 22 October 1918.

[24] 'Today I received notification from Jahoda that he cannot publish my treatise. Allegedly for technical reasons. But I would dearly like to know

The letter may be taken as an indication that Karl Kraus, the satirist, and Adolf Loos, the architect, had been involved in this first effort to find a publisher for Wittgenstein's book.

With the Jahoda episode we enter the long and troubled history of the publication of the *Tractatus*. It is obvious that Wittgenstein was very anxious to publish his book. The many difficulties and obstacles must have depressed him deeply.

On 20 August 1919, only a few days after his return from captivity, Wittgenstein wrote to Russell:

> Ich bin jetzt mit einer Kopie meines MS zu einem Verleger gegangen, um den Druck endlich in die Wege zu leiten. Der Verleger, der natürlich weder meinen Namen kennt, noch etwas von Philosophie versteht, verlangt das Urteil irgendeines Fachmanns, um sicher zu sein, daß das Buch wirklich wert ist, gedruckt zu werden. Er wollte sich deshalb an einen seiner Vertrauensmänner hier wenden (wahrscheinlich an einen Philosophie-Professor). Ich sagte ihm, nun, daß hier niemand das Buch beurteilen könnte, daß *Du* aber vielleicht so gut sein würdest, ihm ein kurzes Urteil über den Wert der Arbeit zu schreiben; was, wenn es günstig ausfällt, ihm genügen wird um den Verlag zu übernehmen. Die Adresse des Verlegers ist: Wilhelm Braumüller. XI. Servitengasse 5 Wien. Ich bitte Dich nun, dorthin ein paar Worte, so viel Du vor Deinem Gewissen verantworten kannst, zu schreiben. [25]

---

what Kraus said about it. If there were an opportunity for you to find out, I should be very glad. Perhaps Loos knows something about it. Do write to me.'

[25] 'I have now been to a publisher with a copy of my manuscript in order to get its printing finally under way. The publisher, who naturally neither knows my name nor understands anything about philosophy, requires the judgement of some expert in order to be sure that the work is really worth printing. For this purpose he wanted to apply to one of the people that he relies on here, probably a professor of philosophy. So I told him that no one here would be able to form a judgement on the book – but that *you* would probably be kind enough to write him a brief assessment of the value of the work, and if this happened to be favourable that would be enough to induce him to publish it. The publisher's address is: Wilhelm Braumüller, XI Servitengasse 5, Vienna. Now please write him a few words, as much as your conscience will allow you to.'

[See also letter to Engelmann of 2 September 1919.]

Wilhelm Braumüller was the publisher of the work of Otto Weininger, which Wittgenstein much admired. In a letter to Ludwig von Ficker written later that autumn Wittgenstein says it was this fact which induced him to approach Braumüller. The copy of the work mentioned in the letter to Russell was neither the typescript which he had sent to Russell, nor the one which he had sent to Frege. For these typescripts had not by then been returned to the author (see pp. 80, 83 below). It could have been the typescript which, a year earlier, he had given to Jahoda.

From Wittgenstein's next letter to Russell (6 October 1919) we learn that Braumüller had received a letter of recommendation from Russell, but had not yet made up his mind whether to publish the book. Soon after, however, this effort to get the book published came to an end. Braumüller made the publication conditional upon the author's paying for the paper and the printing. This humiliating condition Wittgenstein could not accept. He explains his attitude in the above-mentioned letter to Ficker as follows:

> Erstens habe ich nicht das Geld, um den Verlag meiner Arbeit selbst zu zahlen, weil ich mich meines gesamten Vermögens entledigt habe. . . . Zweitens aber könnte ich mir zwar das Geld dazu verschaffen, will es aber nicht; denn ich halte es für bürgerlich unanständig ein Werk der Welt – zu welcher der Verleger gehört – in dieser Weise aufzudrängen: Das Schreiben war *meine* Sache; annehmen muß es aber die Welt auf die normale Art und Weise.[26]

Wittgenstein then, the letter continues, had turned to 'a professor in Germany', who knew the editor of a philosophical periodical. 'Von diesem erhielt ich die Zusage die Arbeit zu übernehmen, wenn ich sie vom Anfang bis zum Ende

---

[26] 'First of all, I haven't the money to pay for the publication of my work myself, because I've got rid of all my property. . . . But secondly, though I could contrive to get the money for that purpose, I don't want to, because I think it's not the decent behaviour, from a social point of view, to force a book on to the world (of which the publisher is a part) in this way. *My* job was to write the book: its acceptance by the world must proceed in the normal fashion.'

verstümmeln, und mit einem Wort eine andere Arbeit daraus machen, wollte.'[27]

The professor in Germany must have been Frege and the periodical *Beiträge zur Philosophie des deutschen Idealismus* in which Frege had himself published. This can be verified from a lapidary annotation by the late Professor Heinrich Scholz to a list of Wittgenstein's letters to Frege. The letters were kept in the Frege-*Archiv* which Heinrich Scholz had collected and deposited at Münster in Germany. The collection was destroyed in the bombings during the 1939–45 war. No copies of the letters had been taken or none were rescued, but a list of the correspondence has been preserved. It mentions two letters from the year 1913, four postcards from the time of the 1914–18 war, three postcards and one letter from Cassino (and six communications from Wittgenstein through one of his sisters to Frege), and four letters from the autumn of 1919. It must have been in reference to these last letters that Wittgenstein wrote in the letter to Russell of 6 October: 'Mit Frege stehe ich in Briefwechsel. Er versteht kein Wort von meiner Arbeit und ich bin schon ganz erschöpft vor lauter Erklärungen.'[28]

The annotation by Scholz refers to a letter of 16 September 1919 and goes as follows: 'Brief W. an Fr. vom 16.9.1919. Inhalt: Dank für "Der Gedanke", kritische Bemerkungen dazu. Bitte um Verwendung für Druck seiner Abh. in den BPhDI.'[29] 'Der Gedanke' is a paper by Frege which was published in 1919 in the *Beiträge zur Philosophie des deutschen Idealismus*. Frege had evidently sent Wittgenstein a copy of his paper.

It was when the efforts to get his book published through

[27] 'The last named sent to me agreeing to adopt the work, provided I would mangle it from begining to end and, in a word, make a different work out of it.'
[28] 'I'm in correspondence with Frege. He doesn't understand a single word of my work and I'm thoroughly exhausted by giving what are purely and simply explanations.'
[29] 'Letter from W. to Fr. dated 16 September 1919. Content: thanks for 'The Thought': critical observations thereon. Request for assistance towards the printing of his *Tractatus* in BPhDI.'

Frege had failed that Wittgenstein turned to Ludwig von Ficker. He did this in the letter from which we have already quoted. The letter is undated. To judge by existing evidence, I should say it was written some time in the middle of October 1919. After having told of his adversities with Jahoda, Braumüller, and Frege, Wittgenstein continues:

> Da fiel mir endlich ein ob *Sie* nicht geneigt sein könnten, das arme Wesen in Ihren Schutz zu nehmen. Und *darum* möchte ich Sie eben bitten: Das Manuscript würde ich Ihnen erst schicken wenn Sie glauben daß überhaupt an eine Aufnahme in den Brenner zu denken ist: Bis dahin möchte ich nur soviel sagen: Die Arbeit ist streng philosophisch und zugleich literarisch, es wird aber doch nicht darin geschwefelt. Und nun bitte überlegen Sie sich die Sache und schreiben Sie mir möglichst bald.[30]

Ludwig von Ficker (1880–1967), who lived at Innsbruck, was editor of *Der Brenner*, a kind of cultural periodical, and head of a small publishing firm. The two men had met in Vienna on the eve of the outbreak of the war. Wittgenstein had arranged for the distribution through Ficker of a considerable sum of money to some Austrian writers and artists, among them Rilke, Trakl, and Oscar Kokoschka. During the war they had some correspondence. Wittgenstein's letters and postcards to Ficker, 29 in all and from the period 14 July 1914 to 26 January 1920, are now in the *Brenner-Archiv* of Innsbruck University.[31] Ficker's letters to Wittgenstein seem to be lost.

Ficker's first reaction to Wittgenstein's request was apparently a friendly letter, in which he asked for the manuscript and expressed mild surprise that Wittgenstein had not approached him in the matter at once. Wittgenstein's reply

[30] 'Then eventually it occurred to me to wonder whether perhaps *you* wouldn't take the poor creature under your wing. And all I want to ask you is this: I'll only send you the manuscript if you think there's any chance of its being accepted for the *Brenner*. For the present I will only say this much: the work is strictly philosophical and at the same time literary: but there's no gassing in it. Now please give the matter some thought and write to me as soon as possible.'

[31] I am much indebted to Dr Walter Methlagl for access to materials in the *Archiv* and for information about Ficker and *Der Brenner*.

is extremely interesting because of the information it contains
of how Wittgenstein viewed his work. The letter, which is
undated, too, is here reproduced *in toto*:

Lieber Herr Ficker!

Zugleich mit diesem Brief geht das Manuscript an Sie ab.
Warum ich nicht *gleich* an Sie dachte? Ja, denken Sie, ich *habe*
gleich an Sie gedacht, allerdings zu einer Zeit, wo das Buch
noch gar nicht verlegt werden konnte, weil es nicht fertig war.
Wie es aber dann so weit war, da hatten wir ja Krieg und da war
wieder an Ihre Hilfe nicht zu denken. Jetzt aber hoffe ich auf
Sie. Und da ist es Ihnen vielleicht eine Hilfe, wenn ich Ihnen ein
paar Worte über mein Buch schreibe: Von seiner Lektüre
werden Sie nämlich – wie ich bestimmt glaube – nicht allzuviel
haben. Denn Sie werden es nicht verstehen; der Stoff wird
Ihnen ganz fremd erscheinen. In Wirklichkeit ist er Ihnen nicht
fremd, denn der Sinn des Buches ist ein Ethischer. Ich wollte
einmal in das Vorwort einen Satz geben, der nun tatsächlich
nicht darin steht, den ich Ihnen aber jetzt schreibe, weil er
Ihnen vielleicht ein Schlüssel sein wird: Ich wollte nämlich
schreiben, mein Werk bestehe aus zwei Teilen: aus dem, der
hier vorliegt, und aus alledem, was ich *nicht* geschrieben habe.
Und gerade dieser zweite Teil ist der Wichtige. Es wird
nämlich das Ethische durch mein Buch gleichsam von Innen
her begrenzt; und ich bin überzeugt, daß es, *streng*, NUR SO zu
begrenzen ist. Kurz ich glaube: Alles das, was *viele* heute
schwefeln, habe ich in meinem Buch festgelegt, indem ich
darüber schweige. Und darum wird das Buch, wenn ich mich
nicht sehr irre, vieles sagen, was Sie selbst sagen wollen, aber
Sie werden vielleicht nicht sehen, daß es darin gesagt ist. Ich
würde Ihnen nun empfehlen, das *Vorwort* und den *Schluß* zu
lesen, da diese den Sinn am unmittelbarsten zum Ausdruck
bringen.

Das M.S., das ich Ihnen jetzt sende, ist nicht das eigentliche
Druckmanuscript, sondern eine von mir nur flüchtig durch-
gesehene Kopie, die aber zu Ihrer Orientierung genügen wird.
Das Druck M.S. ist genau durchgesehen; es befindet sich aber
augenblicklich in England bei meinem Freund Russell, dem ich
es aus der Gefangenschaft geschickt habe. Er wird es mir aber
in der nächsten Zeit zurückschicken. Und so wünsche ich mir
einstweilen viel Glück.

Seien Sie herzlich gegrüßt von Ihrem ergebenen
Ludwig Wittgenstein[32]

As was noted above (p. 73), Wittgenstein had shortly before his release from the prison camp begged Russell to return the manuscript to Vienna. The request was repeated in the autumn, but it was not until 21 November that Wittgenstein could, in a letter to Russell, acknowledge safe receipt of the only corrected and complete copy of his work then in existence.

It was probably on that same day that Wittgenstein received

[32] Dear Mr Ficker,

My manuscript is going off to you at the same time as this letter. Why didn't I think of you *at once*? Now, just imagine! I *did* think of you at once but at a time when the book couldn't be published at all, because it wasn't yet ready. But then, when it was ready, the war was on and there was again no question of help from you. But now I am putting my hopes in you. And in that connection it will probably be a help to you if I write you a few words about my book. You see, I am quite sure that you won't get all that much out of reading it. Because you won't understand it; its subject matter will seem quite alien to you. But it isn't really alien to you, because the book's point is an ethical one. I once meant to include in the preface a sentence which is not in fact there now but which I will write out for you here, because it will perhaps be a key to the work for you. What I meant to write, then, was this: My work consists of two parts: the one presented here plus all that I have *not* written. And it is precisely this second part that is the important one. My book draws limits to the sphere of the ethical from the inside as it were, and I am convinced that this is the ONLY *rigorous* way of drawing those limits. In short, I believe that where *many* others today are just *gassing*, I have managed in my book to put everything firmly into place by being silent about it. And for that reason, unless I am very much mistaken, the book will say a great deal that you yourself want to say. Only perhaps you won't see that it is said in the book. For now, I would recommend you to read the *preface* and the *conclusion*, because they contain the most direct expression of the point of the book.

The MS that I'm sending you now isn't the actual one intended for printing but one that I've only glanced through: it will serve to orientate you, though. The MS intended for printing has been carefully revised. At the moment it is in England with my friend Russell. I sent it to him from the prison camp. But he will send it back to me in the near future. And so I wish myself, for once, the best of luck.

Best wishes from yours sincerely
Ludwig Wittgenstein

from Ficker the unpleasant news that Ficker too was hesitant to publish the book. In the letter to Russell of the 21st he does not mention this; but in a letter one week later (27 November) he complains: 'Ich habe jetzt erneute Schwierigkeiten wegen meines Buches. Niemand will es verlegen.'[33] And on the 22nd he had written to Ficker:

> Lieber Herr Ficker!
> Ihr Brief hat mich natürlich nicht angenehm berührt, obwohl ich mir ja Ihre Antwort ungefähr denken konnte. Ja, wo meine Arbeit untergebracht werden kann, das weiß ich selbst nicht. Wenn ich nur selbst schon wo anders untergebracht wäre als auf dieser beschissenen Welt. – Von mir aus können Sie das Manuscript dem Philosophie-Professor zeigen (wenn auch eine philosophische Arbeit einem Philosophie-Professor vorzulegen heißt, Perlen . . .). Verstehen wird er übrigens kein Wort. Und jetzt nur noch *eine* Bitte: Machen Sie's kurz mit mir und schmerzlos. Sagen Sie mir lieber ein rasches Nein als ein gar so langsames; das ist österreichisches Zartgefühl, welches auszuhalten meine Nerven momentan nicht ganz stark genug sind.
> > Ihr ergebener
> > Ludwig Wittgenstein[34]

The highly emotional tone of the letter alarmed Ficker and

---

[33] 'The difficulties over my book have started up again. No one wants to publish it.'

[34] Dear Mr Ficker,
   The effect your letter had on me was, of course, not a pleasant one, though I had been more or less able to imagine what your answer would be. I agree with you: I myself don't know where a home can be found for my work. If only I could myself find a home somewhere else, and not in this filthy world. As far as I'm concerned you can show the manuscript to your professor of philosophy (even though showing a philosophical work to a philosophy professor is the same as casting pearls . . .). However, he won't understand a word. And now just one more request: make it quick and painless for me. Tell me no immediately rather than ever so slowly: that's Austrian delicacy and my nerves are at the moment not quite strong enough to endure it.
   > Yours sincerely,
   > Ludwig Wittgenstein

he sent the author a soothing telegram. On 4 December
Wittgenstein replied:

Lieber Herr Ficker!
    Es war sehr schön von Ihnen, daß Sie mir auf meinen
Brandbrief mit einem so freundlichen Telegramm geantwortet
haben. Freilich, lieber wäre es mir Sie nähmen mein Buch, weil
Sie etwas darauf halten als, um mir einen Gefallen zu tun. Und
wie kann ich Ihnen mein eigenes Werk anempfehlen? – Ich
glaube, es verhält sich damit in allen solchen Fällen so. Ein
Buch, auch wenn es ganz und gar ehrlich geschrieben ist, ist
immer von *einem* Standpunkte aus wertlos: denn eigentlich
brauchte niemand ein Buch schreiben, weil es auf der Welt
ganz andere Dinge zu tun gibt. Andererseits glaube ich sagen
zu können: Wenn Sie den Dallago, den Haecker, u.s.w.
drucken, *dann* können Sie auch *mein* Buch drucken. Und das ist
auch alles, was ich zur Rechtfertigung meines Wunsches sagen
kann, denn, wenn man mein Buch mit einem *absoluten*
Maßstab mißt, dann weiß Gott wo es zu stehen kommt.
            Mit vielen Grüßen bin ich Ihr ergebener
            Ludwig Wittgenstein[35]

On the same day as this letter was written Wittgenstein also
received a letter from Ficker, to which he replied the day after:

Lieber Herr Ficker!
    Kaum hatte ich gestern meine Antwort auf Ihr Telegramm
abgeschickt, als Ihr lieber Brief vom 28.11. eintraf. Das Opfer,

---

[35] Dear Mr Ficker,
    It was very nice of you to answer my ferocious letter with such a
friendly telegram. Of course, I'd rather you took my book because you
thought something of it than in order to do me a favour. And how can I
recommend my own work to you? I believe that the way things are in
all such cases is this. Any book, even if it's written with absolute
honesty is from *one* point of view worthless: because really nobody
need write a book, given that there are quite other things to do in the
world. On the other hand I think I can say that if you're going to print
Dallago, Haecker, etc. *then* you can print *my* book too. And, moreover,
that's *all* I can say in justification of my wishes, because, measured by
absolute standards, God knows what my book is worth.
            With many good wishes, I am yours sincerely,
            Ludwig Wittgenstein

daß Sie mir, wenn alle Stricke reißen, bringen wollen, kann ich
natürlich nicht annehmen. Ich könnte es nicht vor mir
verantworten, wenn die Existenz eines Menschen (wessen
immer) durch die Herausgabe meines Buches in Frage gestellt
würde. So ganz verstehe ich es freilich nicht. Denn es haben ja
schon oft Menschen Bücher geschrieben, die mit dem
allgemeinen Jargon nicht zusammenfielen, und diese Bücher
sind verlegt worden und die Verleger sind nicht an ihnen zu
Grunde gegangen. (Im Gegenteil.) – Mein Vertrauen täuschen
Sie durchaus nicht, denn mein Vertrauen, oder vielmehr bloß
meine Hoffnung, bezog sich doch nur darauf, es möchte Ihnen
vielleicht Ihr Spürsinn sagen, daß die Abhandlung kein Mist sei
– wenn ich mich hierin nicht vielleicht selbst täusche – aber
doch nicht darauf, Sie möchten sie, ohne etwas von ihr zu
halten, aus Güte gegen mich und gegen Ihr Interesse annehm-
men. – Kurz, ich bin Ihnen *sehr* dankbar, wenn Sie in meiner
Sache durch Rilke etwas erreichen können; geht das aber nicht,
so lassen wir Gras darüber wachsen. – (Nebenbei bemerkt,
müssen die Dezimalnummern meiner Sätze unbedingt
mitgedruckt werden, weil sie allein dem Buch Übersichtlich-
keit und Klarheit geben und es ohne diese Numerierung ein
unverständlicher Wust wäre.)

Und nun leben Sie wohl und machen Sie sich meinetwegen
keine Sorgen. Es wird schon alles in Ordnung kommen.

Ihr Ergebener
Ludwig Wittgenstein

6.12.19 à propos: giebt es einen Krampus, der die schlimmen
Verleger holt?[36]

---

[36] Dear Mr Ficker,

Scarcely had I sent off my answer to your telegram yesterday when
your kind letter of 28.11 arrived. Of course I cannot accept the sacrifice
that you are willing to make for me if the worst comes to the worst. I
couldn't answer for it to myself if the existence of any human being
whatsoever was endangered by the publication of my book. Though I
must admit that I'm not completely convinced. Because, people have
often written books that didn't fall in with the jargon of the day and
those books have been published and the publishers haven't been ruined
by them. (Quite the contrary.) – You haven't shown my trust in you to
be an illusion, because my trust – or rather my hope – was simply that
your nose would tell you that the treatise was not rubbish – unless I am
myself under an illusion: I didn't trust or hope that you would accept it
without thinking it any good, out of kindness towards me and contrary

In the letter there is a reference to the poet Rainer Maria Rilke. The background to Rilke's entering the stage of the publication history of the *Tractatus* is as follows.

In order to help the author in his efforts to find a publisher, Ficker had written to Rilke. Apparently without disclosing to Rilke the identity of the anonymous donor of 1914 he asked whether Rilke could find a publisher for that donor's *'Logisch-philosophische Abhandlung'*. Rilke replied with the question whether Ficker thought the Insel-Verlag (Rilke's own publisher) suitable and with a request for names of German publishers to whom he might write. Rilke's reply to Ficker is dated 12 November 1919. He said he had received Ficker's letter the day before. There is no indication that either Ficker or Rilke did anything further to pursue this line.

In the letters to Russell during the autumn we can see how the plans (first mentioned in the letter from Cassino in April 1918) for a meeting of the two friends made progress. They eventually met in The Hague in the middle of December 1919, probably from the 13th to the 20th. On the 15th Wittgenstein wrote from Holland to Engelmann: 'Russell will meine Abhandlung drucken und zwar vielleicht deutsch und englisch (er wird sie selbst übersetzen und eine Einleitung zu ihr schreiben, was mir ganz recht ist).[37]

The tone of the last letter is quite euphoric. Wittgenstein

---

to your own interest. In brief, I'll be *very* grateful to you if, with Rilke's help, you can achieve anything on my behalf. But if that doesn't come off, we can let the grass grow over the whole project. (By the way: the decimal numbers of my remarks absolutely must be printed alongside them, because they alone make the book perspicuous and clear: without the numbering it would be an incomprehensible jumble.)

And now: all best wishes, and don't fret yourself on my account. Everything is going to turn out all right.

Yours sincerely,

Ludwig Wittgenstein

6.12.19 By the way, is there a *Krampus* (devil) to haul off naughty publishers?

[37] 'Russell wants to print my treatise, possibly in both German and English (he will translate it himself and write an introduction, which suits me).'

obviously was very pleased with the meeting. In his first letter
to Russell after his return to Vienna (8 January 1920) he says:
'Ich habe unser Beisammensein *sehr* genossen und ich habe das
Gefühl, daß wir in dieser Woche sehr viel wirklich gearbeitet
haben. (Du nicht auch?)'[38] And in a letter to Engelmann, dated
29 December, he says: 'Mein Zusammensein mit Russell war
sehr genußreich.'[39]

From the meeting with Russell in The Hague Wittgenstein
also wrote to Frege, announcing a visit on the way home to
Austria.[40] The visit, however, had to be cancelled, because
Wittgenstein's companion on the journey to Holland, Mr
Arvid Sjögren, had fallen seriously ill. Wittgenstein arrived
back from the meeting with Russell on 26 or 27 December.

It was thus at the meeting in The Hague that the plan came
up that Russell should write an Introduction to the book.
Wittgenstein was quite optimistic that with this authoritative
support his book would find a publisher. He wrote to
Engelmann (29 December 1919): 'Mit einer Einleitung von
Russell ist das Buch für einen Verleger gewiß ein sehr geringes
Risiko da Russell sehr bekannt ist.'[41] He also wrote about the
forthcoming Introduction to the publishers whom he had
contacted. In a letter to Russell of 8 January 1920 he writes:
'Von meinen vorhabenden Verlegern habe ich noch keine
Antwort auf die Mitteilung, daß Du meinem Buch mit einer
Einleitung nachhelfen willst.'[42]

The publishers (in the plural) to whom Wittgenstein is here
referring were Ficker, and perhaps, Braumüller and/or Reclam. To Ficker he wrote (28 December):

[38] 'I enjoyed our time together *very* much and I have the feeling (haven't
you too?) that we did a great deal of real work during the week.'

[39] 'My meeting with Russell was most enjoyable.'

[40] Annotation by Scholz: 'Brief an Fr. vom . . . Zeit des Treffens mit
Russell mit der Unterschrift R's Ankündigung des Besuchs von W.' ('Letter
to Fr. of . . . time of meeting with Russell, with Russell's signature, notice
of a visit by W.')

[41] 'Surely, with an introduction by Russell, the book will be a very small
risk for a publisher, as Russell is very well known.'

[42] 'I've not yet had any answer from my prospective publishers to the
notification that you are willing to give my book a helping hand with an
introduction.'

Lieber Herr Ficker!
Vorgestern bin ich aus Holland zurückgekommen, wo ich
Prof. Russell traf und mit ihm über mein Buch sprach. Falls ich
es nicht in Österreich oder Deutschland verlegen kann, so wird
Russell es in England drucken lassen. (Er will es übersetzen.)
Dies würde ich natürlich als die ultima ratio ansehen. Nun
steht die Sache aber so: Russell will zu meiner Abhandlung eine
Einleitung schreiben und damit habe ich mich einverstanden
erklärt. Diese Einleitung soll ungefähr den halben Umfang der
Abhandlung selbst haben und die schwierigsten Punkte der
Arbeit erläutern. Mit dieser Einleitung nun ist das Buch für
einen Verleger ein viel geringeres Risiko, oder vielleicht gar
keines mehr, da Russells Name sehr bekannt ist und dem
Buch einen ganz bestimmten Leserkreis sichert. Damit will ich
natürlich nicht sagen, daß es so in die rechten Hände kommt,
aber immerhin ist dadurch ein günstiger Zufall weniger
ausgeschlossen.
   Schreiben Sie mir bitte so bald als irgend möglich, was Sie
von der Sache halten, da ich Russell Bescheid geben muß.

>   Besten Gruß
>   Ihr
>   Ludwig Wittgenstein[43]

---

[43] Dear Mr Ficker,
   The day before yesterday I got back from Holland, where I met Prof.
Russell and talked to him about my book. If I can't publish it in Austria
or Germany, then Russell will have it printed in England. (He wants to
translate it.) Naturally I should regard this solution as the last resort.
But at present the matter stands as follows: Russell wants to write an
introduction to my treatise and I have declared myself in agreement
with this. The introduction is intended to be about half the length of the
treatise itself and to elucidate the most difficult points in the work.
Now, with this introduction, the book is a much smaller risk for a
publisher, or possibly no longer a risk at all, because Russell's name is
very well known and will guarantee a quite definite public for the book.
Of course, I don't mean that this will bring it into the right hands, but at
any rate it will render a happy accident less out of the question.
   Please write as soon as you possibly can what you think of the matter,
because I must give Russell an answer.

>   Kind regards,
>   Yours,
>   Ludwig Wittgenstein

We do not know whether Ficker had replied to this letter, when suddenly a new prospective publisher appeared in the picture. This was the well-known German publishing house Reclam in Leipzig. It seems to have been Engelmann who had suggested this new possibility to Wittgenstein.[44] Engelmann evidently made some inquiries on the author's behalf. It must be with a reference to these inquiries that Wittgenstein on 19 January 1920 wrote to Russell: 'Heute erhielt ich die Nachricht, daß der Verlag von Reklam in Leipzig aller Wahrscheinlichkeit nach mein Buch nehmen will. Ich werde also mein MS aus Innsbruck kommen lassen und es an Reklam schicken. Wann aber kommt Deine Einleitung?! Denn ohne sie kann ja der Druck nicht beginnen.'[45]

Wittgenstein wrote to Ficker the very same day:

Lieber Herr Ficker!

Bitte seien Sie so gut mir umgehend mein Manuscript zu schicken, da ich es an Reklam in Leipzig senden muß, der aller Wahrscheinlichkeit nach gewillt sein dürfte, mein Buch zu verlegen. Ich bin neugierig, wieviele Jahre es noch dauern wird, bis es erscheint. Hoffentlich geht es noch vor meinem Tod.

Ihr
Ludwig Wittgenstein[46]

One week later, when the book had not yet arrived, he wrote another letter, a last one, to Ficker:

[44] See Wittgenstein's letter to Engelmann of 29 December 1919.

[45] 'I have had word today that the publisher Reclam in Leipzig is in all probability prepared to take my book. So I will get my manuscript from Innsbruck and send it to Reclam. But when is your introduction going to arrive?! Because the printing can't begin without it.'

[46] Dear Mr Ficker,

Please be so kind as to send me my manuscript by return, because I have to send it to Reclam in Leipzig, who may in all probability be willing to publish my book. I am curious to see how many more years will elapse before it appears. Let's hope it will come out before my death.

Yours,
Ludwig Wittgenstein

Lieber Herr Ficker!

Es ist traurig zu hören, daß es Ihnen mit dem Brenner so schlecht geht. Ich bin davon überzeugt, daß es nicht Kleinmut Ihrerseits ist, daß Sie mein Buch nicht nehmen. Ich schrieb Ihnen vor einigen Tagen und bat Sie um umgehende Rücksendung meines Manuscripts, da ich es an Reklam schicken muß, der die Arbeit wahrscheinlich übernehmen wird. Welche Art von Beruf werden Sie dann ergreifen? Es würde mich freuen, wenn er uns irgendwie wiederum zusammenführte. Benachrichtigen Sie mich bitte davon, was Sie zu tun gedenken.

Ihr
Ludwig Wittgenstein

P.S Auch ich kämpfe jetzt mit großen Widerwärtigkeiten.[47]

As this letter shows, Wittgenstein must have received a letter from Ficker, in which Ficker had complained of financial difficulties with the *Brenner* and evidently also expressed some uneasiness at his refusal to print Wittgenstein's book. Thus ended this chapter in the publication history of the *Tractatus*. But 34 years later, in the final issue of *Der Brenner*, Ficker wrote an epilogue to the story which must also be mentioned.

Ficker's essay is called 'Rilke und der unbekannte Freund. In memoriam Ludwig Wittgenstein.'[48] In it we are told that Wittgenstein in the autumn of 1919 had come to visit Ficker in Innsbruck. It is not quite clear whether the author of the essay has in mind one or several visits. For he also says that Wittgenstein came to see him on his way back to Austria from the meeting with Russell in Holland. He says, moreover, that

---

[47] Dear Mr Ficker,

It is sad to hear that things are going so badly for you as regards *Der Brenner*. I am convinced that it's not because of cowardice on your part that you're not accepting my book. I wrote to you some days ago and asked you to send back my manuscript by return, because I have to send it to Reclam, who will probably take the work in hand. What sort of occupation are you going to take up now? I'd be very pleased if it brought us together again somehow or other. Please keep me informed of what you mean to do.

Yours,
Ludwig Wittgenstein

P.S. I too have considerable vexations to struggle with at present.

[48] 'Rilke and the unknown friend. In memory of Ludwig Wittgenstein.'

Wittgenstein had taken the route *via* Hamburg in Germany, where he ran short of money and had to spend the night in a Salvation Army hostel (*Nachtasyl*) by the harbour. It was on the occasion of this visit on the way home that he allegedly brought with him and left Ficker a typed copy ('*Durchschlag*') of his book. Ficker never saw Wittgenstein again, he says.

There is nothing in the letters to Ficker which would confirm this story. Some details are easily shown to be false. We know, for example, that the manuscript was sent to Ficker before the meeting with Russell in Holland in December – and that Ficker's request to Rilke for assistance with publishing it was made in November. But there are several details of the story, as told by Ficker, which make it highly improbable that it is unconscious invention. Such details concern, for example, the way Wittgenstein was dressed and how he declined Ficker's hospitality for the night. I think the truth in the matter is as follows.

Wittgenstein, on all reliable evidence we have, did *not* visit Ficker in the autumn of 1919, nor on his way back from the meeting with Russell in Holland in December. Their only contact during this period was by letter. But some two and a half years later, in August 1922, Wittgenstein and Russell met at Innsbruck (see p. 106 below). In a letter to Engelmann (10 August 1922) Wittgenstein tells about the meeting and also mentions that he had seen Ficker on the same occasion. My conjecture is that Ficker, when writing down his recollections of Wittgenstein more than 30 years later, was not relying exclusively on the letters but was also served by defective memory – thus conflating his correspondence with Wittgenstein in 1919–20 concerning the publication of the *Tractatus* with the author's actual visit to him some years later, when the book was already on the point of being published by Kegan Paul in England.[49] The Hamburg episode belongs to a journey to Norway which Wittgenstein undertook in the summer of 1921 in the company of Arvid Sjögren.

[49] It must be mentioned, however, that Ficker in a letter to F.A. Hayek of 4 December 1953 expressly says that Wittgenstein's visit was in *October* 1919 and that he knows nothing of a visit to Innsbruck a few years later and a meeting there with Russell.

Ficker eventually returned the typescript, but Russell's Introduction was not yet there. Somewhat impatiently Wittgenstein wrote to Russell on 19 March 1920: 'Wie steht's mit der Einleitung? Ist sie schon fertig?'[50] And at the very end of the letter: 'Schreib mir bald einmal und schicke auch Deine Einleitung.'[51]

By the beginning of April the Introduction was there. Letter of 9 April:

> Besten Dank für Dein Manuskript. Ich bin mit so manchem darin nicht ganz einverstanden; sowohl dort, wo Du mich kritisierst, als auch dort, wo Du bloß meine Ansicht klarlegen willst. Das macht aber nichts. Die Zukunft wird über uns urteilen. Die Einleitung wird jetzt übersetzt und geht dann mit der Abhandlung zum Verleger. Hoffentlich nimmt er sie![52]

Wittgenstein's satisfaction with Russell's Introduction did not last long, however. Letter of 5 May 1920:

> Deine Einleitung wird nicht gedruckt und infolgedessen wahrscheinlich auch mein Buch nicht. – Als ich nämlich die deutsche Übersetzung der Einleitung vor mir hatte, da konnte ich mich doch nicht entschließen sie mit meiner Arbeit drucken zu lassen. Die Feinheit Deines englischen Stils war nämlich in der Übersetzung – selbstverständlich – verloren gegangen und was übrig blieb war Oberflächlichkeit und Mißverständnis. Ich schickte nun die Abhandlung und Deine Einleitung an Reclam und schrieb ihm, ich wünschte nicht daß die Einleitung gedruckt würde, sondern sie solle ihm nur zur Orientierung über meine Arbeit dienen. Es ist nun höchst wahrscheinlich, daß Reclam meine Arbeit daraufhin nicht nimmt (obwohl ich noch keine Antwort von ihm habe). . . . Und nun sei nicht

[50] 'How are things with the introduction? Is it ready yet?'
[51] 'Do write to me soon, and also send me your introduction.'
[52] 'Thank you very much for your manuscript. There's so much of it that I'm not quite in agreement with – both where you are critical of me and also where you are simply trying to elucidate my views. But that doesn't matter. The future will pass judgement on us. The Introduction is in the course of being translated, and will then go with the treatise to the publisher. I hope he will accept them.'

bös! Es war auch vielleicht undankbar von mir, aber ich konnte
nicht anders.[53]

Wittgenstein's misgivings were justified. Reclam did not
accept the book. To judge from a letter to Engelmann, dated
30 May 1920, Wittgenstein had by then received the negative
news from the publisher. But it was not until some six weeks
later, on 8 July, and the day when he received his diploma
from the teachers' training college (*Lehrerbildungsanstalt*) he
had been attending, that he wrote about this to Russell (8 July
1920): 'Reclam hat mein Buch natürlich nicht genommen und
ich werde vorläufig keine weitere Schritte tun, um es zu
publizieren. Hast Du aber Lust es drucken zu lassen, so steht es
Dir ganz zu Verfügung und *Du kannst damit machen, was Du
willst.* (Nur wenn Du am Text etwas änderst, so *gib an, daß die
Änderung von Dir ist.*)'[54]

Wittgenstein's efforts to find a publisher for his book had
thus come to an end. He withdrew from Vienna and became a
schoolmaster in the country. Exactly how he disposed of the
typescripts and manuscripts at that time, we do not know. At
least one typescript must have been in the hands of Bertrand
Russell. This evidently was the same one which Russell had
received through Keynes from Cassino and of which Wittgenstein had then said that it was his only corrected copy.

[53] 'Your Introduction is not being printed and consequently it's probable
that my book won't be either. – You see, when I actually saw the German
translation of the Introduction, I couldn't bring myself to let it be printed
with my work. All the refinement of your English style was, obviously, lost
in the translation and what remained was superficiality and misunderstanding. Well, I sent your Introduction to Reclam and wrote saying that I didn't
want it printed: it was to serve only for his own orientation in relation to my
work. It is now highly probable that Reclam will not accept my work
(though I haven't had an answer from him yet). . . . And now, don't be
angry with me. Perhaps it was ungrateful of me, but I couldn't do anything
else.'

[54] 'Reclam has, naturally, not accepted my book and for the present I
won't take any further steps to have it published. But if you feel like getting
it printed, it is entirely at your disposition and *you can do what you like with it.*
(Only, if you change anything in the text, *indicate that the change was made by
you.*)'

5

In the autumn of 1920 Russell went to China and he did not
return until the end of August in the following year. Before
leaving England he gave the typescript of Wittgenstein's work
to Miss Dorothy Wrinch and asked her to try to get it
published.[55] She offered the book to the Cambridge University Press. The Syndics of the Press, at their meeting on 14
January 1921, declined the offer.[56]

After the Cambridge Press had refused to publish the book,
Miss Wrinch wrote to three German periodicals offering them
the book and, evidently, Russell's introduction as well. All
three editors replied during February.[57] F. Schumann of the
Zeitschrift für Psychologie und Physiologie der Sinnesorgane said
that he could not take the work unless it were psychological
rather than philosophical in content. Ludwig Stein of the
Archiv für systematische Philosophie was quite willing to publish
work by a pupil of Russell's but said there would be some
delay in printing and asked Miss Wrinch to write to him again
in May before sending the manuscript. These two letters are
dated 12 February 1921. The date of the letter from Wilhelm
Ostwald is not clear[58] but must have been about the same
time. He wrote:

> In jedem anderen Falle würde ich auf die Aufnahme des
> Aufsatzes verzichtet haben. Ich schätze aber Herrn Bertrand
> Russell so ungewöhnlich hoch als Forscher und als Persönlich-

[55] I am indebted to Miss Wrinch for information relating to this stage in
the publishing history of the *Tractatus*. In his *Autobiography 1914–1944*, pp.
99–100, Russell says that he had been discussing the book with Miss Wrinch
and the French philosopher Jean Nicod (probably in the autumn of 1919).

[56] The Secretary of the Syndics, Mr R. W. David, tells me in a letter that he
thinks, on the evidence of the minutes of the meeting for 14 January 1921,
that the work had been offered to the Press *without* the Introduction by
Russell.

[57] Their replies are in the Russell Archives at McMaster University,
Hamilton, Ontario.

[58] It appears to be 52 21 (for 5.2.21?) but he apologizes for his delay in
replying. 15 or 21 February 1921 (the 52nd day of the year) would fit in
better with the date of dispatch of the manuscript; see below.

keit, daß ich den Aufsatz von Herrn Wittgenstein gern in
meinen *Annalen der Naturphilosophie* veröffentlichen werde: die
Einleitung von Herrn Bertrand Russell wird besonders will-
kommen sein.[59]

He went on to say that the next issue of the periodical would
not be for a couple of months but that, if it were not too
expensive, offprints could be produced earlier. Miss Wrinch
sent off the manuscripts on 24 February and in a postcard
postmarked 10 March 1921 Ostwald acknowledged receipt of
the *Tractatus* and his intention to publish it. It did in fact duly
appear in the final issue of *Annalen der Naturphilosophie*[60] and,
as will be seen, some offprints were available.

Russell seems to have been unaware of these developments
when he returned from China at the end of August and began
to discuss publication of Wittgenstein's book in England with
C.K. Ogden. Ogden had that very year assumed editorship of
the International Library of Psychology, Philosophy and
Scientific Method, a series published by Kegan Paul, Trench,
Trubner & Co., Ltd. It is not known whether the idea that
Wittgenstein's book might be included in that series came
from the editor or from Russell. The earliest documents we
have relating to this new turn in the history of how Wittgenstein's work was published is an undated letter from Miss
Wrinch to Russell and a letter of 5 November 1921 from
Ogden to Russell. The first refers to Ogden's interest in the
matter, of which Russell evidently had told Miss Wrinch in an
earlier letter. Ogden's letter to Russell, printed in Russell's
Autobiography, reads as follows:

> Kegan Paul ask me to give them some formal note for their files
> with regard to the Wittgenstein rights.
> I enclose, with envelope for your convenience, the sort of
> thing I should like. As they can't drop less than £50 on doing it I

[59] 'In any other case I should have declined to accept the article. But I have
such an extremely high regard for Mr Bertrand Russell, both for his
researches and for his personality, that I will gladly publish Mr Wittgenstein's article in my *Annalen der Naturphilosophie*: Mr Bertrand Russell's
Introduction will be particularly welcome.'

[60] *Annalen der Naturphilosophie*, Verlag Unesma G.m.b.H., Leipzig, ed.
by Wilhelm Ostwald, *Band* 14, *Heft 3–4* (1921), pp. 184–262.

think it very satisfactory to have got it accepted – though of course if they did a second edition soon and the price of printing went suddenly down they might get their costs back. I am still a little uneasy about the title and don't want to feel that we decided in a hurry on *Philosophical Logic*. If on second thoughts you are satisfied with it, we can go ahead with that. But you might be able to excogitate alternatives that I could submit.

Moore's Spinoza title which he thought obvious and ideal is no use if you feel Wittgenstein wouldn't like it. I suppose his *sub specie aeterni* in the last sentences of the book made Moore think the contrary, and several Latin quotes. But as a selling title *Philosophical Logic* is better, if it conveys the right impression.

Looking rapidly over the off print in the train last night, I was amazed that Nicod and Miss Wrinch had both seemed to make so very little of it.[61] The main lines seem so reasonable and intelligible – apart from the Types puzzles.

. . .

P.S. On second thoughts, I think that as you would prefer Wittgenstein's German to appear as well as the English, it might help if you added the P.S. I have stuck in, and I will press them further if I can.

As Ogden's letter shows, by the beginning of November he had studied an offprint of Ostwald's printing of the *Logisch-philosophische Abhandlung*. The words 'Moore's Spinoza title' in the letter must refer to the title *Tractatus Logico-Philosophicus*, which seems first to have been suggested by G.E. Moore. As is clear from his letter of 23 April 1922 to Ogden, Wittgenstein preferred this Latin title to the alternative suggestion *Philosophical Logic*.

Ogden's letter indicates that Russell was decidedly in favour of printing the original German side by side with an English translation. We know from a letter from Wittgenstein to Engelmann (15 December 1919) that the question of publication in both languages had in fact already been discussed between Wittgenstein and Russell in December 1919 when they met in The Hague.

Russell replied three days later to Ogden:

[61] See *The Autobiography of Bertrand Russell 1914–1944*, pp. 99–100.

I dare say I could part with Wittgenstein's MS without consulting him, but I thought it better to tell him what was being done. I wrote some days ago, and if I hear nothing by the end of next week I shall assume he has no objection. He certainly won't make a fuss anyhow, but I have as yet nothing definite *in writing* giving me the rights.

As for 'philosophical logic', it seems to me all right, but if you like I will write to Wittgenstein and put alternatives before him.

The words 'part with Wittgenstein's MS' are slightly puzzling. They can hardly mean anything else than that Russell permitted Ogden to go ahead with publication. As far as we know, the only typescript which had been with Russell was the one Miss Wrinch had sent to Ostwald in February. It is possible that Ostwald returned it to Russell when the printing was completed. It was not, however, used for the printing in England. We do not know by whom and exactly when it was sent back to Wittgenstein.

It seems that Wittgenstein had not heard even about the publication by Ostwald when he received the news from Russell about the plans for publication in England. His reply to Russell's letter is dated Trattenbach, 28 November:

Dank Dir vielmals für Deinen lieben Brief. Ehrlich gestanden: es freut mich, daß mein Zeug gedruckt wird. . . . Liest Du die Korrekturen? Dann bitte sei so lieb und gib acht, daß er es genau so druckt, wie es bei mir steht. . . . Am liebsten ist es mir, daß die Sache in England erscheint. Möge sie der vielen Mühe die Du und andere mit ihr hatten würdig sein. . . . Von Ostwald habe ich keinen Brief erhalten.[62]

After receipt of this letter, Russell wrote again to Ogden on 5 December, telling him that Wittgenstein had agreed to the publication plans:

[62] 'Thank you very much for your kind letter. To be honest, I must confess that I am pleased that my stuff is being printed. . . . Are you going to read the proofs? If so, please be so good as to see that he prints it exactly the way I have it. . . . What pleases me most is that the thing is going to come out in England. I hope that it may be worth all the trouble that you and others have had with it. . . . I have received no letter from Ostwald.'

Enclosed from Wittgenstein gives all the authority needed for going ahead, so you can tell the publishers it is all right. Please return Wittgenstein's letter to me, and let me see proof or typescript of Ostwald's stuff[63] if you have it. I am much relieved that W. takes the whole affair sanely.

A student of the Ostwald edition of Wittgenstein's work is struck by a number of oddities in the use of logical symbols. For example, exclamation marks '!' are used for the Sheffer stroke, a slanted stroke '/' for the negation sign (occasionally also for the Sheffer stroke) and the capital letter C for material implication. The explanation of these eccentricities is as follows.

The typewriter which was used for making the typescript of the book did not have the proper symbols. Rather than having them inserted by hand, Wittgenstein let them be typed with signs that were available. Russell made no changes – and so it was that the text became printed with the odd symbols.[64]

In the 'Prototractatus' manuscript Wittgenstein uses, for example, '|' for the Sheffer stroke, '~' for negation, and the horseshoe '⊃' for implication. But in the second part of the manuscript he uses '/' for negation (in 5.254). This gives strong support to the idea that the second part of the manuscript is a draft of additions to a typescript which had just been made (cf. p. 73 above). It should also be noted, that the words '*6 Zeilen frei*' in 6.241 on p. 118 of the manuscript sound like a directive from the author to a typist – to leave six lines free. The space reserved was for the proof of the proposition that $2 \times 2 = 4$.

It seems to me intrinsically unlikely, indeed impossible, that Wittgenstein would have left unchanged the symbolism of the typescript which Ostwald was printing if he had checked the

---

[63] 'Ostwald's stuff' can hardly mean anything else than the *Logisch-philosophische Abhandlung*. The way Russell expresses himself here would indicate that *he* had not seen the offprint to which Ogden was referring in his letter of 5 November.

[64] This is established by Wittgenstein's own comments on the symbols in a letter to C.K. Ogden dated 23 April 1922. Wittgenstein says he was 'too lazy' to put the proper Russellian symbols in afterwards.

proofs. The printing of the eccentric symbolism and the occurrence of a very considerable number of uncorrected misprints constitute by themselves conclusive evidence that Wittgenstein had no hand at all in the production of the Ostwald edition. (It is also evident from the account given above that Russell never saw the proofs.) We have, moreover, evidence that the production greatly annoyed Wittgenstein. In a letter, dated 5 August 1922, he tells Engelmann that the book is shortly to appear in England, with a translation. Of the Ostwald edition he now says: 'Diesen Druck betrachte ich aber als Raubdruck, er ist voller Fehler.'[65] It is difficult to see why Wittgenstein calls the printing 'pirated', considering that he had left the question of its publication in Russell's hands and had even expressed pleasure when he heard that the work was being printed. But he had reason to be annoyed at the errors and the barbarous typography which, we must assume, he would not himself have let pass uncorrected.

Ostwald also printed a German translation of Russell's Introduction ('Vorwort von Bertrand Russell').[66] He placed it *after* Wittgenstein's *Vorwort*. This translation is most probably *not* the one referred to in the Russell–Wittgenstein correspondence of 1920, but one which Ostwald had made or allowed to be made for his printing.

Ogden wanted to print the original Introduction with the new publication and wrote to Ostwald – only to find that he had destroyed the original. Ostwald's reply is dated 11 November:

Das Manuskript von B. Russells Einleitung kann ich leider nicht schicken, da ich es nicht mehr besitze. Ich hatte es aufbewahrt, bis ich die Korrektur der deutschen Übersetzung gelesen hatte; da es weiter nicht nötig war, ist es in den Papierkorb gewandert. Ich muß mit dem Entfernen von entbehrlichem Papier streng sein, da ich sonst in der Papierflut untergehen würde. Hätten Sie mir geschrieben, daß Sie das

[65] 'However, I consider this a pirated edition. It is full of errors.'
[66] It is not listed in the Bibliography of the Writings of Bertrand Russell in P.A. Schilpp (ed.), *The Philosophy of Bertrand Russell* (Tudor Publishing Company, New York, 1944).

englische Manuskript zurück haben wollten, hätte ich es
natürlich geschickt.[67]

Russell fortunately found a second copy and notified Ogden of
this in an undated letter evidently of mid-November.[68]

Later in the winter, however, Ogden seems to have
returned the Introduction to Russell. For in a letter to Ogden
of 9 May from Penzance Russell writes: 'I return herewith the
Introduction to Wittgenstein. I have added a date on p. 1, as
you suggested.' The printed Introduction is dated 'May 1922'.

A comparison between the 1921 German version and the
1922 English version of the Introduction shows that the two
for the most part correspond sentence by sentence although
there are a number of errors of translation in the German.[69]
Only at the beginning are there some significant discrepancies,
consisting of substantial additions to or expansions of the
earlier German text. The most expanded passage is the one
dealing with Wittgenstein's concern with the conditions for a
logically perfect or ideal language. This passage in the
Introduction is well known and has, I am afraid, contributed
to some current misunderstandings about Wittgenstein's
concern with language in the *Tractatus*.

Another difference of interest between the two versions is
the following. The early version refers to some passages in the
book by their decimal numbers but the passages are not
quoted. In the later version some passages referred to are also
quoted in English translation. The translation is not always
exactly like the translation in the main text of the book. It

[67] 'I regret that I cannot send the manuscript of B. Russell's Introduction,
as I no longer have it. I kept it until I had read the proofs of the German
translation; when it was no longer needed, it went into the wastepaper
basket. I have to be strict in disposing of unnecessary paper, since otherwise I
should be drowned in the flood of paper. Had you written to me that you
wanted the English manuscript back, I should of course have sent it.'

[68] Ogden's reply in which he thanks Russell for the duplicate copy of the
Introduction is likewise undated but refers to the arrival on the day of
writing of Ostwald's letter above.

[69] For a detailed study of Russell's Introduction and its two versions, see
M. Teresa Iglesias, 'Russell's Introduction to Wittgenstein's "Tractatus"' in
Russell: The Journal of the Bertrand Russell Archives **25–28**, 1977.

seems that the translation of the passages had been made by
Russell – and that Wittgenstein had approved of them. We
gather this from a letter written to Professor Max Black and
signed by Mr Colin E. Franklin of the publishing house
Routledge & Kegan Paul, but largely composed, it seems, by
C.K. Ogden. In this letter it is said: 'It seems that the German
text, as corrected by Wittgenstein, reached us from Wilhelm
Ostwald in January 1922 with instructions from the author to
treat the translations in Russell's Introduction as having equal
authority with the original.' This letter was written in 1954
and the long lapse of time since the printing of the *Tractatus*
may count for what must be a conflation of two different
things in the memory of the letter writer. What Ostwald
might have sent to Ogden in January 1922 was the typescript
from which he had printed the paper of which at least one
offprint had been in Ogden's hand since November the year
before. The 'instructions' concerning translations by Russell
can hardly mean anything but the references to Russell which
occur in Wittgenstein's comments, in letters to Ogden from
April–August 1922, on the text and the translation of the
Tractatus when the book was in the process of being printed in
England. These comments indicate that Russell too had a
share in the translation. Exactly what his role was, it seems
impossible now to determine.

The translation of the *Logisch-philosophische Abhandlung* into
English was made in the course of the winter and completed
by March. It seems that the first draft of the translation was
produced by F.P. Ramsey alone. According to a statement by
Ramsey's father in a memorial album composed and written
after Ramsey's death in 1930, 'he had been shown Wittgenstein's "Tractatus" in MS or typescript and it interested him
greatly. Then Ogden asked him to translate it for publication.
His knowledge of German was so good that he used to go into
Miss Pate's office and translate the book to a shorthand
writer.' Miss Pate was the head of the University Typing
Office in Trinity Street, Cambridge. It is impossible to tell
whether the typed text of the translation which still exists is
the one produced in Miss Pate's office on the basis of Ramsey's
dictation. The typescript was sent to Wittgenstein in March.

In a letter dated Trattenbach, 28 March, Wittgenstein acknowledges its receipt. It is plain from his letter that the typescript of the English translation was sent to him without the German text. Wittgenstein had at that time no typescript of his work with him. He could get one from Vienna, he says. But this would be an uncorrected (and hence incomplete) copy. The only corrected one, he reaffirms, is the copy he gave Russell, that is, the copy I have called the Engelmann TS. Wittgenstein wonders where it is now. He has heard nothing from Ostwald and even thinks Ostwald will not publish it. This is surprising, since it ought to have been plain from Russell's letter to him in November that Ostwald *was* printing the *Logisch-philosophische Abhandlung*. (Russell's letter is not preserved; perhaps it was unclear on this point.)

Wittgenstein's comments on specific points in the English translation show that he started correcting the translation before he had the German text in front of him. But he evidently had access to the original at a later stage of the work.

We know that before returning the translation with his corrections and comments Wittgenstein had received an offprint of the Ostwald printing. Whether it was sent to him by Ogden or by Ostwald we do not know; probably he got it from the former. This offprint he returned to Ogden with his corrections at the same time as he returned the translation on 23 April. That he had taken great pains with this double task is clear both from his letter to Ogden of that date, from his 20 pages of attached comments on specific points in the translation, and from the physical marks on the German and English texts he returned.

The author must have found revising the corrupt Ostwald text an exasperating job. A detailed comparison of the German of the Ostwald edition and of the (first) Kegan Paul edition shows, beside the alterations to the symbols and the correction of numerous misprints, also several changes of a more substantial nature. Sometimes a word or short phrase is added to the Ostwald text, sometimes another word is substituted for the one originally printed, sometimes a factual mistake in a logical formula has been corrected. The most important changes are in 4.003, the last paragraph of which does not occur in the Ostwald text, and in 6.2341, which in the *Annalen* has nearly the same formulation as 6.211 of the 'Prototracta-tus'. Finally, the following puzzling matter should be men-tioned.

At 4.0141 in the Ostwald text stand only the words '(Siehe Ergänzung Nr. 72)'. The remark itself is missing. Nor does it occur in the 'Prototractatus' or in the second part of the manuscript.

In the typescript of the English translation which Ogden sent to Wittgenstein for revising, the words '4.0141 (See supplement No. 72)' are typed. In the offprint of the Ostwald edition which Wittgenstein returned to Ogden with his revisions, Wittgenstein has crossed out the printed words 'Siehe Ergänzung Nr. 72' and written instead 'Insert from MS attached'. This evidently is a directive to the English printer. Attached to the same page is a slip of paper with the actual remark in Wittgenstein's handwriting. In the Engelmann TS, finally, there are the words '4.0141 (Siehe Ergänzung Nr. 72)' in handwriting, and also the *Ergänzung* itself typed on two small slips of paper.

From this it must be concluded, I think, that the 'Ergänzung Nr. 72' existed at the time when the Engelmann TS was finally left with Russell. When was this? As noted above (p. 83), the typescript Wittgenstein had sent to Russell from the prison camp Russell returned to Vienna in the autumn of that same year (1919). After the two friends had met in The Hague in December, Russell wrote the Introduction. When writing it, he must again have had a typescript of the book. It is reasonable to think that this was the Engelmann TS which Wittgenstein had given back to Russell at, or soon after, the meeting in Holland. We have no evidence that Russell returned the typescript, which he had in 1920 before going to China, when he gave it to Miss Wrinch. If this is right, the *terminus ante quem* of the *Ergänzungen* would be December 1919.

One is struck by the relatively high number – 72 – given to this particular supplement. This is much greater than the number of remarks, or paragraphs in remarks, which appear in the *Tractatus* but which are neither in the 'Prototractatus' nor in the rest of the manuscript book. There is some reference to these supplements in a letter from Wittgenstein to Ogden of 5 May 1922. Ogden had evidently asked the author, whether he was not willing to let more '*Ergänzungen*' be printed. Wittgenstein firmly declined this proposal. He mentioned that there were about a hundred supplements, but we do not know what happened to the rest of them. Probably Wittgenstein destroyed them, not having found any use for them in the final text.

If the '*Ergänzung Nr.* 72' was attached to the typescript used by Ostwald's printer, it is surprising that the supplement was not printed. This must then have been due to carelessness – a hypothesis which does not seem to me too unlikely. It is also surprising that Ogden did not originally translate the supplement. This fact constitutes additional evidence for the hypothesis that the translation too, and not only the printing in England, was done from an offprint (or from proofs) of the Ostwald edition.

It is noteworthy that Wittgenstein, both in the letter of 28 March and in that of 23 April and in the comments added to the second letter,[70] speaks of 'the translators' of his book in the plural. Since Ogden's letters to Wittgenstein have not been preserved, we do not know what Ogden had told Wittgenstein about the translating of the book. By 'the translators' Wittgenstein can hardly have meant Ramsey and *Ogden*, since in the letter from April he asks Ogden to communicate his thanks to the translators. It must remain an open question whether there was someone else, who can no longer be identified, assisting with the translating. It is evident from the correspondence, however, that besides Ogden and Ramsey, Russell also had been active in the translation.

In his letter to Engelmann of 15 December 1919, Wittgenstein had hinted that Russell was going to translate the book (and write an introduction to it). There is no direct evidence,

[70] For these comments, and my comments on them, see Ludwig Wittgenstein, *Letters to C.K. Ogden with Comments on the English Translation of the* Tractatus Logico-Philosophicus, edited with an Introduction by G.H. von Wright. Basil Blackwell, Oxford and Routledge & Kegan Paul, London, 1973.

however, that Russell had assisted in the production of the first draft of the translation in 1922. For it, Ramsey alone was probably responsible. But in the typescript of the translation which was sent to Wittgenstein in March there are some changes which evidently had been made by Russell. Wittgenstein's comments to Ogden show that he was aware of this (cf. p. 102 above). But we have no contemporary evidence that Wittgenstein had discussed directly with Russell details of the translation. It is therefore surprising that Russell, in letters of a *much* later date, 1951 and 1960, explicitly refers to discussions with Wittgenstein about the translation. In the first letter, to C.K. Ogden, Russell says: 'All that I do remember about the translation in general is having arguments with Wittgenstein on various points, which involved his sanctioning unliteral translations.' The second letter, to F.K. Ogden, reads as follows:

> I learn that questions have arisen as to the authenticity and authority of the English version of Wittgenstein's *Tractatus*. I know that this version was sanctioned point by point by Wittgenstein. There are places where it is not an exact translation of the German. When I pointed this out to him, he admitted it, but said that the translation as it stood expressed what he wished to say better than a more exact translation. It is, of course, open to anybody to make a new translation in a more modern idiom, but it would be misleading to suggest that such a translation gave a more accurate rendering of Wittgenstein's thought at the time than that which was published. I say this from recollection of careful and minute discussion with Wittgenstein as to what he wished the English version to say.

The question arises when and where did this 'careful and minute discussion with Wittgenstein' take place? It can hardly have been in the The Hague in 1919 when the translation had, for all we know, not even been begun. For the first time after their meeting in Holland, Russell and Wittgenstein met again at Innsbruck in Austria between 6 and 11 August 1922. At that stage Wittgenstein had already read and dispatched the proofs of both the German and the English texts back to Ogden. We do not know the topics of discussion at the meeting in Innsbruck. But it is at least a possibility that they concerned the translation and the forthcoming publication of the book in England.

The next exchange of letters between Ogden and Wittgenstein took place early in May. Ogden then sent Wittgenstein a questionnaire, relating to specific points in the translation. (There are also indications that he returned the typescript of the whole translation.) Wittgenstein sent back the questionnaire with his annotations and comments. In a letter a few days earlier Wittgenstein had replied to Ogden's request for more supplementary material to be printed with the book. It is not quite clear to me whether Ogden's request had been made in the same letter with which he sent the questionnaire, or in a separate one.

In June, Wittgenstein, at Ogden's request, sent Ogden a declaration whereby he gave the publisher Kegan Paul all the publication rights in his book. In the accompanying letter he discussed the question of complimentary copies. He asked Ogden to send one copy to the mother of David Pinsent, the friend to whose memory Wittgenstein had dedicated his work. The agreement concerning the publication is between C.K. Ogden and Kegan Paul Ltd, and is dated 11 July 1922.

The next exchange of letters with Ogden dates from July. Wittgenstein had left Trattenbach and was in Vienna. In his letter to Ogden, dated 17 July, he refers to Ogden's 'good news' about the book. Perhaps the news was that proofs were now ready.

The proofs must have been dispatched some time in June or July. They were sent to Vienna, but forwarded from there to Hallein near Salzburg, where Wittgenstein was staying with relatives. He returned the proofs, duly corrected, on 4 August with a letter and a number of comments written on special sheets.

The final printing was evidently not made from the proofs Wittgenstein had corrected, but from a special set of proofs which somebody, probably Ogden himself, had prepared for the printer. This was natural, considering that the proofs which were sent to Austria contained comments and exchanges of questions and answers between Ogden and Wittgenstein in addition to the actual corrections.

Russell had been sent proofs of the book in June. In a letter, dated Penzance, 29 June, he says he is returning 'the proofs of Wittgenstein'. 'I have corrected the Introduction but not his stuff, as I supposed you didn't need my help over that,' he adds.

The book was published in November. Ogden sent him the news and also some copies of the work. In a letter of 15 November Wittgenstein acknowledges receipt. He seems to have given all the copies away. One was given to a schoolmaster by the name Josef Putre, with whom Wittgenstein had made friends during his time in Trattenbach; another went to Rudolf Koder, a schoolmaster at Puchberg; and a third to Arvid Sjögren: these last two remained lifelong friends of Wittgenstein. Through Ogden Wittgenstein also arranged for a copy to be sent to David Pinsent's mother and to J.M. Keynes. When, in December 1924, Moritz Schlick in a letter asked the author for advice and help in obtaining copies of either the Ostwald or the Kegan Paul edition for Schlick's circle of students in Vienna, Wittgenstein replied (7 January 1925) that he himself had *no* copy of the book.

When Wittgenstein submitted the *Tractatus* as a Ph.D. thesis after his return to Cambridge in 1929, Ogden helped him to obtain a free copy of the book from the publishers.

6

Ramsey visited Austria in 1923 and again in 1924. On both visits he met Wittgenstein, who was at that time a schoolteacher at Puchberg, a village at the foot of the Schneeberg. When on his visit to Austria in 1924 Ramsey wrote from Vienna to Wittgenstein:

> . . . Ogden also asked me to get from you, if possible, while I was here any corrections in case there should be a second edition of your book. (This is not really likely.) I have got marked in my copy a lot of corrections we made to the translation, and 4 extra propositions you wrote in English. Obviously I think the corrections to the translation should be made in a new edition, and the only doubt is about the extra

propositions; and also you might have had something else you would like altered. . . .

The letter tells of a previous occasion on which the two had met and made 'a lot of corrections' to the translation. This evidently was in September 1923, when Ramsey had spent a couple of weeks with Wittgenstein discussing the *Tractatus*. Ramsey's copy of the book has been preserved and contains a number of corrections in Wittgenstein's hand.[71] Many, though not all of them, were incorporated into the second edition of the work which appeared in 1933. The four 'extra propositions' were *not* incorporated. They appear, in the margin of Ramsey's copy, in English, in Wittgenstein's hand.[72] Their German version, if they had one, has not been preserved.

[71] A detailed study of this copy of the *Tractatus* has been made by Dr Casimir Lewy, 'A Note on the Text of the *Tractatus*', *Mind* **76**, 1967, pp. 416–423.

[72] They are printed ibid., pp. 421–422.

THE ORIGIN AND
COMPOSITION OF THE
PHILOSOPHICAL
INVESTIGATIONS

My research on the origin and composition of Wittgenstein's *Philosophische Untersuchungen* (*Philosophical Investigations*) was begun in 1973 and has lasted to the present day (see the Introduction to this volume). In the course of this research I have relied heavily on the help given to me by my two assistants, Dr André Maury and Mr Heikki Nyman. I am also indebted to Mr Rush Rhees who read an earlier draft of the essay and to the numerous persons, some but not all of whom are mentioned by name in the text, who answered my inquiries in correspondence.

The study was first published in *Wittgenstein: Sources and Perspectives*, edited by C.G. Luckhardt (Cornell University Press, Ithaca, NY, 1979). It has been extensively revised for the present collection. On certain points I regard it as still unfinished.

SUMMARY

I THINK the reader will find it helpful if I begin this paper with
what usually goes at the end, namely a summary.

The *Philosophische Untersuchungen* (*Philosophical Investigations*) was published posthumously two years after Wittgenstein's death. Wittgenstein did not regard it as a finished work.
It consists, in its printed form, of two parts. If Wittgenstein
had published his work himself, he would presumably have
formed the two parts into a more unified whole.

In August 1936, Wittgenstein began to work on a revision,
in German, of the Brown Book which he had dictated at
Cambridge in the academic year 1934–35. He had then
withdrawn to solitude in Norway, where he remained, with
interruptions, until towards the end of the following year. He
called the revision '*Philosophische Untersuchungen, Versuch einer
Umarbeitung*'.[1] Before finishing it he became dissatisfied with
what he was doing and wrote at the end 'Dieser ganze
"Versuch einer Umarbeitung" – ist *nichts wert*'.[2] Thereupon he
set himself to writing, in November and December of that
same year, 1936, a new version which he also called '*Philosophische Untersuchungen*'. What he then wrote is, broadly
speaking, the beginning of the book, as we have it. It
corresponds, roughly, to the first 188 numbered remarks of
the printed text (see p. 116 below). However, in the course of
the years which followed, Wittgenstein made many additions
and changes even in this first part of his work.

About one year later, from mid-September to mid-November 1937, Wittgenstein wrote the main part of a continuation
to this manuscript. Again a year later, in August 1938, at
Cambridge, he dated the Preface to a typescript essentially
based on what he had written in Norway in the two periods

[1] Published under the title *Eine philosophische Betrachtung*, ed. by Rush
Rhees, Suhrkamp, Frankfurt am Main, 1970 (Ludwig Wittgenstein,
Schriften 5).
[2] MS 115, p. 292. I refer here to the manuscripts and typescripts of
Wittgenstein using the catalogue numbers given in 'The Wittgenstein
Papers' above.

mentioned. This typescript constitutes what I call the early
version of the *Investigations*. Some time later, presumably at
the beginning of 1939, Wittgenstein added another 16 pages to
this typescript.

The early version of the *Investigations* thus consists of two
parts written, mainly, in the autumn of 1936 and the autumn
of 1937 respectively. The two parts form a consecutive whole.
For this reason and because they are of almost equal length,
they could also be described as the two halves of this early
work. The first half, as mentioned, corresponds to the first 188
remarks of the printed final version. The second half, however, does not belong in the final version. A rearrangement,
made by Wittgenstein himself, of its main content was
published posthumously as Part I of the work called, by the
editors, *Remarks on the Foundations of Mathematics*.

In the seven years from 1937 to 1944 Wittgenstein's chief
preoccupation was with the philosophy of mathematics. It
was only in the second half of 1944, it seems, that he resumed
work on what was eventually to become the final version of
the *Investigations*. In that same year he produced what I call the
intermediate version of the work. For it he wrote the Preface,
dated Cambridge, January 1945, which is printed with the
final version.

The intermediate version of the *Investigations* consists,
substantially, of a revision of the first half of the early version
and of a continuation to it of remarks written in 1944. The
continuation is about half as long as the part written earlier. Its
content is in the final version dispersed over the remarks from
189 to 421.

In the summer of 1945 Wittgenstein prepared a typescript,
called by him 'Bemerkungen I' (Remarks I).[3] A considerable
proportion of the remarks in this collection had been written
after the completion of the intermediate version. But the
major part of them Wittgenstein had selected from earlier
manuscripts, dating back as far as 1931. Presumably in the
academic year 1945–46 Wittgenstein expanded the intermediate version of the *Investigations* with more than 400 remarks

[3] TS 228.

from *'Bemerkungen* I' into what is essentially the final version of Part I of the printed work.[4]

This means that of the 693 remarks which make up Part I of the *Investigations* much more than half are new relative to the first and second versions of the work.

The manuscripts from which the remarks forming Part II of the *Investigations* were selected were written in the three-year period from May 1946 to May 1949.

The names *'Teil I'* and *'Teil II'* for the two parts composing the printed version of the *Investigations* were given to them by the editors.

THE MANUSCRIPT SOURCES

The primary task set for the research embodied in this study was to trace the remarks in the *Investigations* back to their sources in Wittgenstein's manuscripts. It was possible to find manuscript sources for all but 99 of the remarks in Part I and for all but 27 remarks in Part II of the *Investigations*. In Part II every paragraph, or group of paragraphs, separated from other paragraphs by a 'space', that is, by an empty line, has been counted as a remark.

In some cases the sources are for a part of a remark only. In other cases different parts (paragraphs) of a remark have their sources in different manuscripts.

Sometimes a remark passed through several manuscript versions before it was dictated for a typescript. Frequently Wittgenstein made further changes in handwriting to the typescripts, but on the whole the assignment of a manuscript source to a printed remark is *univocal* and the changes *slight* from the formulation in manuscript to the final formulation.

One of the 99 remarks in Part I, for which no manuscript source is known, occurs in an early typescript (213) prepared by Wittgenstein. It is possible that some of the remarks for which no manuscript source has been found were dictated extempore by Wittgenstein to the typist. It is, of course, also

[4] TS 227.

possible that the sources of some remarks have simply escaped
the searcher's notice. A further, more important, possibility is
that the sources are in manuscripts which no longer exist. This
last calls for a comment.

It is reported that when he was on his last visit to Vienna in
the early months of 1950, Wittgenstein had ordered a great
many papers, belonging to all periods of his work, to be
burned.[5] It is also reported that when living in Ireland after his
retirement from Cambridge, he destroyed old material which
he considered useless.[6] It seems to me unlikely that there were
several manuscripts containing unidentified source material
for the *Investigations* among the material destroyed by him.
Perhaps there were *no* such manuscripts at all.

One most important manuscript, however, is missing – and
perhaps destroyed. This is a big manuscript book written in
Norway late in 1936 and containing most of the content of
remarks 1–188 of the printed text of the work.

This manuscript[7] Wittgenstein gave to his sister, Mrs M.
Stonborough, as a Christmas present. To the dedication he
had added '*ein schlechtes Geschenk*' ('a poor gift'). I saw and
studied the manuscript when I visited Mrs Stonborough at
Gmunden in 1952. After her death in 1958, several manuscripts were with her son, Mr T. Stonborough, in Vienna. In
1965 I went there to check the material. Much to my surprise, I
found none of the material I had seen at Gmunden 13 years
earlier – but I did find some items, among them the
'Prototractatus', which had until then been unknown to me. A
subsequent search in the house at Gmunden brought to light
some hitherto unknown typescripts – but not the 1936
manuscript of the *Investigations*. I cannot regard it as out of the
question that it has been destroyed.

It has been possible to identify manuscript sources for 104 of
the first 188 remarks in the *Investigations*. About 25 of the
identified remarks go back to the attempted revision in
German of the Brown Book, about 40 to earlier manuscripts

---

[5] See Editors' Preface to *Notebooks 1914–1916*, Basil Blackwell, Oxford,
1961, 2nd edition, 1979. The report is from Miss Anscombe.

[6] Report from Mr Rush Rhees to G.H. von Wright.

[7] MS 142.

from the years 1930–34, more than 20 to a notebook from 1936, some 15 to manuscript writings from 1937 and 1938, and one – added in pencil to the final typescript – to 1945. It is also possible to trace to manuscripts all *Randbemerkungen* (notes), which appear at the bottom of a page in the printed version of the work. It is a reasonable conjecture that of the 84 unidentified remarks among the first 188 the vast majority, perhaps all, have their source in the now lost manuscript (MS 142). Accepting this conjecture as true, we could say that the manuscript sources for only some 15 of the 693 remarks in Part I of the *Investigations* are completely unknown, or never existed.

THE EARLY VERSION OF THE *INVESTIGATIONS*

The Preface to the printed version of the *Investigations* is dated Cambridge, January 1945. But, as we have seen, there existed an early version of the work with a Preface dated Cambridge, August 1938. Incidentally, the early Preface does not differ very substantially from the printed one.

This early version is based on material written in the years 1936–39. Wittgenstein had it typed. The typescript comprises in all 272 pages. It falls into two parts. The first, of 137 pages and 161 numbered remarks, is that part which is, broadly speaking, identical with the first 188 remarks of the printed version. The second, of 135 pages, contains 281 remarks not, however, as in the first typescript numbered by Wittgenstein himself.

The first typescript, TS 220 of the catalogue, is, as far as we can tell, based directly on the lost manuscript (142) which had been written in Norway in November and December 1936. Two copies of this typescript have been preserved – a top copy and a second copy. Roughly the first half of the top copy (pp. 1–65) and the second half of the other copy (pp. 66–137) were used by Wittgenstein for a thorough revision of TS 220 undertaken during the war years. The existence of this revised copy, now registered as TS 239, was not known to me until 1977 when it unexpectedly turned up in the United States. The unrevised TS 220 which was always present in Wittgenstein's *Nachlass* thus consists of two halves which originally belonged to two different copies of the same typescript. Calling it 'unrevised' should be taken with a grain of salt: it contains in fact a good many changes and insertions in Wittgenstein's hand.

The second part of the early version, TS 221, also exists in two copies. One of the copies contain some, but rather few, marks in Wittgenstein's hand. The other is entirely clean. Originally there was also a third copy. This Wittgenstein cut up into '*Zettel*'. The cuttings he clipped together in a large number of bunches. There are numerous changes and annotations in handwriting on the cuttings. This typescript of cuttings, listed in the catalogue as TS 222, was printed posthumously as Part I of the *Remarks on the Foundations of Mathematics*.

TS 221 was evidently dictated at two different times. There is a first – the main – part of it comprising pages 1–119 and a second part consisting of pages 120–135. The immediate reason for calling them two 'parts' is that they were typed on different typewriters. The first part is extracted from MSS 117, 118, and 119. The selections from 118 and 119, which make up 50 pages of the typed text, were written during the period from 10 September to 9 October 1937. The selections from 117, which comprise the first 69 pages of the whole thing (221), were written beginning on 11 September 1937. We cannot give them a definite *terminus ante quem*, but the writings in 117 which were dictated for TS 221 precede writings which Wittgenstein continued in a manuscript (121) begun in April 1938. It is my conjecture that the part of MS 117 which was used for TS 221 was also written in Norway in the autumn of 1937.

It is of some interest to note that the greatest part of what I have called the early version of the *Investigations* was the result of two relatively short periods of concentrated writing – one in November–December 1936 and another in September–November 1937, both periods in Norway.

The second part of TS 221 is extracted from three MS sources separated by several years. Pages 120–130 are based on sections in MS 115 which were probably written early in 1934. The remaining pages, 131–135, are based on writings in MS 121 and MS 162a, written at the turn of the year 1938 to 1939.

It is an open question whether TSS 220 and 221 (up to page 120) were dictated at the same or at different times. But it is noteworthy that they seemed to have been typed on the same typewriter – with the exception of some 20 pages in TS 220 which were typed on a different typewriter, *not*, however, the same as the one used for typing pages 120–135 of TS 221. TS 221 cannot have been dictated until some time in 1938; but TS 220 Wittgenstein *may* have dictated on a visit to Cambridge from Norway the year before.

It is known that Wittgenstein had a typescript with him in Norway in the autumn of 1937, which most probably was a typescript of what he had written one year earlier. But there is some evidence which points to it *not* being the typescript (TS 220) which has been preserved of the first half of the early version. I would therefore conjecture that the entire 'early version', that is, both TSS 220 and 221, were made at Cambridge in 1938 – and that the concluding part of 221 was added some time after January 1939.

When did Wittgenstein cut up TS 221 into '*Zettel*', composing TS 222? This we cannot tell with certainty. It is noteworthy that pages 120–135 were not cut up. This might indicate that the cutting up happened before these pages were even dictated. Pages 120–130, based on the much earlier MS 115, were clipped together and added as a separate bunch to the collection of '*Zettel*'.

In MS 124 we find, for 18 March 1944, two references 'to the Typscript'. They can easily be identified as referring to TS 221 (or 222), and have the character of additions. They were included, by the Editors, in their proper places in the printed text of Part I of the *Remarks on the Foundations of Mathematics*, but Wittgenstein did not himself insert them in the typed text. It is interesting to note that as late as in 1944 he was still making additions to the second half of the early version of his work.

I incline to think that the cutting up of TS 221 into '*Zettel*' took place in connection with a revision of the *entire* early version. Wittgenstein then decided to continue the revised TS

220 in a new direction – leading eventually to what is now Part I of the *Investigations*. This decision he probably made in 1944. Having made it, Wittgenstein laid aside the cut-up version of TS 221, i.e. TS 222, and never again returned to further work on it.

In MS 117 there are several drafts of a preface to a book. They are from the period June–August 1938. Their typed and final version is dated 'Cambridge, August 1938'. This preface was typed on the same typewriter as the second part of TS 221. This is an indication, I think, that the first and main part of TS 221 was typed not later than June or July 1938.

EARLY PLANS FOR PUBLICATION

Wittgenstein left Norway in mid-December 1937 and travelled to Vienna, where he seems to have stayed until the middle of January 1938, when he went to Cambridge. In the first half of February he moved to Dublin and late in March back to Cambridge. This was the time of the Nazi invasion of Austria, which for obvious reasons much troubled Wittgenstein and made him decide to apply for British citizenship. It seems that it was not until late April that he was again able to do concentrated philosophical work.

In February 1938, evidently before going to Dublin, Wittgenstein deposited with Trinity College Library a number of manuscripts and typescripts and gave to the college the publication rights in the event of his death. It has not been possible for me to identify the papers then deposited in the Library. In 1944 Wittgenstein withdrew the entire deposit.

In 1938, but presumably later in the year, perhaps at the time of writing the Preface, Wittgenstein also approached the Cambridge University Press about publication.[8] According to their minutes, the Syndics of the Press on 30 September 1938 offered to publish the German original with a parallel

---

[8] For information relating to Wittgenstein's contacts with the Cambridge University Press I am greatly indebted to Mr Jeremy Mynott. However, no correspondence with Wittgenstein has been preserved; there are only a few records in the Syndicate's minutes.

English translation of a work referred to as Wittgenstein's *Philosophical Remarks*. In spite of the somewhat puzzling reference to the title, there can be little doubt that the work meant was what I have here called the early version of the *Philosophical Investigations*.

Wittgenstein, however, hesitated. In the minutes of the Syndics for 21 October 1938 we read that 'the Secretary reported that Wittgenstein was uncertain about the publication of his *Philosophical Remarks* but was making arrangements with a translator'. The translator referred to was evidently Mr Rush Rhees, who at that time produced a translation of a considerable part of the text.

It is a reasonable conjecture that Wittgenstein's hesitation then about publication was connected with his continued work on the part of the book dealing with the philosophy of mathematics. As noted above, the concluding pages of the existing TS 221 are based on manuscript sources written at the turn of the year 1938–39.

Wittgenstein's next contact with the Press was in September 1943. What prompted him to make it then is not quite clear to me. One circumstance of importance, however, seems to have been his conversations in 1943 with Nicholas Bachtin. The two were together reading the *Tractatus*[9] – and, as Wittgenstein says in the printed Preface to the *Investigations*, it then suddenly seemed to him that he 'should publish those old thoughts and the new ones together'. The work now offered to the Press is referred to in the minutes under the title *Philosophical Investigations* and the Syndics 'agreed to the author's condition that a reprint of the *Tractatus* should be included in the volume'. The acceptance was confirmed on 14 January 1944. Permission for the reprinting had then been obtained from the publishers of the *Tractatus*, Routledge and Kegal Paul. (This permission was later withdrawn.)

A question of interest is how the work offered by Wittgenstein to the Press in 1943 was related to the work the

---

[9] From the printed Preface one would conclude that the reading of the *Tractatus* with Bachtin happened in 1941. This, however, is an error. The correct year is 1943. Cf. 'The Wittgenstein Papers' above, note 13.

publication of which was being discussed in 1938. TS 221, which in 1938 was still incomplete, had been finished (cf. p. 119). TS 220 had undergone drastic changes as a result of work which Wittgenstein is known[10] to have done at the end of 1942 or beginning of 1943. Traces of these revisions had survived in the form of 12 pages of the revised text, corresponding to 16 consecutive pages in the earlier typescript (220). Then, as already mentioned, the entire revised type-script came to light in 1977. The revisions and rearrangements are considerable – in relation both to the early version and to existing later versions. Also the numbering of the remarks (by Wittgenstein himself) in this version of 1942–43 differs from earlier and later versions.

It is possible that the work, as conceived by Wittgenstein in 1943, consisted of revised versions of *both* halves of the early version. Some evidence for this can be found in TS 222. Another possibility is that Wittgenstein had already then decided to separate the writings on the philosophy of mathematics from the *Investigations*. In any case it is a fact that the version of the *Investigations* which Wittgenstein in 1943 was offering the Cambridge University Press cannot with certainty be reconstructed.

THE BIG MANUSCRIPT BOOK (MS 116)

A major difficulty confronting the dating of the manuscript sources for the *Investigations* is caused by MS 116. This is the biggest of all Wittgenstein's preserved manuscript books. The number of written pages in it is 347. There is only one date in the book. It occurs on page 316 and reads (in English) 'May 1945'. There is every reason to think that the part from page 316 to the end was written in May or in May and June 1945. Of the remarks in this part of the manuscript, 29 occur in the *Investigations*.

When had the rest of MS 116 been written? This remaining and major part of the manuscript can be divided into three

---

[10] I am indebted to Mr Rush Rhees for this information.

sections. The first covers pages 1–135, the second pages 136–264, and the third pages 265–315.

As far as its content goes; the first section clearly stands apart from the rest. An examination reveals that pages 1–135 in fact consist of selections with revisions from the beginning (pages 1–197) of the typescript with the number 213. This so-called Big Typescript of in all 768 pages was probably dictated in 1933. It in turn is based on a typescript (TS 211) which Wittgenstein cut up into *'Zettel'* and rearranged before dictating TS 213. The underlying manuscript writings are from the years 1929–32.

In manuscripts from 1933 and 1934 Wittgenstein revised parts of the content of TS 213. His efforts were evidently aimed at the composition of a work representing his position in philosophy at that time. These efforts he abandoned – under the influence, it seems, of the new developments of his thoughts which first manifested themselves in the Blue Book and then were continued in the Brown Book. Pages 1–135 of MS 116 were perhaps a last effort to revise the earlier work. When was this revision undertaken?

The big manuscript book had been purchased in Bergen (Norway). After the end of the academic year 1935–36 Wittgenstein went to stay in his hut in Norway for the greater part of the period from August 1936 to December 1937. Here he started (August 1936) a translation into German, with important revisions and additions, of the Brown Book which he had dictated at Cambridge in the year 1934–35. He was then writing in the manuscript book MS 115. Later in the autumn he abandoned the efforts at an *'Umarbeitung'* (revision) and proceeded to the writing of the now lost manuscript book (142) which was the first version of the beginning of the final *Investigations*. This he finished in December. Preliminary materials for it are found in the notebook MS 152. For the sections 151–188 (including the long passage on *'Lesen'*) he used materials in the *Umarbeitung* which were new relative to the Brown Book.

Two pocket notebooks, MS 157a (second half) and MS 157b, are all that we possess of writings by Wittgenstein which can be dated with certainty to the first half of 1937. They relate to the beginning of the *Investigations* and some of the remarks were selected and revised for the typescript of the first half of the early version (TS 220) which Wittgenstein dictated in 1937 or 1938.

It may seem intrinsically unlikely that Wittgenstein had written the first section of MS 116 *after* having written the beginning of the *Investigations* in the autumn of 1936. Nor is there much reason to believe that he wrote it simultaneously with either the revision of the Brown Book or the beginning of the *Investigations*. These facts speak in favour of the view that Wittgenstein began writing in MS 116 *before* going to live in Norway in 1936. It would follow that he must have acquired the book in Norway on some previous visit. (It is improbable that he had ordered the book or that it was sent to him from Norway.) Since he called it 'Band XII' and the manuscript book in which he was writing in the beginning of 1934 was Band XI (MS 115), it is reasonable to assume that the earliest date of the writings in MS 116 is 1934.

It is not known, however, that Wittgenstein visited Norway in the period between his return to Cambridge in 1929 and the year 1936. His pocket diaries, of which there exists an unbroken sequence from those years, contain no indication of a visit to Norway prior to 1936. (The diaries record appointments to see people and occasionally also some dates relating to travels.)[11] For this and other reasons one must, I think, keep open the possibility that Wittgenstein's revision, in MS 116, of the beginning of the Big Typescript (TS 213) was, after all, made in 1936 or 1937. If this is the truth, the writings in the first part of MS 116 would thus be *later* than the writings for the first part of the early version of the *Investigations*. It is a fact that Wittgenstein later selected 47 remarks (and a few *Randbemerkungen*) from pages 1–135 of MS 116 to be included in the final version of Part I of his great work.

The second part of MS 116, pages 136–264, is a revision of

[11] In Rush Rhees (ed.), *Ludwig Wittgenstein: Personal Recollections*, Basil Blackwell, Oxford, 1981, there is a suggestion that Wittgenstein had been in Norway in 1931 (p. 135). In view of the testimony of the pocket diaries I think this extremely unlikely. The context on the page in the book suggests to me the year 1937 rather than 1931.

MS 120, a manuscript written late in 1937 and in the first third of 1938. At the very end of this part there are, however, a couple of remarks which had originally been written in MS 121 in July 1938 and five remarks which are selected from MS 115.

The third part of MS 116, pages 265–315, cannot be directly related to any other writings by Wittgenstein. But it is noteworthy that it deals to a large extent with topics which are also dealt with in MS 128. This latter MS contains a sketch of a Preface for a new version of the *Investigations* (in fact for the preface to the work as printed). MS 128 was most probably written in 1944, and it seems that this was also the year in which MS 116, pages 265– 315, was written.

It would then follow that the second part of MS 116 was written between 1938 and 1944 inclusive. I should hazard a conjecture that it was actually written late in that period, perhaps as late as 1944. There is internal evidence – closeness of the thoughts to those in MS 129 written in the autumn of 1944 – to support this conjecture.

THE INTERMEDIATE VERSION OF PART I OF THE *INVESTIGATIONS*

Even with due regard to the uncertainties pertaining to the dating of MS 116, it seems safe to say that only a very minor part of the *Investigations* stems from the years 1937–43 inclusive. During those seven years Wittgenstein's main concern was with the philosophy of mathematics. In 1937–38 he wrote what was originally the second half of the early version of the *Investigations* printed as Part I of the *Remarks on the Foundations of Mathematics* (see p. 118 above). In the beginning of 1944 Wittgenstein was still writing about the philosophy of mathematics – but then he shifted to work on the philosophy of psychology, which was to become a source for a new version of the *Investigations*. After 1944 he did not write anything about mathematics.

An examination of the final typescript of Part I of the *Investigations* (TS 227) reveals that there must have existed an intermediate typescript between it and the typescript of the early version. This one can see from the fact that the page numbers and the numbers of remarks on some pages have been crossed out and changed in handwriting.

Sometime in 1949, or possibly 1950, Wittgenstein put in my hands some 20 typed pages and said that I could destroy them, since they were no longer of any use. This I did not do, but put them aside in an envelope. This was fortunate. For it turns out that the pages with a changed page number in the final typescript *and* those discarded pages together, without gaps, make up pages 144–195 of one and the same typescript. The first 143 pages are pages 1–143 of the final typescript (TS 227). Page 195 has only four lines typed on it. It may very well be the last page of the entire typescript. The last remark has the number 300. It is identical with remark 421 in the printed work.

An examination of pages 144–195 of that earlier typescript shows that almost all remarks on them are from the first 89 pages of manuscript MS 129. The exceptions are only eight in number. One is from the beginning of MS 130, one from the end of MS 129, five remarks stem from pages 90–132 of MS 129, and finally there is one which begins with a paragraph from MS 124 while the rest of it cannot be identified in the manuscripts. MS 129 was begun on 17 August 1944 and MS 124 was probably finished by that time. The beginning of 130 is undated. The later parts of that manuscript are from the period May–August 1946. There is independent evidence, as we shall see, for thinking that the beginning of MS 130 was written considerably earlier.

The remarks from MS 129 were not, however, sifted directly into the typescript pages 144–195. They made the passage by the route of another, preparatory typescript, TS 241. This typescript was not known to exist until 1976. There are, moreover, two copies of it. In both copies there are (different) corrections and insertions in handwriting. The typescript has 33 pages and 114 numbered remarks. (The occurrence of the number '115' after the last remark *could* indicate that Wittgenstein had thought of continuing it – but I think this possibility unlikely.) All remarks on pages 144–195 with the exception of only five remarks correspond to remarks in TS 241. TS 241 is thus virtually a first typescript version of the new material which, together with the revised TS 220 and a brief section (pages 135–143) of remarks taken from TS 221, make up what I proposed to call an intermediate version of the *Investigations*.

It seems to me very likely that there existed in January 1945, or soon after, a typescript consisting of 195 pages and containing 300 remarks. It was for this intermediate version that Wittgenstein wrote the preface dated Cambridge, January 1945, which remains, with this somewhat misleading dating, the preface of the final, printed version of the *Investigations*.

The fact that Wittgenstein had rewritten the preface to the early version and dated the new preface January 1945 would indicate that he was again thinking of publishing. I do not know of any records, however, which show that he had then been in contact with Cambridge University Press or any other publisher. We can only conjecture the reasons that kept Wittgenstein from proceeding with the publication plans. Presumably they have something to do with the fact that, soon after Wittgenstein had dated the preface for the intermediate version, we find him busy at work composing yet a further version of that which is now Part I of the printed *Investigations*.

BEMERKUNGEN I

On 13 June 1945, Wittgenstein wrote to Rush Rhees: 'I've been working *fairly* well since Easter. I am dictating some stuff, remarks, some of which I want to embody in my first volume (if there'll ever be one). This business of dictating will take roughly another month, or 6 weeks.'

This interesting record gives rise to a number of questions. Which are the writings Wittgenstein was then in the process of dictating? Can we identify the typescript the dictating resulted in? And what does he mean by the phrase 'my first volume'?

Wittgenstein says that he has been working 'fairly well since Easter'. This would mean April to May. As we know, the last part of the big manuscript book MS 116 was dated May 1945. There are no other writings of Wittgenstein which can be dated with *certainty* to this period, nor to the earlier months of 1945. The most reasonable candidates are the later part of MS 129, the undated beginning of MS 130, and possibly some other portions of MS 116.

The time allowed for the dictating would indicate that there was a considerable amount of material to be typed. The resulting typescript, however, was neither the final nor yet another typescript of Part I of the *Investigations*. For all we can judge, the dictation resulted in a collection of 698 remarks, called by Wittgenstein *Bemerkungen* I. A comparative study of remarks which appear both in *Bemerkungen* I and in the final typescript of the *Investigations* establishes beyond doubt that *Bemerkungen* I must be the earlier of the two typescripts.

The first 231 remarks of *Bemerkungen* I, i.e. roughly the first third of the whole work, are selected – in order of entry – from the first three parts of MS 116. Among them is included one single remark from MS 115. Then follow some 130 remarks from MS 129 (and one from MS 124), that is, from the period 1944–45. Then there is a jump back in time: after some 25 remarks in mixed order from TS 213, MS 114, MS 117, and MS 119, more than 100 consecutive selections from MS 115 and more than 60 from MS 114 follow. All these latter sources are pre-war. But from remark number 563 to the end the selections are again mainly, though not exclusively, from later manuscript sources: chiefly from the beginning of MS 130 and from the concluding part, dated May 1945, of MS 116. Unless *Bemerkungen* I was dictated at different periods – for which there is *no* evidence – it was dictated *in toto* after May 1945 but, as mentioned, before the final typescript of Part I of the *Investigations*.

THE FINAL VERSION OF PART I OF THE *INVESTIGATIONS*

Wittgenstein selected about 400 of the 698 remarks in *Bemerkungen* I to be included, occasionally with some changes, in the final typescript of Part I of the *Investigations*. Seventeen additional remarks from *Bemerkungen* I are included as *Randbemerkungen*. It should be noted that these inclusions amount to many more than half of the total number (693) of remarks in the printed Part I. (Of the remaining remarks in *Bemerkungen* I, about 220 are printed in *Zettel*, occasionally with some cuts.)

There is a list, made by Wittgenstein himself, of the selections from *Bemerkungen* I for the book. In the catalogue it has the number MS 182. The list also makes reference to pages where the selected remarks were to be inserted. A comparison with the intermediate typescript of the *Investigations* shows that the page references are to this. After the last page reference (to page 194) a long list of remarks from *Bemerkungen* I follows. They correspond, in their order, *fairly well* with the remarks from number 421 to the end of Part I of the printed text of the *Investigations*.

It is possible that the long list of remarks following the last page reference was composed later. The handwriting gives some support for this conjecture. If this end part of MS 182 is later, this would indicate that Wittgenstein had in the first instance contemplated an expansion of the existing intermediate version into yet another intermediate version.

The final typescript of Part I was evidently composed on the basis of the intermediate typescript and the *Bemerkungen* I with the aid of the list. When composing the new typescript Wittgenstein changed the order of the remarks, omitted a good many of them, and also included some new ones. Since many of the omitted remarks occur in *Zettel* this throws light on the history and composition of that particular collection.

There is no indication that the final typescript contains remarks from manuscript sources of a later date than that of the composition of *Bemerkungen* I, that is, approximately June 1945. The version that existed in January 1945 had 195 pages, as against the 324 pages of the final typescript.

When was the final typescript of Part I made? It *could* have been made immediately after the production of *Bemerkungen* I. *For* this conjecture speaks the time allowed for the dictations and perhaps the words in the letter to Rhees that Wittgenstein was dictating 'stuff' (evidently *Bemerkungen* I) *some of which* he wanted to embody in his 'first volume'. On existing evidence I find it likely that the typescript was made either immediately after *Bemerkungen* I or in the academic year 1945–46. But

Wittgenstein must have continued to work on the typescript after that and as late as in 1949 or 1950. The fact that he then gave me the loose typescript pages mentioned above can hardly mean anything else than that he was then still revising from the intermediate to the final typescript of Part I of the *Investigations*.

| | | Number of selected | |
| | | Bemerkungen (or parts of them) | Randbemerkungen (or parts of them) |
MS	Year of writing		
108	1930	2	
109	1930–31	1	
110	1931	8	
112	1931	5	
153a	1931	1	
114	1933–34	38	4
115 (1)	1933–34	79	2
110	1933–34	1	
116 (1)	1934? (1937?)	47	5
115 (2)	1936	26	
152	1936	34	
157a	1937	11	
157b	1937	13	
117	1937	14	
119	1937	10	
121	1937–38	1	
162b	1939–40	4	
163	1941	3	
116 (2)	1938–44	46	
116 (3)	1944?	28	1
124	1944	16	
127	1944	1	
128	1944	3	
180a	circa 1945		1
129	1944–45	201	3
130	1945?	15	
116 (4)	1945	29	
Total		637	16

The table shows how the remarks are distributed over the manuscript sources.

Comments on the table

1   When one and the same remark in the *Investigations* has several manuscript sources, we have in the statistics taken notice only of the source which has the *latest* date and which therefore, in time, is closest to the printed remark. Then it should be remembered, however, that a majority of the identified MS sources for the first 188 remarks in the book were presumably sources, *immediately* for the now lost MS 142, and only *remotely* for TSS 220 of the early version and 227 of the final version. It must be left to future research to try to trace all MS sources back to their *earliest* appearance in the manuscripts.

2   The total number of remarks in Part I of the *Investigations* for which a MS source has been found is 594. The sum of figures given in the third column in the table is considerably higher, 637. This is due to the fact that many remarks have partial sources in several manuscripts (cf. p. 115 above).

3   The remarks in MS 114 (from the part paginated 1–228), those from the beginning part of MS 115, and those from the first of the four distinguishable parts of MS 116 (cf. pp. 122–125 above) are revisions, sometimes containing considerable additions and changes, of the writings in TS 213 (the Big Typescript). This TS was probably dictated in 1933 and had a predecessor in a TS probably dictated the year before. The chief MS sources (MSS 109–114) for these typescripts are writings from the years 1930–32. As a consequence, the remarks in the *Investigations* which were selected from MS 114 and from the first parts of MS 115 and MS 116 respectively have remoter MS sources in writings from 1930–32 – in some few cases even in writings from 1929.

4   The second half of MS 115 was written in Norway in 1936 and is (see p. 123 above) a revision, with additions, in German of a substantial part of the Brown Book. Wittgenstein broke off the work before finishing it and then started to write the now lost MS 142, which became the beginning of the present *Investigations*. As seen from the table, there are 26 remarks in the *Investigations* for which we have indicated a MS source in the 1936 part of MS 115. They were presumably 'lifted' from MS 115, with many revisions, into MS 142 (see p. 123 above). In addition, the beginning of the printed text (*roughly* remarks 1–21) is close in content and sometimes

also in formulation to the beginning of the 1936 part of MS 115. It would not, however, be correct to regard *these* passages in MS 115 as MS sources for remarks in the beginning of the final *Investigations*. They are therefore not included in the statistics of the above table.

BEMERKUNGEN II

What do the words 'my first volume' in the letter to Rhees refer to?

In a letter to Moore (designated M 40) from February 1939 Wittgenstein also refers to 'my first volume'.[12] And in a letter to me from September that same year he mentions 'the first volume of my book'.[13] There can be little doubt that he means the first half (TS 220) of the early version of the *Investigations*. It seems to me obvious that in the letter to Rhees six years later he uses the phrase to refer to the revision and enlargement of this first volume, i.e. to what I have here termed the intermediate version of the *Investigations*.

But which is the other volume or volumes referred to by implication? Was Wittgenstein in 1945 contemplating a second volume dealing with the philosophy of logic and mathematics? This volume would presumably have embodied a new version of the second half of the early version of the *Investigations*, with additions from his many writings on those topics during the period 1937–44. This is *one* possibility – and the one I consider most likely. But it must remain a conjecture. The conjecture would get considerable support if it could be shown that Wittgenstein had done the cutting up of the second half of the early version roughly at this time (1944–45). We have no direct evidence for this (see p. 119 above). But the fact is that Wittgenstein made additions to the cut-up version from writings from the year 1944, and this at least shows that he was still working on it then.

Another possibility is that Wittgenstein had then already planned the continuation to Part I of the *Investigations* which

[12] Ludwig Wittgenstein, *Letters to Russell, Keynes and Moore*, ed. by G.H. von Wright, Basil Blackwell, Oxford, 1974, rev. edit. 1977, p. 176.
[13] Cf. the Introduction to this volume.

eventually resulted in what is now Part II of the printed work. Against this, however, speaks the fact that Wittgenstein did not begin the writings which are the manuscript sources for Part II of the *Investigations* until about one year after the letter to Rhees, or in May 1946 (see below).

Sometime after the completion of *Bemerkungen* I, but before the commencement of the writings for Part II of the *Investigations*, Wittgenstein composed a typescript (230), called by him *Bemerkungen* II. It contains 542 remarks, practically all of which are also in *Bemerkungen* I. Furthermore, practically all remarks from *Bemerkungen* I which were selected for Part I of the *Investigations* also occur in *Bemerkungen* II. Therefore it seems out of the question that *Bemerkungen* II was a projected second volume – assuming that Part I was the first volume.

Why did Wittgenstein compose *Bemerkungen* II at all? The remarks in *Bemerkungen* I had been selected from manuscript sources mainly in chronological order of writing, though with some 'jumps' back and forth in time among the manuscripts. *Bemerkungen* II is definitely an arrangement with a view to subject matter. With some justification *Bemerkungen* II may be regarded as an independent and final work by Wittgenstein.

Wittgenstein must have worked hard on the composition of *Bemerkungen* II. Three typescripts of it are preserved. All three contain further corrections and additions in Wittgenstein's hand – not always the same in the three copies. Wittgenstein also made a list of correspondences between the remarks in *Bemerkungen* I and *Bemerkungen* II.

PART II OF THE *INVESTIGATIONS*

The undated beginning of MS 130 was evidently written mainly in the first half of 1945 and several remarks from it were selected for *Bemerkungen* I. About halfway through the book there appears the date 26 May 1946. After this the rest of the book, 293 pages in all, is dated. Continuous with this manuscript are MSS 131–138. These consecutive writings end in MS 138 with the date 22 March 1949. There is an additional entry dated 20 May of that year.

It is from these manuscripts, covering a period of almost exactly three years, that practically all the remarks in Part II of the *Investigations* are selected. There are also some remarks selected from the pocket notebook MS 169. They probably date from the spring of 1949, when Wittgenstein visited Vienna from Dublin in April, returning to Dublin in May. It is possible that he wrote the pocket notebook in Vienna and that this piece of writing thus bridges the gap between the penultimate and the ultimate insertions in MS 138.

On the basis of selections from MSS 130–135 Wittgenstein dictated a typescript (229). Its pagination continues that in *Bemerkungen* I. The numbers of the remarks also continue those in *Bemerkungen* I – with the exception of an intermediate 'zone', where the numbers start with 699 but then drop back to 670. The zone is somewhat longer than the overlap of numbers of remarks; it ends with remark 701. Of the 33 remarks constituting the zone all but the first five can be traced to the undated part of MS 130. They were thus probably written in 1945. I find the existence of the zone somewhat puzzling.

The last remark in TS 229 has the number 1804. The typescript is a collection of in all 1,137 remarks. Only some 70 of them were selected for Part II of the *Investigations*. 142 are (sometimes with cuts) printed in *Zettel*.

On the basis of the concluding part of MS 135, from 9 November 1947, and up to the entry of 23 August 1948 in MS 137, Wittgenstein made selections for another chronologically arranged typescript, TS 232. It has 736 numbered remarks. The page numbers are from 600 to 773 – a fact for which I can offer no explanation. Of the 736 remarks, about 40 were used for Part II of the *Investigations*; 242 are (*in toto* or with cuts) printed in *Zettel*.[14]

Some time in 1949, probably before he went to visit Norman Malcolm and his wife in the United States in July, Wittgenstein composed a handwritten selection of remarks from all his writings from the three-year period 1946–49 (beginning with the latter part of MS 130). This manuscript,

[14] See Appendix in *Remarks on the Philosophy of Psychology*, Vol. II, ed. by G.H. von Wright and Heikki Nyman, Basil Blackwell, Oxford, 1980.

MS 144, is, save for a small number of omitted remarks, identical in content with Part II of the *Investigations*.

There existed also a typescript, based on this manuscript. The printing of the book took place from the typescript which is now, unfortunately, lost. It is not known when the typescript was made nor even whether it was dictated by Wittgenstein himself. It is at least a possibility that it was made by a typist who tried to follow the numerous instructions in the manuscript concerning the reordering of the written remarks. In two places the printed order disagrees slightly with the order indicated in the manuscript. The order indicated in the handwritten text seems to me to fit better the trend of thought; perhaps the order ought to be amended in future printings of the work. But it also seems certain that Wittgenstein must have seen the typescript even if he had not himself dictated it. This is plain, I think, from the numerous minor differences in the spelling of words which exist between MS 144 and the printed text.

The last section of the printed book (Part II, section xiv) is written on a separate sheet in MS 144 which is placed in between two sheets with consecutive text on them. This section also seemed 'displaced' in the typescript. The editors decided to place it at the very end of the book and said so in their Preface. There is no reason to think that Wittgenstein himself would have disagreed with this editorial decision.

THE UNITY OF THE *INVESTIGATIONS*

How did Wittgenstein himself view the relation between the two parts, which now jointly make up the *Investigations*? Did he regard them as being essentially *one* work – and was it his intention, if possible, to knit the two parts together so as to form a more complete whole? The editors of the *Investigations*, Anscombe and Rhees, indicate in their Preface that they think this was so. Perhaps they are right – and perhaps this was one reason why Wittgenstein could not bring himself to publish the book in his lifetime. One would then be justified in calling the *Investigations* an unfinished work.

I am not sure, however, that this is the right view to take. I lean, myself, towards the opinion that Part I of the *Investigations* is a complete work and that Wittgenstein's writings from 1946 onwards represent in certain ways departures in *new* directions. But this fact, which seems to me interesting and noteworthy for a full understanding of Wittgenstein's achievement, need not exclude the possibility that he himself had wanted the two parts of the work to form a more integrated whole than they actually do.

In this connection it is also worthwhile to contemplate the position of the work of Wittgenstein published under the title *Zettel*. It is not known with what end in view Wittgenstein kept this collection of cuttings from various typescripts. Well over half of the remarks which occur in *Zettel* were written in the period May 1946–August 1948. Of the remaining number the overwhelming majority belong to the typescript *Bemerkungen* I (TS 228), which seems to have been composed in 1945 and from which Wittgenstein selected about 400 remarks to be included in Part I of the *Investigations*.[15] It is not an implausible hypothesis that Wittgenstein's plan was to use the *'Zettel'* for 'bridging the gap' between the present Part I and Part II of the *Investigations*. In any case it seems safe to say that *Zettel* belongs between the two disconnected members of the *chef d'oeuvre* of Wittgenstein's 'later' philosophy and thus constitutes the middle part of what could also be thought of as a trilogy.

[15] See p. 128 above and André Maury, 'Sources of the Remarks in Wittgenstein's *Zettel*', *Philosophical Investigations* 4, 1981.

WITTGENSTEIN ON
PROBABILITY

This essay is based on a paper given at the Wittgenstein Symposium at Aix-en-Provence in 1969. It appeared with the title 'Wittgenstein's Views on Probability' in *Revue internationale de Philosophie* **23**, 1969. I am indebted to Brian McGuinness for having later pointed out to me an error in my account of how probabilities may vary with changes in the bulk of our knowledge. This has occasioned a substantial revision of section 5 of the paper for the present volume.

I

A SINGULAR 'holisticity' and integratedness characterizes Wittgenstein's philosophy. Everything in it is connected with everything else. This is true of the *Tractatus Logico-Philosophicus*, and to an even greater extent of the *Philosophical Investigations*. This, I think, is *one* reason why Wittgenstein never succeeded in giving to his later philosophy the shape of one completed literary achievement.[1] The *Investigations* is a torso. In most cases it is next to impossible to select a problem or topic and tell what were Wittgenstein's views of *this*, without trying at the same time to interpret and understand the *whole* of his thinking.

There are a few exceptions to this rule. One is the topic of probability. But it is characteristic that Wittgenstein wrote systematically on this topic only in the years before he began work on the *Investigations*. There are only two mentions of probability in that book, as we have it.[2] And in the selected writings from roughly the same period which were published under the title *Remarks on the Foundations of Mathematics* there is no mention of probability at all.

There are three main sources for a study of Wittgenstein's views of probability. The first are propositions 5.15–5.156 of the *Tractatus*. The second is section XXII of the *Philosophische Bemerkungen (Philosophical Remarks)* written in 1929 or 1930.[3] The third is a typescript of 18 pages, presumably composed in the academic year 1932–33 on the basis of manuscripts from the immediately preceding years. The typescript is essentially a somewhat changed version of the section of the *Philosophical Remarks* just mentioned. It forms two chapters, with the headings *Wesen der Hypothese* ('The Nature of Hypothesis') and *Wahrscheinlichkeit* ('Probability') respectively, of a typescript of 768 pages in all. This – the Big Typescript[4] – has not

[1] Cf. the Preface to the *Investigations*.
[2] Sections 482 and 484.
[3] Ed. by Rush Rhees, Basil Blackwell, Oxford, 1964 in German, 1975 in English.
[4] TS 213 of the catalogue.

been published *in toto*. But a very considerable part of it, including the two chapters on hypotheses and probability, is printed in the work by Wittgenstein called *Philosophische Grammatik (Philosophical Grammar).*[5]

The more or less verbatim recordings of conversations with Wittgenstein by Friedrich Waismann include two fragments on probability.[6] Their dates are January and March 1930. The contents of these fragments are very close to the sections on probability in the *Philosophical Remarks* and *Philosophical Grammar.*

Wittgenstein's writings in the period beginning 1929 and ending, roughly, with the composition of the so-called Blue Book in 1933–34, can be said to constitute a period of transition from his position in the *Tractatus* to his views in the *Investigations*. It seems to me true to say that the writings on probability from this transition period are closer to the spirit of the *Tractatus* than to the later philosophy of Wittgenstein.

I shall not here try to make a detailed exposition of everything that Wittgenstein said on probability. As far as the *Tractatus* is concerned the reader can be referred to Black's *Companion*[7] which also makes incidental reference to material in the *Philosophical Remarks*. My aim is to examine rather than merely to present Wittgenstein's views, to try to understand how his ideas 'work', and to see whether they can be related to one another so as to form a coherent and intelligible whole.

2

Wittgenstein's definition of probability – the only one he ever explicitly proposed – is in *Tractatus* 5.15. The definition can be paraphrased as follows:

[5] Ed. by Rush Rhees, Basil Blackwell, Oxford, 1969 in German, 1974 in English. The sections dealing with probability are on pp. 219–235.

[6] F. Waismann, *Wittgenstein and the Vienna Circle*, ed. by B.F. McGuinness, Basil Blackwell, Oxford, 1967 in German, 1979 in English, pp. 93–96, 98–99.

[7] Max Black, *A Companion to Wittgenstein's Tractatus*, Cambridge University Press, Cambridge, 1964. The section on probability is on pp. 247–258.

Consider a set S of n logically independent propositions. Consider further two propositions, $f_1(S)$ and $f_2(S)$, which are truth-functions of these n propositions in the set, also called truth-arguments (cf. 5.01). By the truth-grounds (5.101b) of the truth-functions we mean those of its truth-possibilities (4.41), that is, combinations of truth-values in the truth-arguments, for which the functions assume the value 'true'. Let the number of truth-grounds of $f_1(S)$ be m and the number of truth-grounds of $f_2(S)$ which are also truth-grounds of $f_1(S)$ be k_m. ($k_m \leqslant m$ and $0 \leqslant m \leqslant 2^n$.) The ratio $k_m : m$ then measures the probability which the proposition $f_1(S)$ gives to the proposition $f_2(S)$, or briefly: the probability of $f_2(S)$ *given* $f_1(S)$.[8]

The notion of logical independence is problematic, and some of its problems crop up in connection with Wittgenstein's definition of probability. It may be regarded as a lacuna of the *Tractatus* that it does not define or make precise this notion, although it is of great importance to the argumentation throughout the book. The closest thing to a definition is the remark 5.152a which says that 'propositions which have no truth-arguments in common with one another are called independent'. If this were the definition of independence, we should have to say, for example, that $pv\sim p$ and $q\&\sim q$ are logically independent. Another way of defining independence would be to say that n propositions are logically independent if and only if it is logically possible that they are true or false in any of the 2^n different combinations. By this definition of independence, $pv\sim p$ and $q\&\sim q$ are not logically independent. But, for example, pvr and $qvrvs$ are independent although they have a truth-argument in common. (They would thus *not* be independent according to 5.152a.)

In the first, or 1921/22, edition of the *Tractatus* Wittgenstein said (5.152b) that independent propositions give one another the probability 1/2. But, by his own definition of probability, the probability of $q\&\sim q$ given $pv\sim p$ is 0, and the probability of $pv\sim p$ given $q\&\sim q$ is undetermined (0/0). The probability of pvr given $qvrvs$ is again 11/14 and the probability of $qvrvs$

[8] The condition $m > 0$ should be added. Wittgenstein does not mention it.

given *pvr* is 11/12. So, by neither one of the two definitions of independence which we have mentioned would it be true that independent propositions give one another the probability 1/2.

Wittgenstein must have realized that everything was not in order here. For in the second (1933) edition of the book he changed the formulation of 5.152b so as to become, simply, 'two elementary propositions give to one another the probability 1/2'. Whether this is true or not depends upon the view one takes of elementary propositions. As I understand Wittgenstein's view it is such as to make the statement true according to either of the two definitions of independence.

The *Tractatus* concept of probability is *relative* to a set of propositions which are truth-arguments of the truth-functions under consideration. – If *p* and *q* and *r* are independent[9] propositions, the probability of *p* given *pvqvr* is 4/7. If *p* and *s* are independent, the probability of *p* given *pvs* is 2/3. These assumptions of independence are compatible with the possibility that *s* is a truth-function of *q* and *r*. Assume that it is their disjunction (*s = qvr*). The same proposition then gives *p* both the probability 4/7 and the probability 2/3, depending upon how it is analysed, that is, conceived of as a truth-function of some truth-arguments.

In order to guarantee the uniqueness of probability values we must single out *one* way of exhibiting propositions as truth-functions. This is done in the *Tractatus* by means of the doctrine of elementary propositions. The elementary propositions are logically independent of one another (1.21 and 4.27). Every proposition is a truth-function of elementary propositions (5). It is not said that the number of elementary propositions is finite. This it need not be. But unless we assume that every proposition is a truth-function of a finite number of elementary propositions, we cannot compute all probability values on the basis of Wittgenstein's definition without modifying it somehow.

Wittgenstein's notion of probability is further dyadic or

---

[9] Henceforth in this paper, by calling *n* propositions independent I mean that they can be true and false in 2^n different combinations of truth-values.

conditional. It is the probability which one proposition gives to or confers upon another proposition.

One could define a notion of probability *simpliciter* as the probability given to a proposition (which is a truth-function of the members of a set of propositions) by the tautology (of the propositions in the set). On this definition, the probability *simpliciter* of a proposition is the number of its truth-grounds divided by the total number of its truth-possibilities.

If we take this notion of probability *simpliciter* as fundamental, we can introduce the notion of conditional probability by definition. The probability of p given q is then simply the probability (*simpliciter*) of $p\&q$ divided by the probability (*simpliciter*) of q. This method is alternative to the one employed by Wittgenstein in the *Tractatus*.[10] Whether we calculate the value of the probability of p given q directly on the basis of Wittgenstein's definition, or determine it as a quotient of two probabilities *simpliciter*, defined as above, we get the same result.

3

According to the classical definition proposed by Laplace, probability is a ratio of the number of possibilities which are favourable to the occurrence of an event and the number of possibilities which are either favourable or unfavourable to the occurrence of the same event – all possibilities being equal.[11] This definition stands at the peak of a mighty tradition in the mathematics and philosophy of probability.

Wittgenstein's definition is a late descendant of this tradi-

---

[10] This alternative way of treating probabilities is used by T. Hailperin in 'Foundations of Probability in Mathematical Logic', *Philosophy of Science* **4**, 1937.

[11] *Essai philosophique sur les probabilités* (1814). It is natural to state the definition in terms of 'occurrences of events' or 'outcomes of experiments'. Laplace states the definition in very general terms, speaking only of 'possibilities' without mention of the things considered possible. But elsewhere in the text Laplace speaks of *événements* as being possible or probable.

tion. The analysis of a situation, which affords an opportunity for the occurrence of an event, into a set of alternative possibilities is a special case of the choice of a set of independent truth-arguments for the purpose of expressing truth-possibilities. The alternatives pronounced 'favourable' to the occurrence of an event are a species of truth-grounds of a proposition (which is a truth-function of the truth-arguments). In these respects Wittgenstein's definition is a generalization of the Laplacean one.

It was always felt that the weak spot of Laplace's definition is the requirement that the possibilities be equal. This requirement is not embodied in Wittgenstein's definition. In this regard it represents a 'purification' of the Laplacean view of an obscure ingredient.

It is illuminating to compare the role of the idea of equipossibility for the Laplacean definition with the role of the idea of analysability in terms of elementary propositions for Wittgenstein's definition of probability. Neither idea is essential to the logico-mathematical fabric which may be erected on the basis of the definitions. Both serve the same purpose of ensuring that the values of probabilities computed with the aid of the definitions are, somehow, 'uniquely correct' values. The problem of the existence and nature of elementary propositions can hardly be regarded as relevant to probability theory. But the question of the grounds on which alternatives should be pronounced equally possible (or probable), *is* one of considerable interest to the philosophy of probability.

A definition of probability which in all essentials answers to Wittgenstein's had been proposed nearly a century earlier by Bolzano in his *Wissenschaftslehre* of 1837.[12] Bolzano also calls probability the relative validity (*vergleichungsweise Gültigkeit*) of a proposition in relation to another proposition. The propositions he regards as functions of variable parts which he calls ideas or thoughts (*Vorstellungen*). This comes very near the notion of a truth-function. As in Wittgenstein's definition, the requirement of equipossibility is not worked into the distinction of truth-possibilities. It seems appropriate to speak

---

[12] Vol. 2, sections 161–168.

of *one* definition of probability here and call it the Bolzano-Wittgenstein definition.[13]

Bolzano's achievements in logic fell into oblivion and were ignored for about a hundred years. In this Bolzano recalls another great figure in the history of logic, Leibniz. I doubt that Wittgenstein had ever read Bolzano or even heard of his views of probability. The same apparently holds, surprisingly enough, for the many nineteenth-century philosophers who after Bolzano endeavoured to give the Laplacean definition of probability a foundation in pure logic. These thinkers usually base their definition of the concept on a theory of disjunctive, or hypothetico-disjunctive, judgements. Lange,[14] Sigwart,[15] Fick,[16] Stumpf,[17] and Czuber[18] are writers in this line. Their treatment of probability is much inferior in clarity and fullness to Bolzano's earlier and Wittgenstein's later treatments.

4

As is well known, Wittgenstein withdrew from active work in philosophy after completing the *Tractatus* and became a schoolteacher in the Austrian countryside. Towards the end of his time as a teacher he was in contact with Moritz Schlick. When he was engaged in the Bau Kundmanngasse in Vienna in 1926–28, he had discussions with Schlick and Waismann and also met other members of the Vienna Circle. These contacts continued for some years after Wittgenstein had returned to

[13] Cf. my books *A Treatise on Induction and Probability*, Routledge and Kegan Paul, London, 1951, p. 168, and *The Logical Problem of Induction*, 2nd edition, Basil Blackwell, Oxford, 1957, p. 211, for additional references to the literature.

[14] F.A. Lange, *Logische Studien*, Iserlohn, 1877, pp. 99–126.

[15] C. Sigwart, *Logik*, vol. 2, section 85, Tübingen, 1878.

[16] A. Fick, *Philosophischer Versuch über die Wahrscheinlichkeiten*, Würzburg, 1883.

[17] C. Stumpf, 'Über den Begriff der mathematischen Wahrscheinlichkeit', *Sitzungsberichte d. philos. -philol. u. hist. Classe d. k. b. Akademie der Wissenschaften zu München*, 1892, *Heft* I, pp. 37–120.

[18] E. Czuber, *Wahrscheinlichkeitsrechnung*, Leipzig, 1903.

philosophy and taken up residence at Cambridge from the beginning of 1929. In Wittgenstein's writings of the period 1929–34 we can, I think, often find the sources of ideas which were discussed among members of the Vienna Circle and became diffused through their publications. Wittgenstein's influence and impact on Friedrich Waismann was particularly strong.

In September 1929 Waismann read a paper on probability at a meeting in Prague. The paper, called 'Logische Analyse des Wahrscheinlichkeitsbegriffs' ('Logical Analysis of the Concept of Probability'), was subsequently published in the first volume of *Erkenntnis* (1930–31). The author acknowledges his indebtedness to Wittgenstein, but says that he does not know how far his views agree with Wittgenstein's in detail.[19] He adds that Wittgenstein is preparing a major work in which probability will be treated.[20] Evidently, Waismann is here referring to the *Philosophical Remarks*.

Waismann puts forward in his paper a definition of probability which can be characterized as a generalization of the definition given by Wittgenstein in the *Tractatus*. Like the Bolzano–Wittgenstein definition it defines the *conditional* probability of a proposition relative to another proposition ('*p* given *q*').

Wittgenstein's definition is in terms of *numbers of truth-grounds*, Waismann's in terms of *measures of ranges* of propositions. Waismann introduces a function μ subject to the following three postulates:

(a)   The μ of a proposition is a not-negative real number.
(b)   The μ of a contradiction is zero.
(c)   The μ of the disjunction of two mutually exclusive propositions is the sum of the μ of the one and the μ of the other.

The probability of *p* given *q* is now defined as the μ of the conjunction of *p* and *q* divided by the μ of *q* alone. In Waismann's symbols:

$$p^{\omega}q = \frac{\mu(p.q)}{\mu(q)}.$$

[19] 'Logische Analyse', p. 228.
[20] Ibid.

The notion of a range (in German *Spielraum*) is in the *Tractatus*. This is probably the source from which the notion has risen to prominence in more recent discussion.[21] I do not know whether Wittgenstein's use of it in turn derives from another source. It seems that the notion was first used in a technical sense by von Kries in 1886 in his book on probability.[22] I would not exclude the possibility that Wittgenstein was familiar with this work – and perhaps with other writings by von Kries, who was also one of the classical exponents of sensory physiology. But I have no direct evidence for this.

Wittgenstein introduces and elucidates the notion of a range in 4.463a by saying that the truth-conditions determine the range which is left to the facts by the proposition. The range, in this sense, is thus of the facts, and not of the proposition.[23] The truth-conditions of a proposition again is a partitioning of the set of truth-possibilities into those which agree and those which disagree with the proposition (cf. 4.431a). If the notion of range is reshaped so as to be an attribute of propositions, it seems best in conformity with Wittgenstein's intentions to say that the range of a proposition is the set of its truth-*grounds*, that is, those of the truth-possibilities which verify the proposition (5.101b). We can then say that Wittgenstein's definition of probability too is in terms of the measures of ranges, the measure of the range of a proposition being identified with the number of its truth-grounds. This would be *one* way, and perhaps the simplest, of specifying Waismann's function μ. (It is easy to see that this specification satisfies Waismann's three postulates.)

[21] Cf. Carnap, *Logische Syntax der Sprache*, Springer Verlag, Vienna, 1934, p. 152.

[22] Johannes von Kries, *Die Prinzipien der Wahrscheinlichkeitsrechnung, eine logische Untersuchung*, Freiburg i.B., 1886. It is significant that, although von Kries' work contains interesting references to the history of probability theory, it contains no mention of Bolzano.

[23] This seems indeed to be the most natural way of using the German word *Spielraum*. von Kries too uses it as an attribute of facts in a situation. Waismann vacillates in his use, but he also speaks of the *Spielräume* of propositions (*Sätze*). The English term 'range' is perhaps better suited as an attribute for propositions.

The general notion of the measure of a range is mentioned nowhere in Wittgenstein's writings – neither in the *Tractatus* nor later. It seems to me a plausible conjecture that the introduction of this notion into probability theory is an original contribution of Waismann – and indeed one of considerable historical importance.

Waismann's definition of (conditional) probability in the terms of measures of ranges of propositions is in all essential features identical with Carnap's definition of the degree of confirmation, $c(h,e)$, conferred by some 'evidence' e on some 'hypothesis' h.[24] It seems therefore appropriate to call the generalized form of the Bolzano–Wittgenstein definition the Waismann–Carnap definition of probability.

5

In his paper Waismann introduces an idea of *the* probability of a proposition.[25] This he defines as the probability conferred on a proposition by the totality (conjunction) of all propositions which are known to be true, including, he says, the hypothetically assumed laws of nature.[26] This idea of *the* probability of a proposition does not occur in Wittgenstein. But the case where a probability is considered relative to the bulk of our knowledge plays a central role in the discussion both in the *Tractatus* and in the later writings.

Let us here ignore, as do Wittgenstein and Waismann, the relativity of knowledge to persons (knowing subjects) and times. What one person knows, another may not know; and what a person knows at a certain time he may be ignorant of at another time. We shall also disregard, for the time being, the provision that knowledge should include 'the hypothetically assumed laws of nature'.

Now consider a finite set of propositions $p_1, \ldots, p_n$ which are logically independent and none of which is a truth-function of any other propositions in the set. Assume that the

[24] Carnap, *Logical Foundations of Probability*, Chicago, 1950.
[25] 'Logische Analyse', p. 237.
[26] Ibid.

truth-value, that is, truth or falsehood, of each one of the propositions $p_1, \ldots, p_m$ is known but that the truth-value of none of the propositions $p_{m+1}, \ldots, p_n$ is known.

The conjunction of all propositions which are known to be true is then equivalent with a conjunction of some k of the m propositions $p_1, \ldots, p_m$ and the negations of the $m-k$ remaining ones. We shall call this conjunction the *bulk* of our knowledge (in the range of the propositions $p_1, \ldots, p_n$). We shall abbreviate it 'Q'.

Consider next one of the propositions with unknown truth-value, or some truth-function of these propositions. The probability of any such proposition or truth-function, given (relative to) the bulk of knowledge Q equals its probability *simpliciter*. That the bulk of knowledge increases means that the sub-set $p_1, \ldots, p_m$ grows by inclusion into it of members from the sub-set $p_{m+1}, \ldots, p_n$. But the fact remains that the probability relative to this growing bulk of knowledge of any single proposition or truth-function of propositions with unknown truth-value remains the probability *simpliciter* of this proposition or truth-function. Increase in the bulk of knowledge will, in other words, not affect the probability of any proposition with unknown truth-value. In particular, if there is only one proposition in the set $p_1, \ldots, p_n$ with unknown truth-value, the probability of this proposition relative to the bulk of knowledge is $1/2$, no matter how big or small the bulk is.

This version of the idea of a probability taken relative to the bulk of knowledge cannot therefore be of much interest. In order to make the notion interesting we must ensure that the probability can vary with variations in the bulk of knowledge. In order to achieve this, we must give up the assumption that the bulk of knowledge consists in knowing the truth-values of all individual members of a (sub-)set of logically independent propositions. We must admit the possibility that sometimes a *disjunction* of propositions is known to be true without the truth-values of the disjuncts being known.

That the truth-value of p is unknown is compatible with the possibility that we know the truth of some disjunction of which p is a member (disjunct). Let this disjunction be $p \vee q_1 \vee q_2$.

Knowing that this is true could, in fact, be all that we know. Relative to this bulk of knowledge Q, the probability of p is $4/7$. (The bulk of knowledge Q can now be expressed as a seven-termed disjunction of state-descriptions.) Now assume that our knowledge grows. We get to know, one way or another, that q_2 is false. Adding $\sim q_2$ to the previous Q and calculating afresh the probability of p we find that its value is $2/3$. This illustrates the way in which the probability of a proposition with unknown truth-value can change with a change in our knowledge.

6

We must now examine the notion of 'bulk of knowledge' which we have reached. Its crucial assumption is that disjunctions can be known to be true independently of knowledge of the truth of at least one of the disjuncts.

Can disjunctions be thus known? This is an interesting question in itself, but it is also one which, to the best of my knowledge, Wittgenstein nowhere explicitly discusses. An answer to it can nevertheless be said to be implicit in his writings on probability, both in the *Tractatus* and later. This answer I venture to formulate as follows.

Disjunctions cannot, strictly speaking, be known independently of their disjuncts. But they can be known in the relative sense of being consequences of what Wittgenstein calls 'the hypothetically assumed laws of nature'. This explains the prominent place accorded to this last notion in his discussions of probability.

Laws of nature, often and typically even if not always and necessarily, have the form of so-called universal implications. In the language of unanalysed propositional units p, q, etc., a law could have the form 'whenever p then also q'. In a richer language, using quantifiers and symbols for predicates and things, a law could be, say, that it is true for all x's that, if x is A, then x is also B. In symbols: $(x) (Ax \rightarrow Bx)$. The simpler example also contains a quantifier, namely the temporal quantifier 'whenever'.

As is well known to every student of the *Tractatus*,

quantification presented Wittgenstein with grave problems.[27] What he has to say about quantification is obscure – though, as so often with him, as the same time challenging. The difficulty for Wittgenstein in the *Tractatus* is connected with his thesis (5) that all propositions are truth-functions of elementary propositions. Quantified propositions would have to be truth-functions of an indefinite number of arguments. In the *Tractatus* Wittgenstein appears to accept this. Later he came to regard the *Tractatus* view of quantification as unsatisfactory.[28]

In the *Philosophical Remarks* and other writings from the same period Wittgenstein took a somewhat different view of quantification. According to this, laws of nature and other hypothetical experiential propositions containing quantifiers are not 'genuine' propositions at all, but rules or schemas (Wittgenstein uses the word *Gesetz*) for the construction or derivation of propositions.[29] Thus, for example, 'whenever p then q' does not express a proposition. But I can derive from the schema, for example, the proposition that, if p is now true, then q is also true. This last proposition, moreover, should be understood purely truth-functionally, as meaning the same as the disjunction which says that either p is now false or q is true.

The view that laws of nature are not real propositions, but schemas for the construction of propositions, was adopted by Schlick and Waismann and for some time played a role in the writings of the logical positivists and other philosophers influenced by Wittgenstein.[30] It was then gradually abandoned

[27] Cf. *Tractatus* 5.521, 5.522, 5.523, and Black's *Companion*, pp. 280–287.

[28] In one of the first conversations I ever had with Wittgenstein (in 1939), he said the biggest mistake he had made in the *Tractatus* was that he had identified general propositions with infinite conjunctions or disjunctions of singular propositions. Cf. also Moore, 'Wittgenstein's Lectures in 1930–33', *Philosophical Papers*, London, 1959, p. 297.

[29] Waismann, *Vienna Circle*, pp. 99 and 255. In *Philosophical Remarks*, p. 285 and *Philosophical Grammar*, p. 219 Wittgenstein says: 'Eine Hypothese ist ein Gesetz zur Bildung von Sätzen' (translated as 'An hypothesis is a law for forming propositions'). He contrasts *Hypothese* with *Satz* but he does not here say expressly that a *Hypothese* is *not* a *Satz*.

[30] M. Schlick, 'Die Kausalität in der gegenwärtigen Physik', *Naturwis-*

in favour of more liberal conceptions of the nature of propositions than the strictly truth-functional view. We need not dwell on the history of the subject here.

We can now give an account of the role of the 'hypothetically assumed laws of nature' for the computation of probabilities relative to the bulk of knowledge. If the bulk of knowledge is to be good for calculating probabilities, it must be expressible in the form of a proposition. Since laws of nature and other propositional schemas involving quantifiers are not propositions, *they* cannot appear (directly) in the bulk of knowledge. What appears there, however, are propositions constructed with the aid of these schemas. For example: If it is an assumed law of nature that whenever p is true, then q is also true, the bulk of knowledge would include, in addition to propositions with strictly *known* truth-value, the disjunction $\sim p \vee q$.

Is this 'quantifier-free' view of the bulk of knowledge at all plausible? The question is much too vast to be discussed in detail here. It is related to the question of whether and in what sense the bulk of knowledge, that is, one person's knowledge at a certain time, is *finite*.

In some sense this bulk is obviously not finite. Any proposition has necessarily an infinite number of logical consequences. For example, from p follows $\sim\sim p$, $\sim\sim\sim\sim p$, etc. If I know p, it is reasonable to think that I know all *these* consequences of p as well, even though it may not be reasonable to say that knowledge of a proposition entails knowledge of *all* its consequences.

This kind of 'infinity' of our knowledge, however, is not problematic here. The problem is, rather, whether there is a finite set S of logically independent (singular) propositions such that every proposition in the bulk of knowledge is a truth-function of the propositions in this set. If there is such a set S, the bulk of knowledge Q will be equivalent with a

senschaften **19**, 1931; F.P. Ramsey, 'General Propositions and Causality' (1929), in *The Foundations of Mathematics*, London, 1931; A.E. Blumberg, 'Demonstration and Inference in the Sciences and Philosophy', *The Monist* **42**, 1932.

conjunction of the propositions of this set and/or their negations *or* with a disjunction of such conjunctions (state-descriptions).

Suppose the world contained an infinity of individual things and that the propositions which may occur in the bulk of knowledge attribute properties to these things or relations to n-tuples of things. Perhaps one of the 'hypothetically assumed laws of nature' is that all things which are A are also B, say, all ravens black – to use a well-worn example. In some sense of 'know' which is, of course, rather different from knowledge of propositions it seems feasible to say that at any given moment only a finite number of individual things are known. And the same holds, *mutatis mutandis*, for (logically independent) properties and relations. If therefore I had to state, in a quantifier-free language, what I know about the things (I know), I could do this in a finite number of propositions. If I relied on the hypothetically assumed laws of nature for constructing further propositions and added them to the bulk, the number of propositions thus constructed would also be finite.

Such considerations as these support, I think, the reasonableness of the notion of 'the bulk of knowledge' which is needed for the computation of *the* probabilities of propositions using the Bolzano–Wittgenstein device. The question of reasonableness here, be it observed, is not affected by the peculiar view which Wittgenstein held in the early 1930s that laws of nature are not genuine propositions. For we could, in fact, add quantified propositions to the bulk of knowledge as here defined. This addition would have no effect on the probability values of unknown singular propositions. The effects of the quantified propositions on the probabilities would manifest themselves only through those quantifier-free propositions, already included in the bulk of knowledge, which are their logical consequences. Consider the following example:

Let the proposition (x) $(Ax \rightarrow Bx)$ be a 'hypothetically assumed law of nature' and add it to the bulk of knowledge Q. Assume that only three things x_1, x_2, and x_3 are known to us (to exist). The singular propositions $\sim Ax_1 \vee Bx_1$ and

$\sim Ax_2vBx_2$ and $\sim Ax_3vBx_3$ are then also in Q. The singular proposition p of unknown truth-value is about one or several of the three things and their properties and relations. (If it were about a fourth thing x_4, we should also have $\sim Ax_4vBx_4$ in Q.) It is easy to see that once we have 'drained' the quantified propositions of all their logical consequences for the not-quantified part of Q, the inclusion of these quantified propositions themselves in Q has no further effect on the calculated probabilities of singular propositions.

7

In 5.154 Wittgenstein makes a comment on probabilities and frequencies. Balls are drawn, with replacement, from an urn containing an equal number of white and black balls and balls of no other colour. The probability of drawing a white ball is estimated as 1/2. Wittgenstein says that 'all the circumstances known to me (including the natural laws hypothetically assumed) give to the occurrence of the one event no more probability than to the occurrence of the other'. The experiment shows that the proportion of white balls among all balls drawn tends to the value 1/2 as drawing continues. This, Wittgenstein says, is not a mathematical fact. What this fact shows is that the probability of drawing a white ball is independent of the circumstances which are unknown to us.

Note that Wittgenstein here speaks of the probability 1/2 as being relative to the bulk of our knowledge, including the assumed laws of nature. – We shall now examine in more detail what it is that the experiment tells us and what would follow, if it told us something different.

The experiment is associated with two possible outcomes (results) in the individual performances of it. We do not know whether the ball which is going to be drawn next will be white. But we know that it will be either white or black. This is knowledge of a disjunction. Without straining things, we can say that this knowledge is derived from an assumed law of nature, namely the hypothesis that the constitution of the content of the urn will not change during the experiment. (This, after all, is an induction.)

Now we make the experiment of drawing. Assume we find, *not* that the relative frequency of drawings of white balls approximates to 1/2, but that it tends, say, towards the value 1/3. If the calculated value of the probability of drawing a white ball was 1/2, should we then, according to 5.154, have to conclude that this probability is *not* independent of the unknown circumstances, that is, that it *is* dependent on some circumstances which were not taken into account, and included in the bulk of knowledge, when we calculated the probability?

The answer is that we are under no compulsion to conclude this. We have a choice between two alternatives here. One is to attribute the discrepancy between probability and frequency to *chance*. This possibility is open, however great the discrepancy.[31] Moreover, given the probability of the outcomes in the individual performances of the experiment, we can calculate the probability of any frequency distribution in *n* experiments. The smaller the probability of a frequency, the greater the 'effects' of chance should this frequency come true.

The other alternative open to us is to attribute the discrepancy to the operation of some *law(s)* which, when duly taken into account in the calculation of the probability on the basis of the bulk of knowledge, will lead to a new, 'corrected', value.[32] It is important to see that the factor to which Wittgenstein refers vaguely and perhaps somewhat incorrectly as 'unknown circumstances' must be an assumed law and cannot be a mere fact.

Let us go back to our example of the drawing of balls. Assume that the frequency of white balls among the drawings is near 1/3. If we add this item of information about the frequency to the bulk of our knowledge and calculate afresh the probability of drawing a white ball next time, the value of this probability will be exactly what it was before. If it was 1/2 when the proposition about the recorded frequency was not included in the bulk, it will be 1/2 after it is included. Anyone

---

[31] *Philosophical Remarks*, p. 292.

[32] Cf. ibid., p. 291, and Waismann, *Vienna Circle*, p. 95.

who doubts this is advised to perform the calculation himself in strict accordance with the Bolzano–Wittgenstein definition.

The calculated probability is insensitive to knowledge, as such, about past frequencies. The only way in which the probability can be affected by such knowledge is indirectly, *via* some general assumptions about laws of nature. The relation of these assumptions to the statistical observations (frequencies) can best be described by saying that the former are 'inspired' by the latter.

What sort of generalizations do statistical observations inspire then? The best answer is perhaps that they inspire hypotheses about probability values. We shall, however, put this answer aside for the time being. We consider first the following argument.

The number of experiments (drawings from the urn) which will actually ever be made in the future is finite. Let this number be n. Consider the disjunction of the 2^n possible ways in which the two outcomes, 'white' and 'black', can alternate in a sequence of n experiments. If we added this disjunction, which is a tautology, to the bulk of knowledge at any time, it would not affect the calculated probability that the next experiment or the m:th experiment ($m \leqslant n$) to be made will yield a white ball. But suppose that, for some reason or other, for example because of recorded frequencies in past experiments, we come to think that it is not in fact possible for all the members of this disjunction to materialize. Only a certain number of them can come true, namely those in which the proportion of white balls is near $1/3$. (*How near* need not be made a problem here.) If we then add the 'mutilated' disjunction, which is not a tautology but the consequence of some unknown law of nature, to the bulk of knowledge and calculate the probability that the m:th experiment will yield a white ball, we shall find that this probability is near $1/3$. – It is in this way, I suggest, that we shall understand the logical mechanism according to which recorded frequencies, *via* the assumption of laws, recoil on probabilities which are computed relative to the bulk of our knowledge by means of the Bolzano–Wittgenstein device.[33]

[33] Cf. *Philosophical Remarks*, p. 291.

The following simplified example will be given to illustrate the above argument. Suppose we were going to make only three more experiments. We call them 'x', 'y', and 'z'. Let 'B' denote blackness and 'W' whiteness (as the outcomes of experiments). The disjunction of all the 2^3 or 8 possible ways in which the two outcomes can result from the three experiments is $Wx.Wy.Wz$ v $Wx.Wy.Bz$ v $Wx.By.Wz$ v $Wx.By.Bz$ v $Bx.Wy.Wz$ v $Bx.Wy.Bz$ v $Bx.By.Wz$ v $Bx. By. Bz$. Assume however that, on the basis of past experience or for some other reason, we think that the laws of nature allow only the fourth, the sixth, and the seventh disjunction to come true. In other words, the disjunction $Wx.By.Bz$ v $Bx.Wy.Bz$. v $Bx.By.Wz$ follows from the assumed laws of nature. We add this to the bulk of knowledge Q. Assume finally that Q contains no further item of knowledge about x, y, or z. If we then calculate the probability of Wx (or of Wy or of Wz) relative to Q using the Bolzano–Wittgenstein method, we get the value $1/3$.

It is a function of probabilities, one could say, to demarcate a border between *chance* and *law*.[34] Fixing the border is 'conventional' in the sense that we are always free to choose whether a discrepancy between a calculated probability and a recorded frequency shall be regarded as a chance event or as being due to the operation of unknown laws. But I think it is right to say that we tend to draw this border so as to narrow down the margin of chance and broaden the scope of law as much as is feasible.[35] This is another way of saying that we want close agreement between probabilities and frequencies.[36] But the criteria of 'feasibility' and of 'closeness' of agreement are vague. We are not prepared to correct the probabilities

---

[34] Wittgenstein nowhere uses this expression, but I think it is a correct rendering of his thought (cf. *Philosophical Grammar*, pp. 229–230). Waismann, 'Logische Analyse', p. 247, says: 'Die Angabe des Masses der Wahrscheinlichkeit ist also die Festsetzung, wann wir von Zufall sprechen wollen und wann nicht.'

[35] Cf. Waismann, 'Logische Analyse', p. 244.

[36] Waismann, *Vienna Circle*, p. 95: 'Wir beruhigen uns erst, wenn die relative Häufigkeit übereinstimmt mit der Wahrscheinlichkeit a priori.' ('Our minds are at rest only when the relative frequency coincides with the *a priori* probability.')

whenever there is a disagreement with statistical experience – chance too must be given a chance to operate – and reasons of elegance and mathematical economy guide the way in which observed frequencies influence our choice of new probability hypotheses.

The idea that probabilities fix the border between law and chance works admirably for reconciling the a priori claims of the definition of probability with the a posteriori claims of statistical experience. But having said this in praise of Wittgenstein's idea we must add something which seems to have escaped his notice. It is that the idea makes the Bolzano–Wittgenstein definition superfluous as a method for computing probability values because the essence of the reconciling proposal is that the truth-grounds of the propositions involved should be adjusted so as to yield the desired (degree of) agreement between probabilities and frequencies. The licensed appeal to 'unknown circumstances', that is, to the operations of unknown laws, for the purpose of this adjustment knocks the bottom out of the original definition. Or, to use a simile much beloved of Wittgenstein himself, the definition becomes an *idle* part of the machinery of applying the calculus to experience. It does not perform the function or role for which it was originally designed, namely the role of feeding the calculus with actual values of probabilities. There is no need for this mediating role of a definition of probability. Statistical experiences 'inspire' *directly* hypothetical assignments of probabilities (cf. above).

8

We set out from a certain definition of probability and have ended up with a conception of the notion which makes this definition otiose. In reaching this end we have followed the route between what I propose to call two poles in Wittgenstein's thinking about probability. The one pole is the logical theory of probability, contained *in nuce* in the Bolzano–Wittgenstein definition. The other pole is the conception of probability values as hypothetical demarcations of the border between chance and law. Both poles were inherent in Wittgenstein's thinking from the beginning. Wittgenstein probably never saw them as separate poles. In the *Tractatus* one can say there is an equal emphasis on both of them. But later there is a shift of emphasis, and the writings from 'the period of transition' centre almost exclusively on the second pole. They contain no reference to or discussion of the definition of probability given in the *Tractatus*.

One can, with due caution, call the two poles a logical and an epistemological pole respectively. The logical theory of probability is based on the concept of the range of a proposition and may be called a theory of the relative magnitudes of ranges. The epistemological view of probability again is linked to the notions of imperfect knowledge[37] and of an incomplete description.[38] The bridge between the two poles is the idea of a probability which is considered relative to the bulk of our knowledge or which satisfies what Carnap[39] calls the Requirement of Total Evidence. In order to make this idea work for its set purpose – which, I suggest, was to give an account of the relation between probabilities and frequencies – Wittgenstein had to include in the bulk what he called 'the hypothetically assumed laws of nature'. Through the inclusion of hypotheses in the bulk of knowledge the calculated probabilities too take on a hypothetical character.[40]

[37] *Tractatus* 5.156a(3): 'Nur in Ermanglung der Gewißheit gebrauchen wir die Wahrscheinlichkeit.' ('We use probability only in default of certainty'.)

[38] Waismann, *Vienna Circle*, p. 94: 'Die Wahrscheinlichkeit wird dann gebraucht, wenn unsere Beschreibung der Sachverhalte unvollständig ist. Die Wahrscheinlichkeit hängt mit dem Wesen einer unvollständigen Beschreibung zusammen.' ('Probability is needed when our description of states of affairs is incomplete. Probability is connected with the nature of incomplete description.') Cf. *Tractatus* 5.156d.

[39] *Logical Foundations of Probability*, p. 212.

[40] *Philosophical Remarks*, pp. 290–291: 'Die Gesetze der Wahrscheinlichkeit, d.h. die, die der Rechnung zu *Grunde* liegen, sind hypothetische Annahmen, die dann von der Rechnung ausgeschrotet und in anderer Form von der Erfahrung bestätigt – oder widerlegt – werden.' ('The laws of probability, i.e. those on which the calculation is *based*, are hypothetical assumptions, which are then rehashed by the calculation and then in another form empirically confirmed – or refuted.')

In Wittgenstein's view, moreover, agreement with observed frequencies is the test of independence of the calculated probabilities of the operations of laws of nature other than those hypothetically included in the bulk of knowledge. When we adjust probability values in the light of statistical experience, we adjust the border between chance and law. Speaking in terms of truth-grounds (ranges), the adjustment means that we narrow or widen the sets of truth-grounds (the ranges) of the propositions involved so as to achieve the desired agreement between calculated probability and observed frequency. But it is then no longer the measures of the sets of truth-grounds which *determine* the probabilities. The roles have become reversed from what they were originally. It is the hypothetically assumed probabilities which now determine (hypothetically) the measures of the ranges. This reversal of roles, one can say, is taken note of in Waismann's definition which is, as it stands, *useless* for the purpose of computing probabilities, since it does not specify the measure-function μ. Of the specification of μ Waismann says,[41] consonantly with Wittgenstein's view at the time, that μ should be so chosen as to yield agreement with statistical experience.

The very idea of agreement or disagreement between probabilities and frequencies seems to presuppose that the 'things' to which we attribute probability are *generic*. By this I mean that they can come true or fail to come true on occasions for their truth or falsehood, and that such occasions can occur repeatedly. When we speak of events as occurring and recurring, or of the results (outcomes) in repeated performances of an experiment, we think of the event and of the results (outcomes) as something generic. The view of propositions, too, as generic, that is, as having a variable truth-value, is neither uncommon nor unnatural. But it is hardly the *Tractatus* view of propositions.

Both Wittgenstein and Waismann, when defining probability, speak about propositions (*Sätze*). But when discussing the notion they easily shift to talking about events (*Ereignisse*). Waismann, moreover, says expressly that all uses of the

[41] 'Logische Analyse', p. 242.

probability calculus presuppose that events are repeatable, and that it is on the basis of sequences of such events that relative frequencies are counted and formed.[42] Wittgenstein is less explicit on the question of genericity. In *Tractatus* 5.156 he says that probability is a generalization and that it involves a general description of a propositional form. I do not know exactly how these pronouncements should be interpreted. If we relate them to what is said in 3.315 about variable propositions, one can perhaps read into them the idea that the terms of the probability relation '*p* given *q*' are generic and not individuated, true or false, propositions. This reading could easily be made compatible with everything Wittgenstein has to say about truth-grounds and ranges and their relation to probability (cf. section 3 above).

In the later writings, but not in the *Tractatus*, Wittgenstein makes a distinction between *two* kinds of probability – and Waismann echoes him here. One is the probability of a hypothesis[43] or, as he also says, an induction.[44] The other is the probability of an event.[45]

Of the probability of a hypothesis Wittgenstein says that it is not measurable,[46] or not numerically[47] measurable, or at least not measurable in the same sense in which the probabilities of the calculus are measurable.[48] It seems to follow by implication that the definition and theory of probability which Wittgenstein developed in the *Tractatus* are concerned with the second kind of probability only, the probability of events. This is surely Waismann's view in his paper.[49]

Of the probability of a hypothesis Wittgenstein further says that it has its 'measure' (*Mass*) in the amount of evidence that is needed in order to make it advantageous (*vorteilhaft*) to

[42] 'Logische Analyse,' p. 241.
[43] *Philosophical Remarks*, p. 286; *Philosophical Grammar*, p. 224.
[44] Waismann, *Vienna Circle*, p. 98.
[45] Ibid. This is the only place where Wittgenstein says explicitly that probability of the second kind is of *events*.
[46] *Philosophical Remarks*, p. 289; *Philosophical Grammar*, p. 225.
[47] Waismann, *Vienna Circle*, p. 99.
[48] Ibid., p. 99.
[49] 'Logische Analyse', p. 228.

abandon the hypothesis.[50] The more inductive support a hypothesis has received from past experience, the higher the price of giving it up.[51] In this sense continued confirmation can be said to *increase* the probability of the hypothesis.[52] Wittgenstein also related the probability of hypotheses to considerations about simplicity[53] and convenience (economy of thought).[54]

Are the two senses of probability related or are they totally distinct? Waismann says the latter and adds that it would be good to use two words for the two concepts.[55] Wittgenstein takes a more guarded attitude. The two concepts, though not identical, are related.[56] On the nature of their relationship, however, he says nothing.

[50] *Philosophical Remarks*, p. 286.

[51] Ibid., p. 284; *Philosophical Grammar*, p. 225.

[52] *Philosophical Remarks*, p. 286.

[53] Ibid., p. 284; *Philosophical Grammar*, p. 224; Waismann, *Vienna Circle*, p. 255.

[54] *Philosophical Remarks*, pp. 284 ff., 288; *Philosophical Grammar*, p. 225.

[55] 'Logische Analyse', p. 228.

[56] *Philosophical Remarks*, p. 286; *Philosophical Grammar*, p. 224.

WITTGENSTEIN ON
CERTAINTY

This essay was read at the *Entretiens* in Helsinki, August 1970, of the International Institute of Philosophy and published together with a Reply by Brian McGuinness in the Proceedings of the conference, *Problems in the Theory of Knowledge*, edited by G.H. von Wright (Martinus Nijhoff, The Hague, 1972). It has undergone some revision for the present volume.

I

DURING the last year and a half of his life Wittgenstein wrote almost exclusively about knowledge and certainty, commenting on some of G. E. Moore's views. [1] These writings possess a thematic unity which makes them almost unique in Wittgenstein's whole literary output. One can speculate about the reasons for this. Does it signify a change in Wittgenstein's philosophical style? Or does it only show that the author was losing his power of keeping a thousand threads of thought in his hand at once? There is no indication, however, that the quality of the thoughts was declining. Considering that the remarks constitute a first, unrevised manuscript they seem to me remarkably accomplished both in form and content.

Wittgenstein's treatise on certainty can be said to summarize some of the essential novelties of his thinking. But it does this in a way which is rather different from any which, to the best of my knowledge, Wittgenstein's numerous commentators have tried. The book opens new vistas on his philosophical achievement.

I shall here try to give a brief presentation of its main ideas. I shall not make any attempt to evaluate it critically – nor try to indicate the extent to which I can agree myself with what Wittgenstein has to say. But I shall at the end sketch a few of its implications, as I see them, for further research.

2

A main problem of epistemology since Descartes has been whether any single contingent proposition can be known for

[1] These writings were published, with the German text alongside the English translation, as *Über Gewissheit – On Certainty*, Basil Blackwell, Oxford, 1969, edited by G.E.M. Anscombe and G.H. von Wright; see the Editors' Preface. See also the brief but excellent account of conversations with Wittgenstein in the summer of 1949 in Norman Malcolm, *Ludwig Wittgenstein, A Memoir*, Oxford University Press, London, 1958, pp. 87–92.

certain to be true. Moore claimed that *he knew* a great number of such propositions. He gave as examples, among others, that he was a human being, that the object he was now pointing to was his hand, or that the earth has existed for many years past. Since he knew such things, he could also prove that there existed a world external to his mind – and thereby settle, so he thought, a problem long under dispute. Moore further claimed that such items as those just mentioned were by no means known exclusively by him, but that they were specimens of what most human beings under normal circumstances can rightly claim to know.

Moore thought, moreover, that our knowledge of most of these 'common sense' propositions, as he called them, is founded on some *evidence* for their truth.[2] But what this evidence is we often cannot tell. We are all, Moore said, 'in this strange position that we do *know* many things, with regard to which we *know* further that we must have had evidence for them, and yet we do not know *how* we know them, that is, we do not know what the evidence was.'[3]

In order to appreciate both Moore's position and Wittgenstein's criticism of it, it is important to keep the distinction clear between the 'common sense' propositions which Moore claimed he knew and the philosophical propositions which he thought provable[4] on the basis of them. Moore thought of the members of both classes of propositions as being *contingent* truths.[5] This opinion may seem very natural as far as the

[2] 'A Defence of Common Sense', p. 44. References are to G.E. Moore, *Philosophical Papers*, Allen & Unwin, London, 1959.

[3] Ibid.

[4] The idea of a proof does not appear until the paper 'Proof of an External World'. But it is implicit already in 'A Defence of Common Sense'. The known 'common sense' propositions *imply*, Moore says there (p. 38), the reality of material things, etc.

[5] Neither in 'A Defence of Common Sense' nor in 'Proof of an External World' does Moore use the term 'contingent (proposition)'. In the first paper he says (p. 42) that 'it seems to me quite clear that it *might* have been the case that Time was not real, material things not real, Space not real, selves not real'. In his later paper called 'Certainty', however, Moore employs the term 'contingent proposition' for 'proposition which is not self-contradictory and of which the contradictory is not self-contradictory'

various propositions of the first category are concerned. With regard to the propositions of the second category this view seems much less natural or even quite dubious. Yet Moore was of the opinion that it is a contingent truth that there is an external world, that time is real, or that there exist selves. To deny these things is not to maintain anything which is logically impossible, that is, self-contradictory.

Suppose somebody wanted to dispute some of the things Moore claimed to know for certain, for example, that he, Moore, was a human being or was pointing to his right hand. This critic would then have to adduce some evidence showing that Moore was mistaken. Moore again would have to accept this evidence, if he was going to give up his claim to knowledge. But what could this evidence be, other than some contingent propositions which contradicted the first ones and which Moore, 'on second thought,' would have to admit as true? And then it would still be the case that there existed a great many 'common sense' propositions which he would claim to know for certain – and which could be used to prove the sort of philosophical propositions which Moore was anxious to defend, for example, that time is real or that there exists an external world.

Moore's philosophical position would therefore not be touched by justified doubts about this or that proposition of the first group. For the justification of the doubts would entail accepting that very position. In order to prove the philosophical propositions on the basis of 'common sense' propositions all that is required is that at any time *some* such 'common sense' propositions should be accepted as certain. Moore did not say this. He, on the contrary, was anxious to claim that he

---

(p. 230). He also says that 'from the fact that a given proposition might have been true it always follows that the proposition in question is not self-contradictory' (ibid.). From this we can conclude that, according to Moore, a proposition affirming or denying the reality of time or of material things is contingent. But Moore also says that propositions which he thinks he knows for certain, such as that he is now standing up, are contingent (ibid.). It is therefore safe to attribute to Moore the view that propositions of both the classes which we have here distinguished are contingent.

knew for certain a number of specific things (propositions), of which he had enumerated a great many in his classic paper. But when in his paper called 'Certainty' which was not published until after his death Moore was fighting the sceptic's argument from dreaming, then – so it seems to me – he unsuccessfully tried to articulate thoughts which point to a more 'relaxed' relationship between the two groups of proposition. How this is to be done in order to be successful can, I think, be seen more clearly on the basis of Wittgenstein's comments on Moore's views.

3

So much then for certain things which Moore had said. Wittgenstein thought Moore's rebuttal of scepticism most interesting and original. But he would not have been the philosopher he was, had he declared himself in agreement with Moore. On the contrary, he was anxious to refute Moore's *explicit* philosophical position at practically every point. Moore's claim that he knew this or that was philosophically worthless, Wittgenstein thought; most of the 'common sense' things Moore said he knew are things which nobody can, in fact, be correctly said to *know*. Moore, moreover, was mistaken in thinking that there was *evidence* for the truth of the propositions in question; mistaken also in thinking that they could be used for *proving* such things as the existence of the external world; and mistaken finally in holding the allegedly proved theses to be *contingent* truths. But, while disagreeing with what Moore had said, Wittgenstein was at the same time in sympathy with the tendency implicit in Moore's efforts. I think we can say that what Wittgenstein did was to give to this tendency a clearer and truer expression.

Let us look briefly at some of the reasons Wittgenstein gave for disagreeing with Moore.

An assurance, however sincere, that one knows something cannot by itself establish that this is so (§§13, 14). Moore, therefore, cannot attack the sceptics 'by assuring them that *he* knows this and that. For one need not believe him. If his opponents had asserted that one could not *believe* this and that, then he could have replied: "I believe it"' (§520). Wittgenstein is here pointing to an important conceptual difference between belief and knowledge. In order to establish that I believe that p, I need not give grounds for thinking p true. But in order to vindicate a claim to knowledge, grounds must normally be provided, that is, we must be able to tell, *how* we know this. And it must be open to others to accept or to remain unconvinced by our grounds.' "I know" often means: I have the proper grounds for my statement. So if the other person is acquainted with the language-game, he would admit that I know. The other, if he is acquainted with the language-game, must be able to imagine *how* one may know something of the kind' (§18). Wittgenstein says that the situation is *often* of this kind when a claim to knowledge is being raised. Perhaps one could even say that it is always or typically of this kind, when it is open to argument whether a person knows something or not, that is, when the situation is as envisaged in §§13 and 14. And this is the situation which Wittgenstein opposes to the Moorean one. One could call the one 'genuine' and the other 'spurious' and say that in a genuine knowledge situation there must be grounds for knowing – and that where grounds are lacking the situation is 'spurious'.

An answer to the question 'How do you know?' could be, for example, 'I saw it myself', 'I calculated it', or 'He told me so'. These are grounds on which one *can* know things and therefore types of 'proper grounds' for my statement that I know. A person who is given these grounds in support of a knowledge-claim will, 'if he is acquainted with the language-game', realize that they are grounds of the proper *type* – but it does not follow from this that he will accept them. He may voice doubts in the form of a rejoinder 'Did you watch it carefully?' or 'Let's check your calculation' (cf. §50), or 'Is he a trustworthy person?'

To answer the question 'How do you know?' is not the same thing as to produce evidence for the truth of the known proposition. But when we remove doubts about the answer, we produce such evidence. If I watched something carefully, I should be able to tell that I saw this and this and . . ., which, if

true, should establish that it is also true what I claim to know –
say that a man was stabbed in the street. To check a calculation
is to check the truth of a number of statements which jointly
entail that the result was what I claimed it to be. To show that a
person is trustworthy, finally, is to point to a number of
statements which are accepted as true and which speak in
favour of the truth of what we said we knew on the basis of
what he had told us.

The evidence which we produce for the truth of a proposition which we claim to know consists of propositions which
we accept as true. If the question is raised, how we know these
latter propositions, further grounds may be offered to show
how we know them and further evidence given for the truth of
the propositions thus claimed to be known. But the chain of
grounds (evidence) has an end, a point beyond which no
further grounds can be given. This is a thing which Wittgenstein often stressed.[6] The reason, why Moore was mistaken in
thinking that his knowledge of the 'common sense' truths was
founded on evidence, Wittgenstein would have said, was that
they were themselves such 'end-points' in chains of grounds.
They might serve as evidence for other propositions which
somebody claimed to know. But nothing would count as
evidence for them.

Consider for example the proposition that I have two
hands. It would sometimes be said, I think, that it is based on
the evidence of my senses.[7] But this is not, as a general
statement, correct. Sometimes, however, it is correct. I have
undergone an operation and been unconscious. I wake up and
am not quite clear what has happened to me. Was it that one of
my hands was amputated? I look and see them both. Then my
knowledge that I *still* have two hands can be said to rest on 'the
evidence of my senses'. But I did not learn that I have two
hands by looking at them and counting. If under quite normal
circumstances I happened to look at my hands – holding them
up before my eyes – and, to my amazement, saw only one,
then I should doubt *my senses* and not that I have two hands.

[6] *Philosophical Investigations*, Part I, §§326, 485. Cf. also *On Certainty*,
§471.
[7] Cf. Moore, 'Certainty', p. 243.

And this shows that the implicit trust which under normal circumstances I have that I have two hands is *not* founded on 'the evidence of my senses.' (Cf. §125.)

Let it be granted that the proposition 'I have two hands' entails the proposition 'there are material objects'. *One* way of showing that the second is *not* contingent would then be to show that the first is necessary. (For a necessary proposition can entail only other necessary propositions.) But is it not obvious that the first is contingent? For all I know I could have only one hand, or none. Perhaps I can imagine myself having more than two. And yet the truth, as known to me, of the proposition that I have two hands, is peculiar. It is not like the many truths which I have learnt from reading or by being instructed or because I have made investigations. Surely the propositions which Moore claimed are indubitable have 'a peculiar logical role in the system of our empirical propositions' (§136). It is this *peculiar* role, not the question whether we really can be said to 'know' these propositions, which Wittgenstein investigates in his book.

4

The core of Wittgenstein's thoughts on these matters could perhaps be paraphrased as follows. In every situation where a claim to knowledge is being established, or a doubt settled, or an item of linguistic communication (information, order, question) understood, a bulk of propositions already stand fast, are taken for granted. They form a kind of 'system'. If this were not so, knowledge and doubt, judging and understanding, error and truth would not 'exist', that is, we should not have and handle those concepts in the way we do. 'All testing, all confirmation and disconfirmation of a hypothesis takes place already within a system. And this system is not a more or less arbitrary and doubtful point of departure for all our arguments: no, it belongs to the essence of what we call an argument. The system is not so much the point of departure, as the element in which arguments have their life' (§105).

The concept of knowledge does not itself apply to that

which is presupposed in its use, that is, to the propositions which 'stand fast' in any given knowledge situation. This is one reason, why Moore's use of 'I know' was out of place. But perhaps one could call the 'common sense' things to which Moore was referring a pre-knowledge (*Vor-Wissen*). (Wittgenstein himself does not use this term.) It is better, however, to speak of *certainty* here (§511), with the addition perhaps that it is a certainty in our *practice* of judging rather than in our *intellection* of the content of our judgements. (See section 8 below).

Thus, for example, the truth of the proposition that the earth has existed for many years past can be said to be presupposed in all so-called historical knowledge. But it is not itself an item of historical knowledge, that is, it is not anything which one has come to know on the basis of investigations about the past. Through geophysical investigations we may come to know that the earth has existed, say, for at least 300 billion years – or that it could not have existed for more than 500 billion years. These are possible items of genuine (scientific) knowledge. But in all the grounds which we could give for, or against, these scientific propositions it would be presupposed – though not in the form of a geophysical hypothesis – that the earth has existed for many, that is, '*for a good many*,' years past. (Cf. §138.)

The problem of the existence of the external world, one could say, *is* in fact solved before it *can be* raised. – In order to raise the question we must know what ('sort of thing') an external world is – or else we do not know what our question is about. But in order to acquire the notion of an external world we must first acknowledge a huge number of facts, all of which 'entail' (in that Moorean sense) the existence of material objects, that is, of a world external to my mind. I can inquire whether this or that object is in the external world, or is perhaps only an illusion. But whether the result in the individual case is positive or negative, the grounds for the decision will be some facts which stand fast and which entail the existence of an external world. This also explains why there is no procedure for investigating whether or not the external world itself exists. Its existence is, so to speak, '*the logical receptacle*' within which all investigations concerning the mind-dependent existence of various objects are conducted. – 'Material object' is a logical – in the *Tractatus* Wittgenstein would have said formal – concept (§36).

5

The propositions belonging to the system of our pre-knowledge cannot be enumerated and 'laid down' once and for all. Many of the items can – temporarily or permanently – be removed and treated as propositions which are supported, or contradicted, by the propositions of the bulk. 'What I hold fast to is not *one* proposition but a nest of propositions,' Wittgenstein says (§225). (Cf. also §§140–142.)

Imagine the following case. I am the victim of an accident and one of my hands is torn off. Someone comes along and finds it lying in the street. 'Whose hand is that?' he cries horrified. 'It is mine,' I say. Then I presumably know this and have evidence for it. But when set in such circumstances, my knowledge that this is my hand seems quite irrelevant to the philosophical purposes which Moore was pursuing when he said he knew certain things. Here I could initially also have doubted what then I knew. Perhaps a hand was torn from someone else too in the disaster. When I establish that this is *my* hand and settle my doubts, if I have any, *then* part of my evidence are things 'I know for certain' in that other and 'deeper' sense which Moore had been thinking of.

Moore's 'common sense' propositions, one could say, have the form of experiential propositions but perform the function of logical propositions or rules (cf. §§56, 82, 308). Their truth 'is fused into the foundations of our language-game' (§558) – like the truth of mathematical propositions.[8] But the fact that we can, at least for a good many of them, imagine circumstances which turn their use into a *move* (as distinct from a *rule*) of one of our language-games (§622) shows that there is no hard and fast distinction between 'analytic' and 'synthetic,'

[8] Cf. Malcolm, *Memoir*, p. 88.

between logical necessity and contingent truth or falsehood. (Cf. §§308, 319, 401.)

Moore's famous gesture, when he wanted to prove the existence of an external world, was no 'proof' of a contingent conclusion from contingent premisses. It was rather an attempt to say (show) that with our *notion* of an external world we take many *truths* (*facts*) for granted (cf. §§83, 617). We *cannot* question these truths, since they go with the possession of the notion. Therefore it is not a contingent proposition that *there is an external world* – as it is contingent that there are, or are not, lions or unicorns. But it is a contingent fact about us, a fact of 'the natural history of man', that *we have the notion* of an external world.

I should like to call attention here to two features which can be said to pervade the whole of Wittgenstein's philosophy. The one could be called, using pre-*Tractatus* terminology, the idea of Bi-polarity.[9] In the *Tractatus* this idea is reflected above all in the alliance between a proposition's having a *meaning* and it's being contingent(ly true or false). Necessary propositions are 'senseless' (but not 'nonsensical')[10] and therefore not strictly speaking true. They are, to use an expression which Wittgenstein employed later in his writings on the foundations of mathematics, senseless expressions 'on the side of truth.'[11] Epistemic attitudes such as knowing and believing apply in the first instance to contingent matters. That which cannot conceivably be doubted, cannot be known or certain either – except under some 'eccentric' use of the words.[12] In his writings from the years when he was working on the *Investigations*, Wittgenstein sometimes expressed himself with a certain dogmatic flavour on questions relating to this topic. It may look as though he wanted to deny, for example, that a man can know that he is in pain or is seeing a red flash – the very things which so many other philosophers have regarded

[9] See 'Notes on Logic' (September 1913), printed as an Appendix to Ludwig Wittgenstein, *Notebooks 1914–1916*, Basil Blackwell, Oxford, 1961.

[10] Cf. *Tractatus Logico-Philosophicus*, 4.461 and 4.4611.

[11] *Remarks on the Foundations of Mathematics*, Basil Blackwell, Oxford, 3rd edition, 1978, Pt. III, §33.

[12] Cf. *Philosophical Investigations*, Part I, §246.

as the prototype of what *can be known*, if anything can be. But Wittgenstein did not wish to deny this – if by 'deny' one here means that he was casting doubts on things which are regarded as certain by others. He only wanted to draw attention to 'the peculiar logical role' of indubitable propositions in connection with our epistemic attitudes. In *On Certainty* Wittgenstein can be said to extend to the whole field of epistemology things which he had before mainly been discussing in connection with, at the one extreme, our immediate experience and, at the other extreme, the necessary truths of logic and mathematics. This extension should help us to see more clearly also the connection and relatedness of the two extremes.

The idea of bi-polarity is related to another *Leitmotiv* which runs through all Wittgenstein's work. This is his preoccupation with the question of the *limits of the world* (and of what can be said and what can be thought). In the preface to the *Tractatus* he said: 'The book will, therefore, draw a limit to thinking, or rather – not to thinking but to the expression of thoughts; for in order to draw a limit to thinking we should have to be able to think both sides of this limit (we should therefore have to be able to think what cannot be thought).' Very much the same thing he could have said in a preface, had he ever written one, to his last writings, those published under the title *On Certainty*. Beyond everything we know or conjecture or think of as true there is a foundation of accepted truth without which there would be no such thing as knowing or conjecturing or thinking things true. But to think of the things, whereof this foundation is made, as known to us or as true is to place them among the things which stand on this very foundation, is to view the receptacle as another object *within*. This clearly cannot be done. If the foundation is what we have to accept before we say of anything that it is known or true, then it cannot itself be known or true. Moore's common sense propositions can indeed be regarded as proof that certain things can be known, namely all those things which commonly are said to be known on the basis of grounds which we do not question. What Moore called 'common sense' – using this phrase in a rather queer sense[13] – is very much the same thing

[13] What Moore was referring to with the phrase 'common sense' is

as that which Wittgenstein in the *Tractatus* would have referred to as 'the limits of the world'. Wittgenstein's high appreciation of Moore's article must partly have stemmed from the fact that he recognized in Moore's efforts a strong similarity with his own. And his criticism of Moore in *On Certainty* we could, in the language of the *Tractatus*, characterize as a criticism of an attempt to say the unsayable.

6

The bulk of propositions belonging to our pre-knowledge can also be said to constitute a world-picture, *Weltbild*. This latter expression is used frequently by Wittgenstein himself. It does not mean a view of the world in the esoteric sense of a philosopher's *Weltanschauung*. It is not a private possession, but bound up with the notion of a 'culture' and with the fact 'that we belong to a community which is bound together by science and education' (§298). One could also say that it is the common ground which we must share with other people in order to *understand* their actions and words and in order to come to an understanding with them in our judgements. It is, in fact, Moore's 'common sense', *Tractatus*' world-boundary. I know no better way to describe its nature and role than to quote Wittgenstein's own words:

> 94. But I did not get my picture of the world by satisfying myself of its correctness; nor do I have it because I am satisfied of its correctness. No: it is the inherited background against which I distinguish between true and false.
> 95. The propositions describing the world-picture might be part of a kind of mythology. And their role is like that of rules of a game; and the game can be learned purely practically, without learning any explicit rules.
> 96. It might be imagined that some propositions, of the form

---

certainly not what is commonly and naturally called this. The oddity of Moore's usage is exposed and commented on in Norman Malcolm, 'George Edward Moore', in Malcolm, *Knowledge and Certainty*, Prentice-Hall, Englewood Cliffs, N.J., 1963.

of empirical propositions, were hardened and functioned as channels for such empirical propositions as were not hardened but fluid; and that this relation altered with time, in that fluid propositions hardened, and hard ones became fluid.

97. The mythology may change back to a state of flux, the river-bed of thoughts may shift. But I distinguish between the movements of the waters of the river-bed and the shift of the bed itself; though there is not a sharp division of the one from the other.

98. But if someone were to say 'So logic too is an empirical science' he would be wrong. Yet this is right: the same proposition may get treated at one time as something to test by experience, at another as a rule of testing.

99. And the bank of the river consists partly of hard rock, subject to no alteration or only to an imperceptible one, partly of sand, which now in one place now in another gets washed away, or deposited.

7

The system of propositions which constitute a world-picture not only has no fixed boundaries. It also has a very in-homogenous composition. It is an agglomeration of a huge number of sub-systems, each with a fluctuating boundary and a 'mixed' content. These sub-systems are related to what Wittgenstein calls language-games. One could say that every language-game has a foundation which is a fragment of the players' pre-knowledge. (Cf. §§560, 519.)

There is no *rigid* order among the language-games, neither logically nor from the point of view of genetic development. But there certainly is *some* order among them in both these respects. The games are of different age in the development of the individual as well as in the history of the language community ('culture'). Some could not have been learned, until others were already mastered. Among the relatively late ones are the language-games with words like 'know', be-lieve', or 'be certain'. (Cf. §538.) For this reason alone, the fragments of a world-picture which underlie the language-games from the beginning represent only a 'pre-knowledge'.

If this is subsequently honoured by the name 'knowledge', as Moore and some other philosophers have wanted to do, its conceptual character still is very different from those items to which we apply this name in the ordinary language-games with the epistemic words. Wittgenstein's 'builders' cannot *say they know* these are building-stones (slabs, columns, etc.); yet this is nevertheless what they can *be said to know* in knowing how to play the game (§396). Wittgenstein asks: 'Does a child believe that milk exists? Or does it know that milk exists? Does a cat know that a mouse exists?' (§478) and 'Are we to say that the knowledge that there are physical objects comes very early or very late?' (§479). Each of these questions could be answered both Yes and No – depending upon how we understand them.

8

Considering the way language is taught and learned, the fragments of a world-picture underlying the uses of language are not originally and strictly *propositions* at all. The pre-knowledge is not propositional knowledge. But if this foundation is not propositional, what then *is* it? It is, one could say, a *praxis*. 'Giving grounds, however, justifying evidence, comes to an end; – but the end is not certain propositions striking us immediately as true, i.e. it is not a kind of *seeing* on our part; it is our *acting*, which lies at the bottom of the language-game' (§204, cf. also §§110 and 229). And Wittgenstein quotes *Faust*: 'Im Anfang war die Tat' (§402).

How does it show, for example, that I do not doubt that I have a body, that this is something I, in Moore's sense, know for certain? Not in that I say *this* or reflect upon it. But in innumerable things I say, and do, and refrain from doing. Such as complaining of headache or of pain in my leg, avoiding collision with other bodies, not putting my hand in the fire or throwing myself out of the window as if nothing was going to hurt me. It is within this framework of certainties in my behaviour that I learn the names of the parts of my body and of various bodily sensations and also the word 'body'.

Within it I acquire the notions which the various words in the language-game symbolize. But in order that my behaviour should be describable as actions of a certain kind, it must be interpreted in terms of the notions of the language-game itself. So, to this extent the *praxis* at the basis of the language-game is a *pre-praxis*, one could say, and not yet full-fledged *action*.

9

The world-picture in its 'practical,' pre-propositional stage could also be called a *form of life*. 'My life shews that I know or am certain that there is a chair over there, or a door, and so on' (§7). 'Now I would like to regard this certainty, not as something akin to hastiness or superficiality, but as a form of life,' Wittgenstein says (§358).

A world-picture, therefore, is neither true nor false (cf. §§162, 205). Disputes about truth are possible only inside its frame. The presupposition then is that the disputants share the same culture or form of life, play *the same* language-games. They must, for example, *mean* the same by the words they use. But sameness or difference of meaning is possible only if there is already a certain amount of agreement about facts. (Cf. §§114, 126, 306, 456, 486, 506, 507, 523, 624.)

There are some typical cases when this presupposition breaks down or is not fulfilled. One case is when one person denies or doubts that which is part of the world-picture of most other persons in the community. Then it would often be said that the person is mentally deranged rather than that he is in error. (Cf. §§71–73, 155, 156.) What should we, for example, say of somebody who earnestly doubts that the world has existed before he was born and manifests his doubt in everything he does and says? Perhaps we should say that his lunacy consists in that we cannot teach him history. (See §206.) He is not capable of participating in all forms of our life. But we can imagine circumstances under which we should admit that this is not really a 'mental defect', but is due to a difference in 'culture'. 'Why should not a king be brought up in the belief that the world began with him? And if Moore and this king were to meet and discuss, could Moore really prove his belief to be the right one?' (§92). Moore could perhaps convert the king to his view, bring him to look at the world in a different way. This would happen through a kind of *persuasion* (§262) and would not be to convince the king of error. (Cf. also §§608–612.) We should then not be correcting his opinions, but combatting his world-picture.

When we look back on a defeated world-picture we easily do it injustice. We regard it as 'primitive' or 'superstitious'. We think of the change as a transition from darkness to light. This is often an unfair judgement.[14] But we must on the other hand also acknowledge that there are various *reasons* why world-pictures change in the course of history. Simplicity and symmetry are such reasons, Wittgenstein says (§92). Another type of reasons, I would suggest, is diverging interests in the uses of knowledge.

10

Wittgenstein's investigations into the role of the concept of a world-picture have, I think, interesting applications to the sociology of knowledge.

In his influential and justly praised book *The Structure of Scientific Revolutions*,[15] T.S. Kuhn holds that normal science is conducted within the framework of what Kuhn calls *paradigms*. The accepted paradigms set the frame of questions for scientific inquiry and determine the range of possible answers. Partly as a result of the growth of the body of scientific knowledge, these patterns tend to 'wear out', to become unsuited for their role. 'Revolutions' in science consist in an overthrow of established paradigms and the acceptance of new ones. This is a good illustration for Wittgenstein's idea about

[14] In his *Remarks on Frazer's Golden Bough*, ed. by Rush Rhees, Brynmill, Retford, 1979, Wittgenstein wanted to show how shallow and stupid the judgements made by 'civilized' men about 'primitive' cultures are when no account is taken of the *basic* differences in world-pictures and forms of life.

[15] T.S. Kuhn, *The Structure of Scientific Revolutions*, The University of Chicago Press, Chicago, 1962.

the role of world-pictures. But the illustration stands in need of much more elaboration than given to it by Kuhn.[16] One line of elaboration leads us to consider the differences between the natural sciences and the sciences of man.

Even if natural science is not the uniformly growing body of knowledge which sometimes (and traditionally) has been thought, it still is, it seems, at any one time basically *one* body of paradigms. It is only during protracted periods of crisis, such as the transition from Aristotelian to Galilean physics during the late Renaissance and the Baroque, that the unity temporarily gets lost. But does this apply also to the social sciences and to the so-called *Geisteswissenschaften*? Perhaps their history is too short to allow a definite judgement. Kuhn seems to think[17] that the social sciences have not yet reached a stage, when paradigms have been articulated with sufficient clarity to make a confrontation of paradigms possible. I am not sure, however, that he is right – and that he is not looking for the paradigms in the wrong direction, so to speak. The paradigms of social science, I would suggest, are set in the last resort by political and social *ideologies.* Sometimes ideologies try to extend their influence into the paradigmatic background of the natural sciences too. But here the effects of ideology never penetrate deep. Lenin's attack on Mach notwithstanding, there is no serious Marxist alternative to relativity theory. Nor is there a respectable Marxist alternative to Mendelean genetics. But there *are* bourgeois and Marxist economics or sociology in their own rights, I would say. To say that they differ in valuations would not be quite correct. Valuations do not belong *within* the body of a social science, whether 'bourgeois' or 'Marxist'. This is the truth contained in Max Weber's famous postulate of *Wertfreiheit* (value-freedom). But types of social science may differ in paradigmatic conceptions as to what constitutes the social reality and conditions social change. These differences in paradigms may be traced back to differences in interests (valuations) and the articulation of interests to form ideolo-

[16] There are pertinent references to Wittgenstein in Kuhn's book, though not, for obvious reasons, to the late writings which we are considering here.

[17] Ibid., p. 15.

gies. The fight between the interests is therefore a factor which matters to the conversion of men from the world-picture of one type of social science to that of another type, or which makes them anxious to defend the one against the other.

MODAL LOGIC AND THE
TRACTATUS

This study incorporates some sections from an earlier paper of mine, 'Modal Logic and Philosophical Systems', published in *Contemporary Philosophy in Scandinavia*, edited by R.E. Olson and A.M. Paul (Johns Hopkins University Press, Baltimore, 1972).

THE terms 'extensional(ist)' and 'intensional(ist)' are used with a multitude of meanings in philosophical logic. I shall not here attempt to clarify or systematize the various uses.

The logical positivists of the 1920s and 1930s often defended a thesis on the 'extensionalist' nature of all meaningful discourse[1] or, more modestly, on the possibility of constructing a purely 'extensionalist' universal language of science.[2] Support for this attitude was found in Wittgenstein's *Tractatus* – more specifically in its tenet that all significant propositions are truth-functions of elementary propositions.

In what I think was its original formulation[3] the so-called Thesis of Extensionality (*Extensionalitätsthese*) said that in any proposition about a given concept, this concept may be taken extensionally, that is, represented by its extension (class or relation). Wittgenstein's view just referred to might be regarded as a special case or version of this general principle.[4] In the course of time, however, the name Thesis of Extensionality has come to be used frequently as a label for the very idea that every meaningful proposition (sentence) can be construed as a truth-function of some elementary propositions (sentences) which are truth-functions of themselves.[5]

[1] For example, R. Carnap, in *Der logische Aufbau der Welt*, Weltkreis Verlag, Berlin, 1928; English translation *The Logical Structure of the World*, University of California Press, Berkeley and Los Angeles, 1967.

[2] R. Carnap, in *Die logische Syntax der Sprache*, Julius Springer, Vienna, 1934; English translation *The Logical Syntax of Language*, Kegan Paul, London, 1937.

[3] In Carnap, *Aufbau*, p. 57 ff.: 'In jeder Aussage über einen Begriff darf dieser Begriff extensional genommen werden, d.h. durch seine Extension (Klasse oder Relation) dargestellt werden.' (Cf. English translation, p. 72.)

[4] Carnap, *Syntax* (English translation), p. 245: 'Wittgenstein . . . put forward the thesis that every sentence is "a truth-function of the elementary sentences" and therefore (in our terminology) extensional in relation to partial sentences.'

[5] As, for example, in D. Favrholdt, *An Interpretation and Critique of Wittgenstein's* Tractatus, Munksgaard, Copenhagen, 1964, p. 11 and p. 15 ff. Favrholdt puts strong emphasis on the 'extensionalist' nature of

One could say that Wittgenstein's position in the *Tractatus* is 'extensionalist' as far as that which in the *Tractatus* view can be *said* is concerned. What is 'intensional' cannot be spoken of in significant propositions. It may nevertheless *show* itself in language.
The paradigm of meaningful language is the language of natural science (*Tractatus* 4.11; 6.53). Philosophy is not one of the natural sciences (4.111a). It is a paradox, often misunderstood and sometimes even stupidly ridiculed, that the *Tractatus*, in the view expressed in the work, is written in strictly meaningless language. And whereof one cannot speak, thereof one must be silent. The logical positivists and their followers who did not take seriously the *Tractatus* distinction between saying and showing were therefore inclined to deny the sui generis character of the intensional and to neglect the study of concepts and modes of discourse other than extensional ones.

It was not until the late 1950s that the *Tractatus* began to be seriously studied for its own sake – and not only as a source of inspiration for logical positivism. Anscombe and Stenius were two important pioneers in this study. For obvious reasons, much of the discussion has centred on the picture theory of language. Another main topic has been the nature of the *Gegenstände* (objects, things) which constitute the substance of the world. But the important role which intensional notions play in the *Tractatus* has also attracted attention. Wolfgang Stegmüller observed in polemics against the 'extensionalist' interpretation of Wittgenstein's work that the *Tractatus* is, in fact, 'soaked' in intensional concepts.[6]

Wittgenstein's position in the *Tractatus*. Also, Max Black (*Companion to Wittgenstein's Tractatus*, Cambridge University Press, Cambridge, 1964) stresses Wittgenstein's commitment to the ' "principle of extensionality", that all propositions are truth-functions of elementary propositions'. Ibid., p. 298.
[6] 'Eine modelltheoretische Präzisierung der wittgensteinschen Bildtheorie', *Notre Dame Journal of Formal Logic* **7**, 1966, p. 181: 'Gegenüber der wiederholt aufgestellten These, daß der Verfasser dieses Werkes ein rein extensionales Denkschema aufgestellt habe, läßt sich vielmehr behaupten, daß der *Tractatus* mit intensionalen Begriffen "durchtränkt" ist und daß sich mehrere solche intensionaler Schichten unterscheiden lassen.'

2

The truth-functional connectives and the quantifiers may be regarded as the 'extensional' notions *par excellence*. Among the many kinds of 'intensional' notion, the modal concepts hold a prominent place. A logician with 'positivistic' leanings will therefore look at modal logic with suspicion. He will either think it a bogus subject or will try to show that modal propositions (sentences) may be translated into an 'extensional' language.

According to Carnap in *Syntax* (§69), modal sentences are 'quasi-syntactical'. They speak, overtly, about the contents or meanings of some sentences – pronouncing these contents possible, necessary, etc. – but are translatable into propositions about the syntactical properties of those same sentences. Thus, according to Carnap, 'it is necessary that p' may be translated to '"p" is analytical', 'it is impossible that p' to '"p" is contradictory', and 'it is contingent whether p' to 'neither "p" nor "$\sim p$" is contradictory'. The ideas of analyticity and contradictoriness are then assumed to be 'extensional'.

In his later work *Meaning and Necessity*,[7] Carnap calls analyticity and contradictoriness *semantical*, and not *syntactical*, properties of sentences. 'Any simple modal sentence', he now says,[8] is logically equivalent to 'a semantical sentence in an extensional language'.

By a *reductivist* view of modality I shall understand a view to the effect that the modal notions can be defined or otherwise explicated in the terms of some non-modal notions. If these latter are 'extensional', the reduction may be termed *extensionalist*. Not every reductivist position as regards the modal concepts is – at least not in a straightforward sense – extensionalist.

Carnap's view in the works just mentioned is reductivist and aims at being extensionalist. Whether it succeeds in being the latter is not obvious, however. The notion of analyticity may turn out to be an obstacle.

Carnap may have found some support for his reductivist

[7] University of Chicago Press, Chicago, 1947.
[8] Ibid., p. 141.

view of the modalities in the *Tractatus*, 5.525b, which reads: 'Certainty, possibility or impossibility of a state of affairs are not expressed by a proposition but by the fact that an expression is a tautology, a significant proposition or a contradiction.'[9]

If the necessary propositions are the tautologies and the impossible propositions are the contradictions, then necessity and impossibility are 'defined' in truth-functional terms. The contingent could then be characterized 'negatively' as that which is neither tautological nor contradictory.

Such a reductivist reading of 5.525b, however, would be question-begging and a complete reversal of Wittgenstein's thought in the *Tractatus*. If one could regard tautology and contradiction as basic notions, then one could also define the contingent as that which is neither the one nor the other. But the basic notion in the context is that of the *significant proposition*. It is in the terms of the possible truth-values of significant propositions that the various truth-functions, among them tautology and contradiction, are defined. It is of the essence of the significant proposition that it *can be* true and it *can be* false. 'Can be' here means (logical) possibility. The notion of propositional significance in the *Tractatus* is itself a modal notion.[10] Therefore an attempt to define necessity,

[9] It is striking that Wittgenstein in the passage quoted speaks about 'certainty' (*Gewissheit*) and not about 'necessity' (*Notwendigkeit*). In her *Introduction to Wittgenstein's* Tractatus (Hutchinson, London, 1959) Elizabeth Anscombe argues (p. 157 ff.) that it is not the tautologous (contradictory) expression itself which expresses the certainty (impossibility) of a state of affairs, since in the *Tractatus* view (4.462) tautologies and contradictions do not express states of affairs at all. In her view, if '*r*' expresses something we *know* and '*r→s*' is a tautology, then '*s*' expresses a certainty. I find her interpretation ingenious but far-fetched. It is true that Wittgenstein in 5.156c uses 'certainty' (*Gewissheit*) in an epistemic sense which does not mean necessity. I therefore agree with Anscombe when she says (p. 159) that Wittgenstein 'cannot hold that *only* the truth of tautology is certain'. He held, however, that the truth of tautology *is* certain (4.464a) – and its certainty is that of the (logically) necessary.

[10] This point receives deserved attention in André Maury's dissertation, *The Concepts of* Sinn *and* Gegenstand *in Wittgenstein's* Tractatus, North-Holland Publishing Co., Amsterdam, 1977.

possibility, and impossibility in truth-functional terms is doomed to failure as a *petitio principii*.

3

Frege and Russell, the two teachers of the young Wittgenstein, have little to say about the modal concepts. It is interesting to notice, moreover, that both those great logicians inclined to a reductivist view of modality. Thus Frege wrote in the *Begriffsschrift*:

> If a proposition is presented as possible, then either the speaker is refraining from judgment, and indicating at the same time that he is not acquainted with any laws from which the negation of the proposition would follow; or else he is saying that the negation of the proposition is in general false. . . . 'It is possible that the Earth will one day collide with another celestial body' is an example of the first case and 'a chill may result in death', of the second case. [11]

In Frege's first case, possibility is an epistemic notion. Calling a proposition possible is then to say that 'nothing is known to the contrary', that is, nothing is known from which its falsehood would follow. In Frege's second case, possibility can also be expressed in language by means of an existential quantifier 'some' or 'sometimes'. 'It is possible that a cold causes death' then means 'Some colds lead to the death of the patient'.

Like the modalities, the epistemic notions are 'intensional'. Quantificational notions are 'extensional' (cf. above, p. 187). Frege's second case thus amounts to an extensionalist reduction of modal concepts. The type in question of extensionalist reduction is nowadays often called a 'statistical' view of modality. The term was first used by Oskar Becker. [12] It seems to have been recoined by Jaakko Hintikka, who in several publications has argued forcefully for the view 'that the whole

[11] Quoted from *Translations from the Philosophical Writings of Gottlob Frege* by Peter Geach and Max Black, Basil Blackwell, Oxford, 1952, pp. 4–5.

[12] *Untersuchungen über den Modalkalkül*, Verlag Westkultur, Meisenheim am Glan, 1952.

statistical model can be said to have been one of the conceptual paradigms of Aristotle's theory of modality'.[13]

The 'statistical' view was very firmly held by Russell. In 'The Philosophy of Logical Atomism' he wrote: 'It is important, I think, to realize that the whole doctrine of modality only applies to propositional functions, not to propositions.'[14] And, consonant with this, he said in his *Introduction to Mathematical Philosophy*[15] that 'If "φx" is an undetermined value of a certain propositional function, it will be *necessary* if the function is always true, *possible* if it is sometimes true, and *impossible* if it is never true'.[16] This is the 'statistical' view in a nutshell.

It was this view that Wittgenstein criticized in *Tractatus* 5.525a and c when he wrote: 'It is not correct to render the proposition "(∃x).fx" – as Russell does – in words "fx is *possible*". – That precedent to which one would always appeal, must be present in the symbol itself.'

In Russell's view, the (accidental) discovery that there actually existed a thing x with the property f would be *proof* that it is possible that something has this property. Wittgenstein thought that this was not right. In order to be able to judge that there is (exists) something which is f, we must (already) know what it means to say of a thing that it is f. That fa and a fortiori (∃x).fx are *true* presupposes that fa *makes sense*. Meaning is prior. (4.064(1): 'Every proposition must *already* have a sense'.)

The significant proposition is a picture of reality (4.01a). A proposition says (*sagt aus*) something only in so far as it is a picture (4.03d). And only by being a picture can it be true or false (4.06). In a proposition, moreover, a state of affairs is tentatively (*probeweise*) put together (4.031a) – its possibility construed, as it were. Therefore it cannot happen that a new possibility is found afterwards (*nachträglich*), that is, when the

[13] Jaakko Hintikka, *Time and Necessity: Studies in Aristotle's Theory of Modality*, Clarendon Press, Oxford, 1973, p. 103.
[14] Quoted from Bertrand Russell, *Logic and Knowledge, Essays 1901–1950*, ed. by R.C. March, Macmillan, New York, 1956, p. 231.
[15] Allen & Unwin, London, 1919.
[16] Ibid., p. 165.

proposition is confronted with facts of the world (2.0123c). In the comparison of the proposition with reality, the possibility of the state of affairs is already present.

It should be noted that by 'possibility' in the *Tractatus* Wittgenstein means that which is also called *logical* possibility. From among everything logically possible one can single out the *physically* possible, and from this again the *humanly* possible (that which can be achieved through action). One can accept that logical possibility is prior to truth, and at the same time also hold the view that the notion of truth is prior to the notions of physical and human possibility. That is: one can argue that the fact that something is (or happens) proves that this is physically possible (can happen), and the fact that something is achieved in action proves that this is humanly possible (can be done). Since that which is physically or humanly possible is *also* logically possible, a plausible view concerning the relation between existence and truth on the one hand and physical and human possibility on the other hand may induce us to take an incorrect view of the relation between factual truth and logical possibility.[17]

4

Wittgenstein's view of modality in the *Tractatus* is intimately connected with the distinction he makes between *saying* and *showing* (cf. section 1 above).

'The proposition *shows* its sense' (4.022a). 'What *can* be shown, *cannot* be said' (4.1212). 'What expresses *itself* in

[17] Duns Scotus seems to have been the first to think of logical possibility as a distinct notion and on this ground he criticized the 'statistical' view of modality current in the medieval Aristotelian tradition. I rely here on Simo Knuuttila, *Duns Scotus ja mahdollisuuden 'statistisen' tulkinnan kritiikki* (Duns Scotus and the Criticism of the 'Statistical' Interpretation of Possibility), Reports from the Institute of Philosophy 1, University of Helsinki, 1976. Wittgenstein's view of modality in the *Tractatus* thus has an interesting precursor in the work of the Schoolmen's *doctor subtilis*. Modality, incidentally, is not the only subject on which Wittgenstein's views are affined to Scotism.

language, *we* cannot express by language' (4.121c). These sentences, in combination with 5.525b on which I commented above, entail that one cannot *say* (in meaningful language) that something is a (logical) possibility (necessity, impossibility).

In the *Tractatus* view, moreover, every significant proposition has a characteristic bi-polarity in relation to truth and falsehood.[18] A significant proposition *can be* true and it *can be* false (cf. 2.21, 2.23, and 2.24). Whether it is the one or the other has to be determined on the basis of a comparison between the proposition and reality (2.223, 4.05). There are no significant propositions that are true (or false) *a priori* (2.225). Tautologies and contradictions are therefore, as Wittgenstein says (4.461c, 4.4611), meaningless (*sinnlos*) – though not nonsensical (*unsinnig*). It is a minor inconsistency when Wittgenstein, in 4.461b, nevertheless calls the tautology unconditionally *true* ('*bedingunglos wahr*').[19] Much later he gave a better expression to this thought when he said of a tautology that it was a degenerate proposition 'on the side of truth'.[20]

Because of the 'bi-polar' character of the significant proposition in relation to truth, the semantic concept of *Sinn* in the *Tractatus* has an essential relationship to the modal concept of contingency[21] – although this technical term as far as I know occurs nowhere in Wittgenstein's writings. This relationship alone makes it interesting to inquire into the formal logical features of the *Tractatus* notion of contingency and of the other modal ideas which figure in the book.

As is well known, modal logic is not a body of logical truths

[18] The term 'bi-polarity' is used by Wittgenstein himself only in the 1913 'Notes on Logic', published as Appendix I to *Notebooks 1914–1916*, ed. by G.H. von Wright and G.E.M. Anscombe, Basil Blackwell, Oxford, 1961, rev. edit. 1979.

[19] Such inconsistencies are hard to avoid and must be treated for what they are. They are not damaging to the structure of thoughts in the *Tractatus*. *Strictly speaking*, a tautology is not true, nor does it express a state of affairs (see note 9 above). Yet a tautology can be said to express the 'limiting case' of that which counts as a state of affairs.

[20] *Bemerkungen über die Grundlagen der Mathematik (Remarks on the Foundations of Mathematics)*, revised edition, Suhrkamp Verlag, Frankfurt am Main, 1974, and Basil Blackwell, Oxford, 1978, p. 167: 'Ich sehe in ihm einen degenerierten Satz, der auf der Seite der Wahrheit ist.'

[21] Cf. section 2 above and Maury, *The Concepts of* Sinn *and* Gegenstand.

uniformly agreed upon by all who study it. There are several systems of modal logic or several modal logics. Most of them share a common core of 'received' truths about the modal concepts. They differ, mainly, in principles that have to do with the modal status of propositions which are themselves modal.

Can the modal logic which is implicit in the *Tractatus* be related to or identified with any of the various systems of modal logic which logicians have studied? The rest of this essay will try to answer this question.[22]

5

A convenient point of departure for formal considerations of modal logic is provided by what is known as the System M. The axiomatics of this system consists of a substructure which is identical with (classical, two-valued) propositional logic (PL) and a superstructure with the following three axioms:

A1 $\quad M(p \vee q) \longleftrightarrow Mp \vee Mq$
A2 $\quad p \rightarrow Mp$
A3 $\quad \sim M \sim t \, (= Nt)$

The rules of inference are:

R1 Substitution (of well-formed formulas for variables).

R2 Detachment (*modus ponens*).

R3 Rule of Extensionality: formulas which are, in the system, provably equivalent, are interchangeable *salva veritate*.

---

[22] The only attempt known to me to deal with modality in the *Tractatus* from a formal logical point of view is by the Polish philosopher Bogusłav Wolniewicz in a paper published in Polish in 1969 and then in English with the title 'The Notion of Fact as a Modal Operator' in *Teorema* (Número monográfico) in 1972 or the same year as the paper of mine mentioned on p. 184 above. Wolniewicz constructs a modal logic for the *Tractatus* notion of a fact (*Tatsache*) and shows that this modal logic is deductively equivalent with the system of Lewis S5. Cf. below p. 200.

The letter *M* stands for 'it is possible that', and *N* for 'it is necessary that'. The letter *t* is used as an abbreviation for an arbitrary tautology of PL, for example, $pv{\sim}p$. I shall assume that my use of the truth-connectives and my bracketing conventions are self-explanatory.

From A2 (and PL) we immediately prove *Mt*. If we replace A2 by *Mt* as an axiom, we obtain a modal logic slightly weaker than the System *M*.

From A1 (and PL and R3) we prove the theorem $M(p\&q) \rightarrow Mp\&Mq$. If a conjunction of propositions is possible each conjunct is possible too. In the System *M*, this relation of entailment does not hold in the reverse direction.

6

We next consider a modal logic with the sub-structure PL, the rules of inference R1–R3, and the following axioms:

B1   = A1
B2   *Mt*
B3   = A3
B4 $Mp\&Mq \rightarrow M(p\&q)$

B2 is a weaker version of A2. B4 strengthens the theorem $M(p\&q) \rightarrow Mp\&Mq$ of the System *M* to an equivalence.

We substitute ${\sim}p$ for *q* in B4. This gives us the formula $Mp\&M{\sim}p \rightarrow M(p\&{\sim}p)$. For $p\&{\sim}p$ we can write ${\sim}t$. By contraposition we then obtain ${\sim}M{\sim}t \rightarrow {\sim}(Mp\&M{\sim}p)$, and from this, by virtue of B3 (and R2), ${\sim}(Mp\&M{\sim}p)$.

$Mp\&M{\sim}p$ says that it is contingent (contingently true or false) that *p*. We introduce a special symbol *C* for the modal status of contingency. The theorem which we just proved can thus be written simply: ${\sim}Cp$.

Since the variable represents an arbitrary proposition, the theorem says in effect that no proposition is contingent. It says, in other words, that every proposition is either necessarily true or necessarily false (i.e. impossible).

It is easily shown that if we replace B4 by the simpler formula ${\sim}Cp$, we get a system that is deductively equivalent to the original one. If, again, we replace B2 by the stronger A2, the system 'collapses' into PL.

A philosophical position according to which everything that is (true), is a necessity, and everything that is not, is an impossibility, is an extreme version of rationalism. The axiomatic system PL + B1–B4 + R1–R3 can thus be called the modal logic of a (certain type of) rationalist view. I shall label it the modal System R.

$\sim(Mp \& M{\sim}p)$ can easily be transformed into $Mp \to Np$. Thus, in the System R, possibility entails necessity.

From B1 and B2 we derive $Mp \lor M{\sim}p$ which can be transformed to $Np \to Mp$.

In the System R possibility and necessity are thus equivalent notions. Everything which is possible is also necessary, and only that which is necessary is also possible.

7

It is possible to construct a modal logic with C as the only (modal) primitive.[23] Such a logic will, however, in a characteristic sense be void of 'independent interest'. This is so because of the following facts:

Not only can one define the concept of contingency in terms of possibility, one can also define the notion of possibility (impossibility, necessity) in terms of contingency and truth. A proposition is possible if, and only if, it is either true *or* contingent. It is necessary if, and only if, it is true *and* non-contingent. And it is impossible if, and only if, it is false and non-contingent. Thus we have, in addition to the defining identity $Cp = Mp \& M{\sim}p$, also the defining identities $Mp = p \lor Cp$, and $Np = p \& {\sim}Cp$.

Assume now that a formal system contains truth-functional notions and the modal primitive C (and no other primitives). Assume also that the rules of formation of the system allow

[23] Cf. H. Montgomery and R. Routley, 'Contingency and Non-Contingency Bases for Normal Modal Logics', *Logique et Analyse* **9**, 1966.

truth-functional compounds of expressions of PL and expressions involving C – as, for example, the formula $p \vee Cp$. On
these assumptions, we can express everything in our calculus
that can be expressed in a modal logic with truth-functional
notions and M (or N) as sole modal primitive. All truths, or
purported truths, about (logical) necessity and possibility will
be formulatable in this logic too.

For a modal logic which is deductively equivalent to the
System M but uses C as its only modal primitive we can give,
for example, the following axiomatic basis:

> C1 $pvqvC(pvq) \longleftrightarrow pvqvCpvCq$
> C2 $Cp \rightarrow C{\sim}p$
> C3 ${\sim}C{\sim}t$

The rules of inference are R1–R3. From C2 we obtain,
through substitution and cancellation of double negation, the
formula $C{\sim}p \rightarrow Cp$. This formula and C2 are jointly
equivalent to $Cp \longleftrightarrow C{\sim}p$. I shall call this last formula the
Bi-polarity Theorem.

8

It seems feasible to equate the *Tractatus* notion of meaningful-
ness or propositional significance with the modal concept C.
But it would not be correct to maintain that the calculus for
this concept which was outlined above captured the modal
logic of Wittgenstein's work. If this were the case, that modal
logic would, moreover, be 'uninteresting' in the sense that it
would embody only the non-controversial, more or less
universally held principles of the modal System M.

The interesting aspects of the modal logic of the *Tractatus*
have to do with the distinction that Wittgenstein makes
between that which can be *said*, that is, expressed in significant
propositions, and that which cannot be said but only *shown* (cf.
sections 1 and 4 above). The latter category of things is very
heterogeneous. It includes, *inter alia*, all 'logical facts' about
language – for example, the fact that a certain proposition is
significant (contingent) or non-significant, or the fact that a

thing (in the *Tractatus* sense of 'thing') can or cannot occur in a
state of affairs of a certain structure. Such facts are not
contingent, and therefore they are not (in the *Tractatus* sense)
'facts' either. They are grounded in the 'nature of the thing'
(2.0123b). Nothing logical, Wittgenstein says (2.0121c(1)) can
be merely possible (*nur-möglich*). That this or that is a logical
possibility is, if true, a necessity; and, if false, an impossibility,
one could also say. The logical possibilities are, Wittgenstein
says (2.0121c(2)), the *facts*(!) of logic.

Thus any proposition to the effect that a proposition is
significant (meaningful) is not itself a significant proposition.
The same holds true for any proposition about the modal
status of a proposition. We can then summarize an important
aspect of the modal logic of the *Tractatus* in the thesis that
propositions about the modal status of propositions are never
contingently true or false. One could, on that account, call
such propositions 'meaningless'. But one could also say – and
this would be far more informative – that they are either
necessary or impossible.

The thesis about the non-contingent character of modal
propositions we can 'formalize' with the aid of our symbol *C*
and truth-functional symbols and split up into a number of
sub-theses:

(a) ∼*CCp* which says that it is not contingent whether a given
proposition is contingent.
(b) ∼*C*(*p*∨*Cp*) which says that it is not contingent whether a
given proposition is possible.
(c) ∼*C*(*p*&∼*Cp*) which says that it is not contingent whether
a given proposition is necessary.
(d) ∼*C*(∼*p*&∼*C*∼*p*) which says that it is not contingent
whether a given proposition is impossible.

9

How are these four sub-theses mutually related? In particular:
If we add an arbitrary one of them as an axiom to the modal
logic with the axiomatic basis PL + Cl–C3 + R1–R3

(= System *M*), can we derive the rest of them as theorems?

Sub-theses (c) and (d) are, of course, equivalent. We obtain the one from the other through a simple process of substitution (and application of R3 for cancelling double negations).

Sub-theses (b) and (d) (and, a fortiori, (b) and (c) as well) are equivalent if we accept the Bi-polarity Theorem (and R3). By virtue of this theorem we have the equivalences $\sim C(pvCp)$ $\longleftrightarrow \sim C(\sim p\&\sim Cp)$ and $\sim Cp \longleftrightarrow \sim C\sim p$. By virtue of R3 we obtain from them the equivalence $\sim C(pvCp \longleftrightarrow \sim C(\sim p\&\sim C\sim p)$.

In order to clarify the mutual relation of (a) and (b) it will be helpful first to 'unpack' their content in terms of the notions of possibility (*M*) and necessity (*N*).

If we translate (a) into terms of *M*, we obtain in the first place the expression $\sim (M(Mp\&M\sim p) \ \& \ M(\sim Mpv\sim M\sim p))$. We thereupon transform this expression, using successively the following principles: de Morgan's Law, the distribution axiom for *M* (A1), the definition of *N* in terms of *M* and the distribution principle for *N* (the 'dual' of A1), and the principle that a disjunction $\sim fvg$ can also be written in the form of an implication $f \rightarrow g$. The transformations yield the formula $M(Mp\&M\sim p) \rightarrow N(Mp\&M\sim p)$. By partly reverting to use of the symbol *C*, we can write this in the simpler form $MCp \rightarrow NCp$. The thesis $\sim CCp$ which says that the proposition to the effect that a given proposition is contingent is not itself a contingent proposition, is thus tantamount (accepting the laws of PL and the System *M*) to a thesis that if it is possible that a proposition is contingent, then it is also necessary that it is contingent. Since necessity entails possibility, we can strengthen the implication into an equivalence $MCp \longleftrightarrow NCp$. But since (in System *M*) necessity entails truth ($NCp \rightarrow Cp$) and truth entails possibility ($Cp \rightarrow MCp$), we also have the equivalence $MCp \longleftrightarrow Cp$. Herewith it has been shown that sub-thesis (a) is tantamount to the idea that contingency by itself is equivalent to possible contingency, and also equivalent to necessary contingency.

Next we perform a similar 'unpacking' of the content of (b). First we get $\sim (M(p \ v \ Mp\&M\sim p) \ \& \ M\sim (p \ v \ Mp\&M\sim p))$. The first conjunct under the principal negation sign can also be written $Mp \ v \ M(Mp\&M\sim p)$, by virtue of A1. The second conjunct can be written $M(\sim p \ \& \ (\sim Mp \ v \ \sim M\sim p))$. The last expression, after distribution, becomes $M(\sim p\&\sim Mp) \ v \ M(\sim p\&\sim M\sim p)$. But $\sim p\&\sim M\sim p$, which says of a certain proposition that it is both false and necessarily true, is refutable. Hence, by virtue of A3 and R3, $M(\sim p\&\sim M\sim p)$ is also refutable. The disjunction, consequently, reduces to $M(\sim p\&\sim Mp)$. But $\sim p\&\sim Mp$ is equivalent to $\sim Mp$ alone (by virtue of A2). Hence we can simplify $M(\sim p\&\sim Mp)$ to $M\sim Mp$.

Sub-thesis (b) has now assumed the form $\sim((Mp \ v \ M(Mp\&M\sim p)) \ \& \ M\sim Mp)$. Applying de Morgan's Law to this, we get $\sim (Mp \ v \ M(Mp\&M\sim p)) \ v \sim M\sim Mp$, which can be further transformed into $Mp \ v \ M(Mp\&M\sim p) \rightarrow NMp$. This last may be dissolved into the conjunction $(Mp \rightarrow NMp) \ \& \ (M(Mp\&M\sim p) \rightarrow NMp)$.

If in the second conjunct we substitute $\sim p$ for p, the antecedent remains the same (the order of conjuncts being irrelevant) and the consequent becomes $NM\sim p$. The conjunction $NMp\&NM\sim p$ can be contracted into $N(Mp\&M\sim p)$. Hence $M(Mp\&M\sim p) \rightarrow NMp$ is equivalent to $MCp \rightarrow NCp$. But this, as we already know, is just another form of the sub-thesis (a) or $\sim CCp$ (accepting the laws of the System M).

Consider now the first conjunct of the formula above, $Mp \rightarrow NMp$. The antecedent can also be written $Np \ v \ Mp\&M\sim p$. That a proposition is possible means that it is either necessary or contingent. We can thus dissolve $Mp \rightarrow NMp$ into a conjunction $(Np \rightarrow NMp) \ \& \ (Mp\&M\sim p \rightarrow NMp)$. The first conjunct is a theorem of System M (by virtue of A2 and R3). The second conjunct may first be amplified to $Mp\&M\sim p \rightarrow NMp\&NM\sim p$, then contracted to $Mp\&M\sim p \rightarrow N(Mp\&M\sim p)$, and finally abbreviated to $Cp \rightarrow NCp$. But this formula too, as we know, is but another version of (a) (accepting the laws of the System M).

Herewith it has been shown that, within the frame of the System M, sub-theses (a) and (b) are equivalent and hence that all four sub-theses into which we divided the characteristic thesis of the modal logic of the *Tractatus* are equivalent. The simplest form of the thesis is

C4 $\sim CCp$

If we add this as a new axiom to System M, we obtain a system of modal logic which is that of Wittgenstein's *Tractatus*. This system is deductively equivalent to the system of modal logic known as S5. Hence it seems right to say that the modal logic embodied in Wittgenstein's theory of propositional significance is S5.

In the traditional *Aufbau* of systems of modal logic, the formula $Mp \rightarrow NMp$ is the characteristic axiom of S5. It is of some interest to notice that this formula can be given the form of a conjunction, whose one conjunct is a theorem of System M and whose other conjunct is in that system deductively equivalent to $\sim CCp$. What the characteristic axiom of S5 says, over and above things already contained in the System M, is simply that (possible) contingency entails necessary contingency or that no proposition is (only) contingently contingent.

A modal proposition is one which attributes a certain modal status (necessity, possibility, contingency, impossibility) to another proposition. Since all four theses (a)–(d) are logically equivalent (in System M) it follows that in S5 no modal proposition is contingent, that is, all modal propositions are either necessary or impossible. Thus, in the *Tractatus* view, the modal logic of modal propositions is a logic of what I called in section 6 above a *rationalist* type. The modal logic of significant propositions, however, is the System M.

WITTGENSTEIN IN RELATION
TO HIS TIMES

This paper was read at the Wittgenstein Symposium at Kirchberg, Austria, in August 1977, and printed in the Proceedings of the Symposium, *Wittgenstein and his Impact on Contemporary Thought*, edited by Elisabeth Leinfellner *et al.* (Hölder-Pichler-Tempsky, Vienna, 1978). A revised version appeared in *Wittgenstein and his Times*, edited by B.F. McGuinness (Basil Blackwell, Oxford, 1982).

So I am really writing for friends who are scattered throughout
the corners of the globe.

I

THESE reflections on Wittgenstein's relationship with his
times lean heavily on the work of his called by its editor *Vermischte Bemerkungen*, translated into English as *Culture and
Value.*[1] It is a collection of remarks on philosophy, on
architecture, literature and music, on history and contemporary society, and on religion. The remarks were written at
various times in Wittgenstein's life but for the most part
towards the end of it. It is I think, a very beautiful collection
and I wish that everyone interested in Wittgenstein and in the
kind of spiritual endeavour that philosophy is would read it
again and again. Although by no means an autobiography, it
tells us more than any other written source about Wittgenstein's intellectual character and view of life, and also about
how he regarded his relationship with his times. It will be an
indispensable source for any future attempt at assessing
Wittgenstein and his achievement as *geistige Erscheinung*.

2

It is a commonplace that Wittgenstein's impact on contemporary thinking has been at least as great as that of any other single
philosopher of the twentieth century. He is, with Ernst Mach
and Bertrand Russell, the spiritual father of the powerful
movement of thought known as logical positivism or logical
empiricism and to which a great deal of what is nowadays

[1] *Vermischte Bemerkungen*, edited by G.H. von Wright with Heikki
Nyman, Suhrkamp Verlag, Frankfurt am Main, 1977. The work has been
translated into English by Peter Winch under the title *Culture and Value*,
Basil Blackwell, Oxford, 1980, and published alongside the German. Page
references below are to that bilingual edition.

cultivated under the names of philosophical logic and foundation research in mathematics and the theory of science may be considered heir. This influence has stemmed mainly from the *Tractatus*, or, rather, from interpretations placed on that work by others. Wittgenstein's later thoughts inspired a trend which is often called Ordinary Language Philosophy and which had its heyday in Oxford and some other universities in the English-speaking world in the 1950s and early 1960s. Wittgenstein's influence today is felt with increasing intensity in many quarters but is more implicit and indirect and therefore difficult to characterize in a uniform manner. Broadly speaking, one notices an alienation of this influence from the typical logico-analytical philosophy and an affiliation of it to thinking in the traditions of phenomenology, hermeneutics, and even Hegelianism. The unravelling and evaluation of the various forms which Wittgenstein's influence has assumed will constitute a major chapter in the history, yet to be written, of twentieth-century philosophy and ideas.

3

It is, however, well known that Wittgenstein himself strongly repudiated his own influence. He saw in it, on the whole, either distortion and misunderstanding, or empty use of a catching jargon. I should like to tell a story here which I hope nobody will think malicious. In the mid-1940s an able and also very influential book appeared with the title '. . . *and Language*'. Its author had for a long time studied with Wittgenstein at Cambridge – and the two had got on very well together. When I expressed astonishment at how little this book, in my opinion, owed to Wittgenstein he said in his striking and inimitable manner that all this author had learned from him was '. . . and Language'. I think this characterization holds good for much, or most, of the work in contemporary philosophy for which Wittgenstein's teaching or published writings have been a source of inspiration. It is surely part of Wittgenstein's achievement to have made concern for language central to philosophy. But few only of those who shared Wittgenstein's concern for language also shared the peculiar motivation which aroused his concern for it. *One* aspect of Wittgenstein's all too obvious alienation from his times is his feeling that not even those who professed to follow him were really engaged in the same spiritual endeavour as he.

Wittgenstein also had grave doubts whether he was a good teacher:

> Ein Lehrer, der während des Unterrichts gute, oder sogar erstaunliche Resultate aufweisen kann, ist darum noch kein guter Lehrer, denn es ist möglich, daß er seine Schüler, während sie unter seinem unmittelbaren Einfluß stehen, zu einer ihnen unnatürlichen Höhe emporzieht, ohne sie doch zu dieser Höhe zu entwickeln, so daß sie sofort zusammensinken, wenn der Lehrer die Schulstube verläßt. Dies gilt vielleicht von mir.[2]

One can react to these facts about Wittgenstein's attitude to his own influence and teaching by asking two questions.

First, why should one find Wittgenstein's repudiation of his influence disturbing? This influence has been and continues to be a seminal factor in philosophy, and *this* is what is important, not how faithfully it reflects the intentions and the spirit of its originator. These latter things must remain a matter of conjecture and it is not at all certain that speculating about them is philosophically rewarding. I do not wish to dispute this. But I would claim that trying to understand Wittgenstein in relation to his times is a task in its own right, not to be dismissed as either idle or irrelevant. It may not be relevant to the philosophy of others; but it is certainly relevant to understanding the philosophy of Wittgenstein.

The second question I have in mind is whether Wittgenstein's attitude to his contemporaries is at all unique. What

[2] 'A teacher may get good, even astounding, results from his pupils while he is teaching them and yet not be a good teacher; because it may be that, while his pupils are directly under his influence, he raises them to a height which is not natural to them, without fostering their own capacities for work at this level, so that they immediately decline again as soon as the teacher leaves the classroom. Perhaps this is how it is with me' (*Culture and Value*, p. 38).

were the attitudes of other great philosophers? Did not all of them feel that they were ahead of their times and therefore could not be properly understood until an entirely new climate of opinion had come to prevail? How did Plato or Descartes or Kant or Hegel feel about this? I do not think that we have enough evidence for a safe answer to these questions. Plato and Hegel were in any case magisterial teachers. Descartes did not teach, but he lived in intense intellectual communication with the avant-garde of his time. Kant's case is perhaps a little more like Wittgenstein's. But I still think that Wittgenstein's attitude to his times makes him unique among the great philosophers – and I shall try to say something here to substantiate this claim.

4

Late in his life Wittgenstein wrote: 'Ich kann keine Schule gründen, weil ich eigentlich nicht nachgeahmt werden will.'[3] And: 'Es ist mir durchaus nicht klar, daß ich eine Fortsetzung meiner Arbeit durch andere mehr wünsche, als eine Veränder-ung der Lebensweise, die alle diese Fragen überflüssig macht.'[4]

Wittgenstein thus thought that the problems with which he was struggling were somehow connected with the '*Lebens-weise*' or the way people live, that is, with features of the culture or civilization to which he and his pupils belonged. His attitude to this culture was, as we shall see, one of censure and even disgust. He therefore wished these ways of life changed – but he had no faith that he or his teaching would change them. One day, however, there will be another culture with different patterns (p. 64). Then, he says, the questions which had tormented him simply will not arise.

In order to see how Wittgenstein could think thus, one must

[3] 'I cannot found a school because I do not really want to be imitated' (Ibid., p. 61).

[4] 'I am by no means sure that I should prefer a continuation of my work by others to a change in the way people live which would make all these questions superfluous' (ibid., p. 61).

first note that it was his philosophical conviction that the life of the human individual and therefore also all individual manifestations of culture are deeply *entrenched* in basic structures of a *social* nature. The structures in question are what Wittgenstein called '*Lebensformen*', forms of life, and their embodiment in what he called '*Sprachspiele*', language-games. They are 'what has to be accepted, the given', the unquestioned basis of all our judging and thinking.[5] This basis, to be sure, is not eternal and immutable. It is a product of human history and changes with history. It is something man made, and *he* changes. But *how* this happens is, according to Wittgenstein, not to be accounted for by a theory, or foreseen. 'Wer kennt die Gesetze, nach denen die Gesellschaft sich ändert?',[6] he asks, and adds: 'Ich bin überzeugt, daß auch der Gescheiteste keine Ahnung hat'.[7]

5

Wittgenstein's view of the entrenchment of the individual in social reality is intimately connected with his view of the nature of philosophy. The problems of philosophy have their roots in a distortion or malfunctioning of the language-games which in its turn signalizes that something is wrong with the ways in which men live. On the intellectual level this malfunctioning consists in certain unhealthy habits of thought ('*Denkgewohnheiten*') permeating the intellectual culture of a period.

Wittgenstein's philosophizing can to a great extent be seen as a fight against such thought-habits (cf. p. 44). This is perhaps most strikingly true of his philosophy of mathematics. It opposes the influence of set-theory on foundation research and thinking about the subject. It is also true of the

---

[5] Cf. *Philosophical Investigations*, Part II, p. 226; *On Certainty*, §559.

[6] 'Who knows the laws according to which society develops?' (*Culture and Value*, p. 60).

[7] 'I am quite sure they are a closed book even to the cleverest of men' (ibid.).

second main branch of his work, the philosophy of psychology. But here the situation is more complex in that
Wittgenstein wages a war on two fronts: against behaviourism
on the one hand and against mentalism on the other.

It is against this background that we must understand why
Wittgenstein, in the midst of writing about set-theory and the
notion of the actual infinite, should have written the often
quoted remark:

> The sickness of a time is cured by an alteration in the mode of
> life of human beings, and it was possible for the sickness of
> philosophical problems to get cured only through a changed
> mode of thought and of life, not a medicine invented by an
> individual. – Suppose the use of the motor-car produces or
> encourages certain illnesses, and mankind is plagued by such
> illness until, from some cause or other, as the result of some
> development or other, it abandons the habit of driving.[8]

The passage is impressive even when quoted out of context.
But it receives a new dimension when we read it in its own
context. To Wittgenstein set-theory was a cancer rooted deep
in the body of our culture and with distorting effects on that
part of our culture which is our mathematics. Had he lived to
see the role which set-theory has since come to play in many or
most countries as a basis for teaching mathematics to children
he would no doubt have felt disgusted and perhaps have said
that it signalled the end of what used to be known as
mathematics.

6

The ways of thought Wittgenstein is fighting are not,
however, primarily the unwholesome influence on our thinking of certain lofty intellectual creations, such as Cantor's.
Set-theory or behaviouristic psychology are only symptoms
of a sickness, not its cause. The cause is in the language-games
and reflects in its turn the way of life.

It is vain to think that by fighting the symptoms one can
cure the illness. Curing it would mean changing the language-

[8] *Remarks on the Foundations of Mathematics*, 3rd edition, p. 132.

games, reforming language – and therewith the ways of thoughts and way of life of the community. Wittgenstein certainly did not think this possible through the efforts of an individual. He is most emphatic about that. All the philosopher can do is to expose the disorder in the language-games, describe it, and thereby rid his mind of the torments produced by the unrecognized illness. But this intellectual cure – '*Friede in den Gedanken*' ('thoughts that are at peace') which, he says (*Culture and Value*, p. 43), is the aim of philosophy – will have no important consequences of a social nature, either for habits of thinking or for ways of living.

Wittgenstein's attitude to language, therefore, is a fighting but not a reformist attitude. 'Wir kämpfen mit der Sprache. Wir stehen im Kampf mit der Sprache,'[9] he writes. What he means can be further elucidated by a passage of about the same date, the early 1930s, which is not printed in *Culture and Value* because it is embedded in other things he then writes (TS 213) about the nature of philosophy:

Die Menschen sind tief in den philosophischen, d.i. grammatischen Konfusionen eingebettet. Und, sie daraus zu befreien, *setzt voraus*, daß man sie aus den ungeheuer mannigfachen Verbindungen herausreißt, in denen sie gefangen sind. Man muß sozusagen ihre ganze Sprache umgruppieren. – Aber diese Sprache ist ja so geworden, weil Menschen die Neigung hatten – und haben – *so* zu denken. Darum geht das Herausreißen nur bei denen, die in einer instinktiven Auflehnung gegen die Sprache leben. Nicht bei denen, die ihrem ganzen Instinkt nach in *der* Herde leben, die diese Sprache als ihren *eigentlichen* Ausdruck geschaffen hat.[10]

[9] 'We are struggling with language. We are engaged in a struggle with language' (*Culture and Value*, p. 8).

[10] 'Human beings are deeply mined in philosophical, i.e. grammatical confusions. And, to free them from these, would *presuppose* that they became disentangled from the enormously multitudinous network which holds them captive. One would, so to speak, have to rearrange their entire language. – But this language has, to be sure, become like this because human beings had – and have – the inclination to think like *this*. Therefore only those can escape who live in accordance with an instinctive distrust of the language – not those whose whole instinct is to live in accordance with *that* herd which has created this language as its *particular* expression.'

7

When Wittgenstein wrote the above he perhaps did not see as clearly as he did later the connection between language and ways of life. In the perspective of his later philosophy one could say that his 'revolt against language' was an *Abstand-nahme*, the marking of a distance, from the complex web of forms of life which constitute contemporary Western civilization.

Wittgenstein's life testifies to this – and so did his words not only in conversation but also in what he wrote, most explicitly perhaps in the printed Foreword to *Philosophical Remarks* and its different drafts in the manuscripts. The spirit in which he is writing, he says, is 'different from the one which informs the vast stream of European and American civilization in which all of us stand'. The spirit of this civilization is to him 'fremd und unsympatisch' ('alien and uncongenial') (p. 6). Its hallmark is belief in progress (p. 7) – progress above all thanks to the technological applications of science. Wittgenstein deeply distrusted it. Many readers must have been puzzled by the epigraph for the *Investigations*: 'Überhaupt hat der Fortschritt das an sich, daß er viel größer ausschaut, als er wirklich ist.' ('The main point about progress is that it always seems greater than it really is.') If one reads it in its context in Nestroy's play, *Der Schützling*, one will perhaps understand it better. Progress, we are there told, is only the greening fringe of a colonial territory with a vast hinterland of impenetrable wilderness. In 1947 Wittgenstein wrote:

> Es ist z. B. nicht unsinnig zu glauben, daß das wissenschaftliche und technische Zeitalter der Anfang vom Ende der Menschheit ist; daß die Idee vom großen Fortschritt eine Verblendung ist, wie auch von der endlichen Erkenntnis der Wahrheit; daß an der wissenshaftlichen Erkenntnis nichts Gutes oder Wünschenswertes ist und daß die Menschheit, die nach ihr strebt, in eine Falle läuft. Es ist durchaus nicht klar, daß dies nicht so ist.[11]

[11] 'It isn't absurd, e.g., to believe that the age of science and technology is the beginning of the end for humanity; that the idea of great progress is a delusion, along with the idea that the truth will ultimately be known; that there is nothing good or desirable about scientific knowledge and that

Wittgenstein calls this '*die apokalyptische Ansicht der Welt*' ('the apocalyptic view of the world').

A little later Wittgenstein wrote:

> Es könnte sein, daß die Wissenschaft und Industrie, und ihr Fortschritt, das Bleibendste der heutigen Welt ist. Daß jede Mutmaßung eines Zusammenbruchs der Wissenschaft und Industrie einstweilen, und auf *lange* Zeit, ein bloßer Traum sei, und daß Wissenschaft und Industrie nach und mit unendlichem Jammer die Welt einigen werden, ich meine, sie zu *einem* zusammenfassen werden, in welchem dann freilich alles eher als der Friede wohnen wird. – Denn die Wissenschaft und die Industrie entscheiden doch die Kriege, oder so scheint es.'[12]

Had Wittgenstein lived to see the sixties and seventies of our century he would, no doubt, have found plenty to reinforce his view of the dangers of self-destruction inherent in the nature of modern industrial society.

These gloomy prospects notwithstanding, Wittgenstein's world view is anything but 'prophetic'. It has no vision of the future; rather it has a touch of nostalgia about the past. Wittgenstein did not feel himself, like Nietzsche, to be 'ein Pfeil der Sehnsucht nach dem andern Ufer' ('a shaft of longing for the opposite shore'), since this would have presupposed a vision of a distant shore on which shipwrecked man could start a new life. For Wittgenstein the future was something unforeseeable. He has several remarks relating to this topic. 'Wolken kann man nicht *bauen*. Und darum wird die *erträumte* Zukunft nicht wahr,'[13] he writes. 'Wenn wir an die Zukunft

---

mankind, in seeking it, is falling into a trap. It is by no means obvious that this is not how things are' (*Culture and Value*, p. 56).

[12] 'Science and industry, and their progress, might turn out to be the most enduring thing in the modern world. Perhaps any speculation about a coming collapse of science and industry is, for the present and for a *long* time to come, nothing but a dream; perhaps science and industry, having caused infinite misery in the process, will unite the world – I mean condense it into a *single* unit, though one in which peace is the last thing that will find a home. – Because science and industry do decide wars, or so it seems' (*Culture and Value*, p. 63).

[13] 'You can't *build* clouds. And that's why the future you *dream* of never comes true' (ibid., p. 41).

der Welt denken, so meinen wir immer den Ort, wo sie sein wird, wenn sie so weiter läuft, wie wir sie jetzt laufen sehen, und denken nicht, daß sie nicht gerade läuft, sondern in einer Kurve, und ihre Richtung sich konstant ändert.'[14] The philosopher who thinks thus, not only makes no forecasts, he is also under no illusion that there will be a continuation of the work he himself began but was perhaps not able to complete (p. 25; cf. also p. 59).

8

Many readers will no doubt be struck by the strongly Spenglerian nature of Wittgenstein's attitude to his times. The observation would perhaps not be very interesting, were it not for the fact that Wittgenstein's outlook is intimately allied to his philosophy. Wittgenstein was not in his philosophy a critic of contemporary civilization as, for example, Nietzsche was. Nor did he, like Spengler, develop a philosophy of history. But he *lived* the *Untergang des Abendlandes* (the decline of the West), one could say. He lived it, not only in his disgust for contemporary Western civilization, but also in his deep awe and understanding of this civilization's great past. How else could he have written the following words, which I find deeply moving? 'Aus der frühern Kultur wird ein Trümmerhaufen und am Schluß ein Aschenhaufen werden, aber es werden Geister über der Asche schweben.'[15]

Since these affinities with Spengler may not be familiar to many, and may strike some people as strange, the matter requires some further documentation. The fact is that Wittgenstein *was* influenced by Spengler. There is a passage in *Culture and Value* (p. 19) where he mentions those who had

[14] 'When we think of the world's future, we always mean the destination it will reach if it keeps going in the direction we can see it going in now; it does not occur to us that its path is not a straight line but a curve, constantly changing direction' (ibid., p. 3).

[15] 'The earlier culture will become a heap of rubble and finally a heap of ashes, but spirits will hover over the ashes' (p. 3).

influenced him. It is worth giving the list in full here: Boltzmann, Hertz, Schopenhauer, Frege, Russell, Kraus, Loos, Weininger, Spengler, Sraffa. This is Wittgenstein's order of enumeration and I think it answers to the chronological order of influence. The remark was written in 1931, but I doubt that Wittgenstein would have added to the list later in life.

It is not certain, however, that Wittgenstein in the passage referred to meant that Spengler had influenced his view of life; it is rather that Spengler's work had reinforced and helped him to articulate this view. The actual influence pertains, it seems, chiefly to an idea in Wittgenstein's later philosophy, indeed to one of its most characteristic thought manoeuvres. This is the idea of 'family resemblance'.[16] It appears to have its origin in Spengler's notion of the *Ursymbol* (archetype). This characterizes each one of the great cultures and constitutes what Wittgenstein, writing about this, in fact calls (p. 14) a family resemblance between a culture's various manifestations – its mathematics, architecture, religion, social and political organization, and so forth. The decay of a culture is, in many ways, a dissolution of the resemblances which unite the ways of life and makes, as Wittgenstein puts it, that 'das Schauspiel, das dieses Zeitalter bietet, auch nicht das des Werdens eines großen Kulturwerkes ist, in dem die Besten dem gleichen großen Zweck zuarbeiten, sondern das wenig imposante Schauspiel einer Menge, deren Beste nur privaten Zielen nachstreben'.[17]

[16] A German student of Wittgenstein, Mr H.J. Dahms, has drawn my attention to similarities between Spengler's view of language, particularly in his later book *Der Mensch und die Technik* (1931), and Wittgenstein's in the Brown Book and the beginning part of the *Investigations*. I find these similarities noteworthy. 'Un-Wittgensteinian', however, is Spengler's theorizing in the work mentioned about the origin of language and the purpose (*Zweck*) of linguistic communication.

[17] '. . . the spectacle which our age affords us is not the formation of a great cultural work, with the best men contributing to the same great end, so much as the unimpressive spectacle of a crowd whose best members work for purely private ends' (*Culture and Value*, p. 6).

9

Few ideas have been more grossly misunderstood and vulgarized than the Spenglerian notion of a 'decline of the West'. Many people identify it with a prophecy of impending disaster – something like an earthquake or deluge. It is not this. Nor is it a forecast of war or of an ecological crisis due to man's thoughtless exploitation of nature – though both surely are features accompanying the decline of the West, just as they were characteristic of the·vanishing of the Greco-Roman culture preceding ours. The perspective of decline (*Untergang*) is what Wittgenstein, speaking of Spengler, calls a '*Form der Betrachtung*' or '*Prinzip der Betrachtungsform*'.[18] And he criticizes Spengler for a tendency to confuse the *Urbild*, or type, '. . . von welchem diese Betrachtungsweise abgezogen ist'[19] with the 'Objekt, worauf wir die Betrachtung anwenden'.[20] One cannot speak of true and false as attributes of a *Betrachtungsweise* (a way of viewing things). But it gets, of course, its significance from the phenomena it illuminates and its justification from how much it contributes to our understanding of history.

To many people this way of viewing things is simply unintelligible; others will find it artificial or exaggerated. Its appeal for those who find it natural will depend partly on features of character and temperament, partly on background and traditions, partly on experience in life. It is surely deeply significant of the formation of Wittgenstein's view of contemporary civilization that he grew up in that melting pot of nations and ideas strangely loaded with contradictions which was the late Habsburg empire, and that during his lifetime he suffered the barbarianism which extinguished that peculiar ferment of our culture represented by central European Jewry. (Reflections on the Jewish mind are abundant in *Culture and*

[18] The translations (ibid., pp. 14, 27) 'form of discussion' and 'principle determining the form of one's reflections' are not entirely happy.
[19] '. . . from which this way of viewing things is derived'. Cf. *Investigations*, Part I, §131.
[20] '. . . object we are viewing in its light' (*Culture and Value*, p. 14; cf. pp. 26 ff.).

Value.) Wittgenstein was deeply rooted in something which became completely uprooted; in order to appreciate the way he saw the world one must understand this double aspect of tradition and rupture with the past which affected his own life.

10

I have dwelt here on three aspects of Wittgenstein's thought; on two of them quite briefly because they are familiar and on the third which is less well known at some length. The first is the view that the individual's beliefs, judgements, and thoughts are entrenched in unquestioningly accepted language-games and socially sanctioned forms of life. The second is the view that philosophical problems are disquietudes of the mind caused by some malfunctioning in the language-games and therewith in the way of life of the community. The third is Wittgenstein's rejection of the scientific-technological civilization of industrialized societies which he regarded as the decay of a culture.

It can hardly be denied that these three aspects are closely interconnected and deeply integrated in Wittgenstein's intellectual personality. An effort to understand it that does not pay due attention to this fact is doomed to failure. What is problematic, however, is whether or to what extent the three aspects are separable from one another in thought or whether there is also some kind of conceptual connectedness between them. Particularly pertinent is the question whether the third aspect, the Spenglerian one, is only contingently, that is, for historical and psychological reasons, connected with the other two in Wittgenstein's thought. If the connection is only accidental or contingent, then one could say that Wittgenstein's attitude to his times is irrelevant to the understanding of his philosophy, even though it may be quite important to an understanding of his personality.

I wish I knew how to answer these questions. To me they pose a problem. If it were only a question of the relation between the first and the third aspects – the entrenchment of individual life in social reality on the one hand and the rejection of contemporary civilization on the other hand – the matter would be easy. There is not much reason for thinking that *they* are connected. The difficulty arises because of the second aspect, Wittgenstein's peculiar view of the nature of philosophy. It constitutes a link between the two other aspects. Because of the interlocking of language and ways of life, a disorder in the former reflects a disorder in the latter. If philosophical problems are symptomatic of language producing malignant outgrowths which obscure our thinking, then there must be a cancer in the *Lebensweise*, the way of life itself.

I do not think that Wittgenstein would have claimed that his conception of philosophy was valid for all the historical phenomena which we heap under the label 'philosophy'. It is a well-known saying of his that what he did was 'a legitimate heir' related by family resemblance to what philosophers of the past had done. Philosophy is not a 'historical constant', any more than science is, or art. Wittgenstein is much more deeply 'history-conscious' than is commonly recognized and understood. His way of seeing philosophy was not an attempt to tell us what philosophy, once and for all, *is*, but expressed what for him, in the setting of his times, it had to be.

If Wittgenstein had claimed a non-historical, timeless validity for his view of philosophy, then again there could be nothing more than a psychological connection between it and his attitude to his times. Because then the claim would entail that good philosophy went with decline in culture. This is obviously wrong; the great philosophies mark the peak of a culture, or at most the beginning of its decline. But Wittgenstein made no such claim. His conception of philosophy is intimately allied to a '*Form der Betrachtung*' of contemporary civilization. This much we must concede. But whether this had to be the Spenglerian form of seeing our times as a dissolution of traditions in art, religion, science, and philosophy which had constituted the relative unity of the historical phenomenon of Western culture is, of course, another matter. Whatever the answer, the question deserves to be thought about and belongs in a so far almost unexplored problem area which Wittgenstein bequeathed to philosophy.

Index of Names

Figures in italics refer to names which occur in footnotes.